United States Army Depot
Brigades in World War I

United States Army Depot Brigades in World War I

ALEXANDER F. BARNES *and*
PETER L. BELMONTE

McFarland & Company, Inc., Publishers
Jefferson, North Carolina

Library of Congress Cataloguing-in-Publication Data

Names: Barnes, Alexander (Alexander F.), author. | Belmonte, Peter L., author.
Title: United States Army Depot Brigades in World War I / Alexander F. Barnes, and Peter L. Belmonte.
Other titles: United States Army Depot Brigades in World War 1
Description: Jefferson, North Carolina : McFarland & Company, Inc., Publishers, 2022 | Includes bibliographical references and index.
Identifiers: LCCN 2021052639 | ISBN 9781476682051 (paperback : acid free paper) ∞
ISBN 9781476643762 (ebook)
Subjects: LCSH: United States. Army—History—World War, 1914-1918. | Soldiers—Training of—United States—History—20th century. | Military training camps—United States—History—20th century. | United States—National Guard—History—20th century. | World War, 1914-1918—United States. | United States. Army—Military life. | BISAC: HISTORY / Military / World War I
Classification: LCC D570.36 .B374 2022 | DDC 940.4/83—dc23/eng/20211029
LC record available at https://lccn.loc.gov/2021052639

British Library cataloguing data are available
ISBN (print) 978-1-4766-8205-1
ISBN (ebook) 978-1-4766-4376-2

© 2022 Alexander F. Barnes and Peter L. Belmonte. All rights reserved

No part of this book may be reproduced or transmitted in any form or by any means, electronic or mechanical, including photocopying or recording, or by any information storage and retrieval system, without permission in writing from the publisher.

Front cover image: Camp Lewis rifle range in Washington State, Company K, 76th Infantry Regiment, 13th Division, 1918 (author's collection).

Printed in the United States of America

*McFarland & Company, Inc., Publishers
Box 611, Jefferson, North Carolina 28640
www.mcfarlandpub.com*

This book is respectfully dedicated to all Americans who put aside their civilian clothes in exchange for Army khaki; Air Force, Coast Guard or Navy blue; or Marine Corps green.

Bruce Catton wrote of an earlier American generation's soldiers in his 1958 book *America Goes to War*:

> If there is one thing in America we can be sure of, it must be that there is a value in our loose, easy-going, good-natured society here that is worth everything anyone can sacrifice for it.
>
> The American soldier, in short, usually plays it by ear. He never really becomes very military; for better or for worse, he remains to the end a citizen in arms.
>
> He never managed to look like a European-model soldier; incurably, he looked precisely like what he was—a civilian who had put on a uniform and taken up a weapon because there was a job to be done.

Catton, a World War I U.S. Navy veteran, could have very easily written these very same words about his fellow soldiers, sailors and Marines during the Great War.

Lest We Forget

Acknowledgments

As with all military history books, this project would never have been possible without the help of some talented historians and truly good friends: Brennan Gauthier, John Adams-Graf, Colonel (Ret.) James "Sluggo" Ebertowski, Marvin-Alonzo Greer, the Honorable Joan Shkane, Brian Stewart, Jesse Smith at the Virginia War Memorial, and Christopher Garcia at the Virginia War Museum. All gave freely of their own time to ensure the accuracy and readability of the book you are holding. John, Marvin-Alonzo, and Brian also contributed some extremely valuable images from their personal collections to ensure the completeness of this work.

Other important contributors and supporters were Major General (Ret.) Ken Bowra, Major General Timothy P. Williams (Adjutant General–Virginia), Major (Ret.) Kevin Born, Brian Grogan, James Miller, Dr. Lynn Rainville, Craig Alexander Rothhammer, John Simmons, Ed Loyd, Dr. John Metz at the Library of Virginia, the National Guard Educational Foundation, the New York Department of Military and Naval Affairs, the Library of Congress, the National Archives, the U.S. Army Quartermaster School and Museum, the Army Logistics University, and the Virginia National Guard Historical Photograph Archives.

Many thanks are also owed to McFarland for giving us the opportunity to tell this story.

And perhaps most of all, a sincere thank you to our wives and our families. They all have paid their tuition to the "Family of Writers School" and listened somewhat patiently as we explained to them the exciting intricacies of the 1917 Selective Service Act or the incredibly important procedures needed to demobilize a four-million-man army. God bless them all.

Table of Contents

Acknowledgments	vi
Preface	1
1. Building an Army	7
2. What Is a Depot Brigade?	20
3. Depot Brigades by the Numbers	40
4. Lame, Halt and Blind: The Development Battalions	86
5. Silver Chevrons Instead of Gold: The Stateside Divisions	103
6. The Students' Army Training Corps (SATC)	138
7. The "Spare Parts" Brigades: Unique and Unusual Events	155
8. Lost in the Shadows: Women, African Americans, Patriotic Liars and the U.S. Guards	196
9. Biographies from the Hilt of the Sword	219
10. Demobilization	235
11. "When I leave the world behind…"	245
Chapter Notes	249
Bibliography	257
Index	263

Preface

"There has been a tendency for certain writers and critics in foreign publications and books to minimize the effect of America's effort in France."[1] This simple statement, written in 1932 by former Army Chief of Staff General Peyton March, is as true today as it was then. Almost from the moment the Armistice was signed, it became fashionable to denigrate the efforts of the United States military during the Great War. Sadly, we no longer have any living advocates from the five million men and women who served in the U.S. Army, Navy, or Marine Corps during the war to refute such nonsense.

The months between April 1917 and November 1918 are a fascinating study for those interested in American and world history. Those nineteen months were filled with a frenetic and frantic energy which still seems amazing today. At last roused to anger by the actions of the German government and its military, the American people joined in what, to many reluctant citizens, still seemed to be a "European war." Others saw America's participation as rightful and a crusade to save civilization. In fact, Brigadier General Charles Dawes put it in exactly those terms when he testified to the United States Congress in 1921 during their inquiry into "extravagant" spending by the Army. Dawes, later the 30th Vice President of the United States (1925–1929) and Nobel Peace Prize winner in 1925, stated,

> We would have paid horse prices for sheep if sheep could have pulled artillery. It's all right now to say we bought too much vinegar or too many cold chisels, but we saved the civilizations of the world ... we weren't trying to keep a set of books. We were trying to win a war.[2]

Unfortunately, as will soon be obvious, the United States in 1917 was poorly prepared to fight and win a war against any but the weakest foe. Having a small army, with few modern weapons—by World War I standards—and, separated from the battlefield by the wide expanse of the Atlantic Ocean, the United States would have to build, train, equip,

The early days of the U.S. Army's war preparation is symbolized in this studio portrait of two young soldiers in training: well intentioned but not quite right. In spite of the awkwardness of the studio-provided cowboy guns, the mismatch of uniform parts, and the varied shades of clothing, both soldiers smile with enthusiasm and their willingness to make the world "safe for democracy" (private collection).

and deploy an armed force capable of surviving on a lethal battlefield. It was a most daunting task.

For the reader with either knowledge or personal experience of military training in the United States Armed Forces in the last fifty years, it will be necessary to suspend much of that knowledge. The contemporary model of "basic training," followed by some form of specialized or advanced training, and then subsequent assignment to a specific unit does not match the model used during the Great War by the United States. Except for the small handful of Regular Army, National Guard, or Marine Corps units, there were no existing units to which trained recruits could be sent. As a result, the units had to be created at the same time as recruits filling them were being inducted and trained.

What follows is our attempt to tell that story and explain the events as best we can through careful research and analysis of what was happening in the U.S. Army during the period 1917 to 1919. Some of what you will read may seem incredible and cause disbelief, especially that which pertains to the massive confusion of attempting to draft and mobilize four million men, move half of them to France, fight a war, endure an epidemic of massive proportions, return the victorious combat veterans to America, and then demobilize them all in a period of only some two years. And to do it all without a single computer, handheld calculator, satellite phone, or Internet electronic file transfer. In order to do justice to the participants whose efforts we describe, we have chosen to let their words speak for them as written and have only inserted our words to clarify something that may not be immediately obvious to the reader.

In 1917 it was determined that the best "way ahead" to build this massive army was the construction of 32 large training camps at which full combat divisions would be created and each filled with some 28,000 soldiers and officers. With speed being of utmost importance in building the Army, the first step was to mobilize the 100,000 National Guard soldiers of the 48 states and the territories of Hawaii, Alaska, the Canal Zone, and Puerto Rico. These troops were then added to the Regular Army force. Under the provisions of the National Defense Act of 1916, President Woodrow Wilson had two choices for activating Guard units. He could either "call out" a Guard regiment for Federal service thereby allowing it to continue as a National Guard unit on active duty, or he could "draft" the unit into Federal service and thus making it a Federal unit. With the benefit of hindsight, this distinction appears very slight and a simple matter of semantics. At the time, however, there was a great deal of heated rhetoric and partisan discussion regarding the differences of the two statuses. Some governors saw this as a blatant attempt to gain complete control over the Guard units from their states. Ultimately, it made little difference. In most cases, Guard units were activated under the first option as National Guard units on active duty and a short while later moved to the second category of "Federal status" by Presidential decree.

In spite of the patriotic fervor and much pro-war rhetoric, it was also very obvious that there were not enough volunteers rushing to the recruiting stations to build the Army to the required strength and size. Additionally, President Wilson sincerely believed a nationally conscripted Army would be more representative of the American people and the American ideals. The solution was to conscript men into the Army through use of a universal draft. The Selective Service Act of 1917 was designed to fix many of the problems which had appeared during the Civil War when a similar conscription act was established in the northern states. The Act of 1917 authorized a selective draft of all eligible males between the ages of 21 and 31 and specifically prohibited a selectee from buying his way out of service by replacing himself with a substitute. The use of these substitutes had been one of the most despised features of the Civil War conscription act because it allowed those with sufficient money to buy their way out of serving.

So with the expected influx of large numbers of untrained draftees, it became obvious that some organization was required at the training camps to receive, feed, clothe, and manage the fledgling soldiers until they could be assigned to actual units. These reception organizations were officially designated as depot brigades. Over time, the mission for these brigades expanded to include everything from managing replacement centers, maintaining detention centers for enemy aliens and conscientious objectors who were drafted but didn't want to serve, establishing education centers for teaching illiterate or foreign-born soldiers how to read and write in English, and quarantining the sick and potentially sick selectees as they arrived as well as a number of other missions. After the Armistice, these same depot brigades were ordered to serve as the demobilization facilities for the U.S. Army returning from France and the two million men in the Army who were awaiting transportation to France when the war ended. One observer later wrote: "There were moments in the history of mobilization in which the government of the United States looked like a madhouse; during demobilization there was lacking even the madhouse in which the crazy might be incarcerated. They were at large." Although there was certainly plenty of "insanity" to go around, it was among the depot brigades and the other training organizations that much of it was centered.

As will become obvious, there was a very different sense of

belonging between those soldiers serving in Europe in the American Expeditionary Forces (AEF) and those who were still in the United States, either training the newest soldiers or being trained. Besides the obvious fact that the AEF was in a combat zone and facing all sorts of uncertain dangers, soldiers in the stateside units often felt they were considered "second-class" citizens through no fault of their own. This sense was particularly prevalent among the soldiers who had served in the Army before the war and now were, because of that previous service experience, relegated to training other soldiers. It was the same in the Marine Corps. Marines stationed in Haiti and the Dominican Republic believed they were missing the keynote event of their generation: the Great War. Because the focus of this work is on the stateside units, little mention will be made of the AEF, but it is important to note that, even within the AEF, there was a great emotional divide between the men in the combat units and those serving in the logistical Services of Supply (SOS). It reached the point that a song was written telling mothers to take down their "blue star" service flags if their son was in the SOS. This sense of "somebody else has it easier than me" has existed in military organizations throughout history and it's likely that hoplites in the first three rows of Alexander's Phalanx probably complained that the ones in the eighth row had a cushy job. *C'est la Guerre.*

The unkindest act any historian can perform is to judge the actions of the past through the lens of current-day knowledge and beliefs. The past makes an easy target, and judging other periods using current standards is very easy to do and very dishonest. The world and the United States were much different places a hundred years ago than they are today. Nevertheless, some acts or episodes of that period, such as the use of poison gas, the devastation of Belgium, or the genocide of the Armenian people, are so inherently evil that they deserve righteous criticism even today. Likewise, the treatment of conscientious objectors in some of the U.S. Army's camps in 1917 and 1918 was despicable even back then; many people knew it and yet it continued. Similarly, the treatment of immigrant and African American soldiers at times often bordered on criminal and has been rightfully denounced. Other acts will remain open to judgment of the reader. Into this category are such conscious decisions as Army Chief of Staff General Peyton March's edict to continue shipping soldiers to France during the height of the Spanish flu epidemic. He knew full well that for some soldiers, his decision would be a death sentence. Yet, as March explained to President Wilson, the only other option would be to stop the transport of soldiers just as the Meuse-Argonne Offensive had begun. He shared with the President his concern that the news that no more soldiers were coming would both strengthen the Germans' resolve and weaken the Allies' morale just as the end of the war was in sight. Therefore, although he recognized that some soldiers would die, he insisted the shipments continue. He justified the action, to himself as well as to the President, by saying, "Every such soldier who has died has just as surely played his part as his comrade who has died in France."[3] These words, coming from General March, a highly literate and lifelong soldier whose only son had recently died in a military aircraft training accident, must have been spoken sadly. He recognized the actions resulting from his decision would cause mourning and grief for the parents and families of soldiers who would die, not facing the Germans but instead fighting for breath in a training camp hospital or on an overcrowded troopship in the Atlantic.

So with all of this in mind it is now time to turn the page and venture back to an intriguing period in history. Beware, this is a period beset with mammoth problems and challenges, all centered on the United States' effort to enter and win/end the greatest war in history. It was a time where rumors and complaints would abound and a senior Republican Congressman, James R. Mann, would write, "I don't know what is the matter with the War Department, but something is the matter."[4] Let's go see.

1

Building an Army

>Who wouldn't join the army,
>That's what we all enquire,
>Don't we pity the poor civilians
>Sitting beside the fire?
>Oh! Oh! Oh! It's a lovely war,
>Who wouldn't be a soldier, eh?
>Oh, it's a shame to take the pay.[1]

Looking back just over a hundred years to 1917, the United States Army was very different than the one we see today. Yet today's version has far more in common with that 1917 Army than the 1917 version had with its predecessor of just a few years earlier. Prior to the First World War, the Army was regimentally based and very few of its officers had much experience commanding more than a few hundred men at a time. This does not imply that they weren't competent or professional. Just the opposite is true. Almost to a man, they were personally brave and had demonstrated their courage on battlefields ranging from Cuba to the Philippines and China. But when the United States entered the First World War in April 1917, the enemy wasn't Philippine Moros, Spanish draftees, Mexican bandits, Chinese Boxers or Dominican outlaws. This time U.S. Army soldiers and their Marine Corps comrades were going to take on what was undoubtedly the most technologically advanced military force in the world—the Imperial German Army. Equipped with flamethrowers, a multitude of automatic weapons, and proven "Stormtrooper" tactics while supported by gas weapons, artillery barrages, and the best aircraft in the sky, the German Army in 1917 was at its technological zenith. Although three years of fierce fighting on the Western Front had considerably thinned its ranks, it had learned to use technology as a force multiplier, and by the time the American Expeditionary Forces (AEF) began to arrive in meaningful numbers, the Germans had the Allies on the ropes. Stalemate had been reached and the Allied soldiers, with their typical soldiers' sarcastic humor, talked about what would happen when their sons and grandsons took their places in the trench line.

Military forces are inveterate copycats, so when it appeared to the U.S. Army leadership in 1915 and 1916 that participation in the global war was inevitable, they decided to redesign how the Army would look and fight. Taking as many lessons as possible from the warring forces in Europe, they set out to build a force which would contain all of the necessary combat arms and logistical elements which were required to arm and support a large combat unit. This redesign had barely begun when Pancho Villa's March 1916 surprise attack on Columbus, New Mexico, took place. The attack led to the deployment of almost the entire stateside Regular Army to the Mexican border and then down into Mexico in pursuit of Villa. When other cross-border attacks took place, the President mobilized the National Guard of all the states and dispatched them to the Mexican border. While on the border, some Regular Army and National Guard units began to train together, and their leaders began to think in terms of the new formations and unit sizes.

There had been major problems, however, in getting the Guard units from some states to the border and many had to do with what might be considered strategic and operational logistics. The problems included such simple things as not having a designated mobilization site

A step in the right direction. The U.S. Army used trucks and airplanes in the field for the first time during the expedition against Pancho Villa. Overall, the trucks and automobiles performed better than the aircraft in the harsh conditions of the Mexican desert (USAMHI).

for the state's units or having to perform physical examinations on thousands of soldiers with little time and few military doctors. Other more complex problems included shortages of weapons, draft animals, signal equipment, and even ammunition. It was not the Guardsmen alone who were underequipped. Army leadership was unpleasantly surprised to discover that the batteries of the six field artillery regiments serving in Mexico or on the border had only 5,800 rounds of ammunition, enough for just three minutes of sustained fire. Making the matter worse, the Army had to close the Field Artillery School to have enough trained artillerymen to deploy with the regiments.

Some of these problems would be resolved by 1917 when the United States entered the First World War, but others were not and would continue to bedevil Army and Marine Corps leaders in the United States and on the Western Front. Before we move our story in that direction, it is important to look at how the U.S. Army had redesigned and reorganized itself for fighting in Europe.

U.S. Army Organization

The Line. In 1916 the branches of the Army that today are called the Combat Arms branches were referred to as the "Line." The Line consisted of the infantry, cavalry, and artillery units.[2]

Infantry. In the U.S. Army of the period, it was widely accepted that the "infantry is the principal and most important branch. It represents the moral force of the nation and of the Army."[3] Following the historical precedent, the basic unit of infantry was the regiment. In an infantry regiment were a headquarters company, a machine gun company, twelve rifle companies, a medical detachment, and a supply company. The rifle companies were organized into battalions of four companies each. Commanding the regiment was a colonel. His staff and the commanders of the subordinate units numbered some fifty other officers with the vast majority being first and second lieutenants. All total, a full-strength infantry regiment had 3,755 officers and enlisted men assigned. Rifle companies each had six officers and 250 soldiers in the ranks.

Each enlisted soldier was expected to carry between 55 and 75 pounds of equipment including his rifle. For most soldiers in the Regular Army and the National Guard, the rifle of issue was the 1903 Springfield. Doctrinally, the units being raised as part of the National Army were usually equipped with the M1917 Enfield rifle.[4] However, as we shall see, this common-sense solution would founder on the rocky shoals of reality when large scale transfers of men between divisions took place.

Also effecting which rifle was used in a division was the order in which the divisions deployed to France; earlier deployers were armed with 1903s and the later units with Enfields.

Other individual soldier items included canteen and cover, condiment can, bacon can, mess kit, silverware, first aid pouch, shovel and cover, bayonet and scabbard, poncho, shelter-half, tent pegs and pole, and personal equipment including spare clothing. By 1917, the now very necessary gas mask and steel helmet were added to the load.

Cavalry. Doctrinally, the characteristics of the cavalry were rapidity of movement, mobility, and the ability to fight either on horseback or on foot. The horse was meant to serve both as a means of transportation and as a weapon.[5] Each cavalry regiment was comprised of a headquarters troop, a machine gun troop, a supply troop, a medical detachment including a chaplain, and twelve cavalry troops. The cavalry troops were further organized into three squadrons, each with four troops assigned. The cavalry regiment was manned similarly to the infantry regiment and each cavalryman had much the same personal equipment as the infantryman. The main exception was the cavalryman who was also armed with a sabre and a pistol but carried no bayonet.

Artillery. U.S. Army artillery of the period was divided into two

A fully equipped infantry soldier of the 1916 period. Soon, however, his load will be increased significantly with the addition of a gasmask, steel helmet, a second pair of boots, and a full combat load of ammunition (Library of Congress).

1. Building an Army

The second side of the combat arms triangle was the cavalry. Although as a combat force cavalry units played a very small role in the war, knowledgeable care and feeding of horses and mules was a necessity as each U.S. Army division required some 10,000 draft animals as prime movers for artillery, ammunition, supply, and sanitary trains (U.S. Army Quartermaster Museum).

basic types: mobile artillery and coast artillery. Of the mobile artillery there was a further sub-division: Mountain Artillery, Light Field Artillery, Heavy Field Artillery, and Siege Artillery. As the names suggest, the size of the artillery piece and shell fired determined to which division of the field artillery a unit belonged. Although the U.S. Army had a history rich in field artillery operations, the vast majority of the AEF field artillery units were issued French or British artillery pieces on arrival in France. The U.S. Army's basic tenet of field artillery operations was that its role on the battlefield was providing direct support to the infantry. This was particularly true for divisional artillery units. Corps and army-level artillery units also had the assigned mission of destroying hostile defenses and providing counter-battery fire against enemy artillery.[6] Most long-range artillery was assigned to army-level units.

The field artillery regiments were organized along the same lines as the infantry and cavalry regiments, with the individual

The third side of the combat triangle was the artillery. Here a field artillery crew practice shooting their three-inch M1902 field gun. The guns were good enough for the training camps, but they were left behind in the States. Almost all the artillery actually used by U.S. artillerymen on the Western Front was made and provided by the French or British (NYSDMNA).

battery corresponding to the infantry company or the cavalry troop. One important difference was that there was no machine gun unit assigned to an artillery regiment. Mountain artillery and light field artillery battalions were organized to have three firing batteries while heavy and siege artillery battalions usually were organized to have just two firing batteries. Later, a review of the organization of the basic combat division adjusted these numbers so that there were three artillery regiments per division. A mix of cannon types between battalions was acceptable and usually followed a formula of two light or medium batteries to each heavy battery.

The Coast Artillery Corps operated out of fixed sites or with railroad-mobile heavy artillery pieces. The coast artillery units were responsible for anti-submarine and torpedo defenses in their area. Coast artillerymen were also trained to serve as infantrymen should that role be required. Altogether, there were 30,305 officers and enlisted men authorized to serve in the U.S. Coast Artillery Corps. During the Mexican border campaign some Coast Artillery units were sent south to augment the infantry on the border; during the war these units would

1. Building an Army

prove a valuable resource when the AEF reached France as they were able to be trained quickly in some of the larger field artillery pieces or the railroad-mounted cannons.

Others, such as two batteries of the Virginia National Guard Coast Artillery, would find themselves rolled into more urgently needed units. The Virginians, primarily from the Roanoke area, were the soldiers selected to become the 117th Military Police Company of the famed 42nd "Rainbow" Division and were the first from the state to deploy to France. Two other Coast Artillery batteries from Virginia were mobilized and dispatched to serve in France in the Coast Artillery Corps' 60th Regiment. There were similar attachments and detachments throughout the various Guard units in all states.[7]

The Staff. In 1917 the part of the Army that was not assigned to the "line" fell under what was considered "the Staff Corps and Departments" and was most often shortened to just "the Staff." Among these branches were the soldiers we would recognize today as logisticians. In the vernacular of the Army at the end of the 20th century, most of these units would belong to what were called "Combat Support" and "Combat Service Support."

General Staff Corps. The doctrinally defined mission for the General Staff Corps was to develop plans for the national defense and to prepare for the mobilization of the U.S. Army in the event of war. The head of the General Staff was the Army Chief of Staff. The Chief of Staff was directly responsible for supervising the troops of the Line and all departments of the Staff. He reported directly to the Secretary of War. Interestingly and unlike today, this position was not the highest or final job an Army general would have; several former Army Chiefs of Staff were among the first division commanders selected in 1917. In 1918 the General Staff was reorganized into five separate divisions: the Executive Division; the War Plans Division; the Purchase and Supply Division; the Storage and Traffic Division; and the Army Operations Division.

Adjutant General's Department. This department was responsible for maintaining all soldiers' and officers' personnel records. It was also responsible for issuing orders that transferred soldiers between units and for ensuring that units receive the correct number and type of soldiers to maintain their unit strength. As will soon become evident, this was a major job for the Adjutant General Corps soldiers serving in the in the United States and in the AEF; movement of soldiers between units for a wide variety of reasons caused no end of headaches for those required to track these movements and report status. As we will see, so many soldiers got "lost in the system" after the war that some states took to contacting family members to ask if their soldier was home yet or if they knew where he was. This was certainly not much comfort to the families receiving such inquiries.

Inspector General's Department. This department acted as the oversight organization to check each soldier's skills and fitness for serving in the Army. They were responsible for oversight of all purchases made by the Army and to investigate any discrepancies uncovered. They also made recommendations to improve the overall effectiveness of the Army regarding weapons, equipment, and supplies.

Judge Advocate's Department. The Judge Advocate's Department was responsible for maintaining the Army's legal records as well as providing legal representation in military courts of law. It worked closely with the Provost Marshal Department. The Provost Marshal Department included the Military Police Corps and the Provost Guard, the organization responsible for security of military posts. The Provost Marshal department was also responsible for guarding and administering prisoners of war.

Medical Department. The Medical Department was responsible for all aspects of camp health and sanitation and for the same functions when the Army was deployed for either for combat or long-term training operations. It was also responsible for care of the sick, both human

Key to any campaign of the 20th century was efficient medical support. Most Army units had a sizable medical staff but when the Spanish flu epidemic hit the training camps many facilities were overwhelmed by the number of patients for which they were required to care (USAMHI).

1. Building an Army

and animal. Included in this department were the Army Nurses Corps, the Dental Corps, the Hospital (Administration) Corps, the Ambulance Corps, the Sanitary Corps, and the Veterinary Corps.

Ordnance Department. Created in 1812, the Ordnance Department was originally chartered to research, procure, and store ammunition

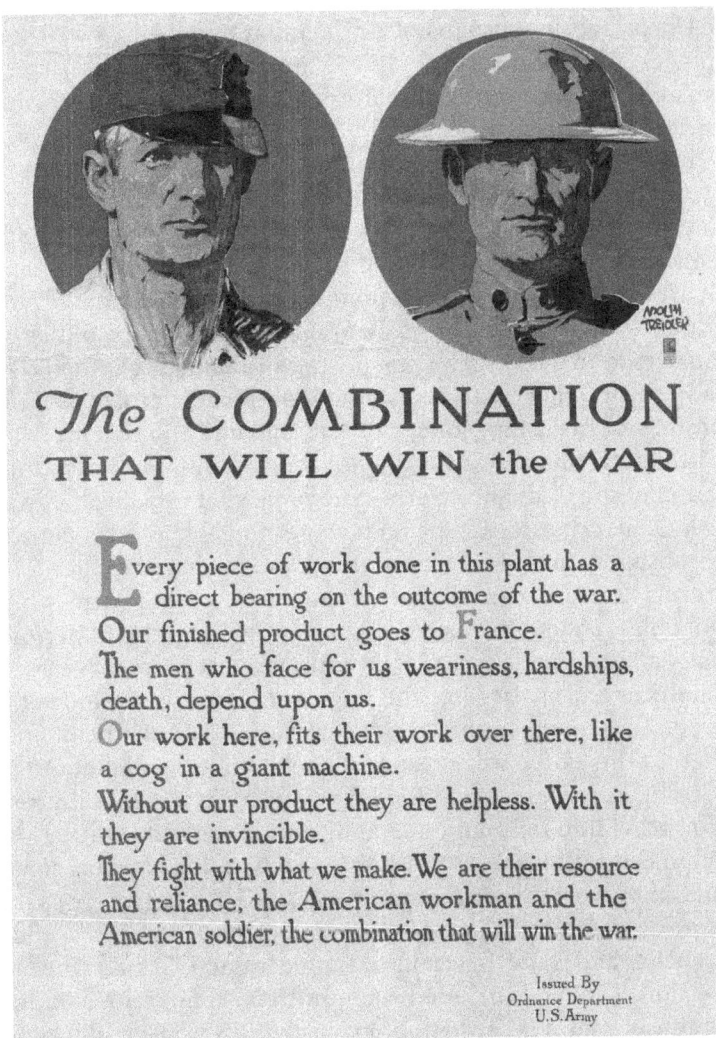

A wartime poster produced by the Ordnance Department lauding the equal efforts of the soldiers and industrial workers. Ordnance Corps soldiers had particular interest in the weapons and equipment being produced in the United States since they were ultimately responsible for maintaining and repairing them (Library of Congress).

and other ordnance materiel for the Army. By 1916 this department was responsible for testing and supplying weapons, ammunition, and ordnance of all types to the other branches of the Army. They were also responsible for maintaining the Army's arsenals and ammunition manufacturing sites. When motor vehicles were added to the Army during the period 1916 to 1918, the officers and soldiers of the Ordnance Corps became responsible for maintaining them as well as artillery pieces. The modern-day U.S. Army's Ordnance Corps remains responsible for ammunition, maintenance, and explosive ordnance demolition (EOD).

Quartermaster Corps. Although quartermaster functions in the Army date back to the Revolutionary War, the Quartermaster Corps did not officially come into existence until 1912. Before that, officers from other branches were detailed to act as quartermasters. By 1916, the Quartermaster Corps was responsible for the movement of soldiers (individual or unit) and supplies. In France, many of these duties would be transferred to either the Transportation Department or the newly formed Motor Transport Corps. The Quartermaster Corps was also responsible for furnishing food, clothing, and unit equipment.

The Quartermaster Corps did not provide ammunition as this was a function of the Ordnance Corps. The same split remains today as the modern Quartermaster Corps remains responsible for distributing all classes of supply except for ammunition and medical supplies. Today's Quartermasters are also responsible for maintaining Army property accountability, conducting petroleum and water operations, performing mortuary affairs functions, and providing aerial delivery services.

Engineer Corps. In 1916, the Engineer Corps was responsible for constructing Army posts as well as fortifications in the field. Soldiers assigned to this corps were responsible for building and maintaining roads, bridges, and railroads. The Engineer Corps was initially responsible for providing railroad units and some watercraft units. Division level engineer units were responsible for preparation of maps, construction and improvement of communications infrastructure, preparation of obstacles, demolition, construction of defensive positions, and providing shelter and water. Specialized engineer units were assigned above the division-level and included such units as "topographical, camouflage, railway, and lumber battalions, bridge and watertank trains and shop companies."[8]

Signal Corps. The Signal Corps was responsible for the transmission and communication of messages by telegraph, telephone, wireless radio, observation balloon, visual signaling techniques such as semaphore, and other communications methods such as aircraft and carrier

1. Building an Army

pigeons. It was this message transmission requirement that caused the Army's early aviation efforts to fall under the Signal Corps. Each of the Army's divisions of the period was assigned a dedicated field signal battalion. In this structure the "signal officer [was] directly responsible for the efficacy of his own system and ... over the systems of subordinate and auxiliary units...."[9]

It is also important to understand a very significant difference between the U.S. Army of 1917 and the modern version. Today's U.S. Army soldier receives his job-specific training at sites designated to provide that training. Quartermaster soldiers receive their specific job-related training at Fort Lee, Virginia, while artillery soldiers receive theirs at Fort Sill, Oklahoma, and so on. After completion of training, the soldier is then assigned to a unit and travels to where that unit is stationed. In the period 1917 to 1918, each of the 32 major training camps was expected to provide almost all of the training for a complete 28,000-soldier division. Certain skills such as field artillery operations for officers, or radio and telegraph installation procedures would be taught at other locations, but the soldier would always return to his unit of assignment for most of his training. This separation of officers or men

Reinforcements and logistics support for the Mexican Punitive Expedition passed through stateside camps such as Camp Columbus, New Mexico, and then across the border to support bases in Mexico. At these bases, such as Casa Grandes seen here, the supplies would be reconfigured and loaded into other conveyances that would carry them further south to the units involved in the search for Villa (USAMHI).

from a unit for periods of time for specialized training is considered the norm for today's soldier but during the period in question, there were some unexpected problems. In some cases, the officers would be gone for considerable periods and would not train together with their soldiers until they reached France. Even after arrival in France, many officers would again be detached from the unit for more staff or tactical training and return to their unit only to find that many of the men under their command had been shipped out as replacements.

One other significant difference between the operations of 1917–1918 and today is way in which logistical supplies are categorized. Today's logistician is used to dealing with ten classes of supply:

Class I: Packaged food, rations, and water.
Class II: Individual clothing.
Class III: Petroleum, oils, and lubricants.
Class IV: Engineer fortification and barrier materials.
Class V: Ammunition.
Class VI: Personal items.
Class VII: Major end items (weapon systems, vehicles, etc.).
Class VIII: Medical supplies.
Class IX: Repair parts.
Class X: Miscellaneous supplies for non-military programs.

The 1917 version was much simpler and only separated supplies into four classes:

Class 1: Food, forage and any material, such as weapons, which was automatically supplied to a unit based on its type and mission.
Class 2: Uniform clothing, shoes, and individual soldier's field gear.
Class 3: Equipment that, although authorized such as trucks, tents, wagons, shovels, etc., would not necessarily impact a unit's mission if missing in some amount.
Class 4: Equipment based on mission-specific requirements such as cold-weather gear, gas alarms, etc.[10]

The very simple structure of the Army Staff Sections, shown above as organized in 1916, had to undergo a rigorous test as the AEF grew into a viable combat force in France. Missions which had long been doctrinally assigned to specific departments or corps were transferred elsewhere. Some branches were reorganized completely, and new departments were brought into being. And by the end of the war, some completely new organizations centered on armor and aviation units were established.

With this basic understanding of how the U.S. Army was organized

1. Building an Army

we now turn to the nation's earnest attempt to build an army for General Pershing to command. To explain the process General Peyton March, the U.S. Army Chief of Staff, created and used a metaphor in which the AEF in France was the blade of the sword and the War Department and its stateside Army training base were "the hilt of the sword."[11] Among the key features of that important hilt was a very unique and fascinating organization which came to life in the major training camps and was officially known as the "Depot Brigade."

2

What Is a Depot Brigade?

"To feed his beloved nephews Uncle Sam had bought the world's output of potatoes, onions, beans, rice, and prunes; and he kept them all at Camp Lee. I had seen 'em."[1]

Before digging into the complex and ever-changing mission assigned to the U.S. Army's newly developed units, the depot brigades, it is necessary to first understand how and where the thirty-two main training camps were set up. With this background information it will then be much easier to appreciate the unique environment in which the depot brigades operated. It's also important to understand that there were two distinctly different categories of divisional training camps: National Army and National Guard.

When the War Department determined that sixteen National Army and sixteen National Guard divisional training camps were needed, the original intention was to make them all the same in form and function. However, the reality of the U.S. Government's budgeting process soon ended that plan. Secretary of War Newton Baker wrote:

> Because of the impracticability of constructing thirty-two cantonments with the fund appropriated, it was decided, as the National Guard had then in its possession a certain amount of tentage, and the War Department could reasonably hope to supply the necessary complement ... to place the National Guard under canvas that their training might not longer be delayed, and to confine cantonment construction to the sites selected in various divisional areas for the National Army.[2]

As the result of this decision, and obviously needing the extended training, the National Army divisions would therefore be quartered in more permanent wooden barracks at their training camps. Since these camps were to be more permanent, weather resistant, and durable in construction, the sixteen sites chosen were almost entirely in northern or central states.

The National Army training sites would become known as

2. What Is a Depot Brigade?

In this cartoon from Camp Lee's newspaper *The Bayonet*, Uncle Sam is turning the crank at the reception station to change variously shaped and differently dressed civilians into identical and sharp-looking soldiers (U.S. Army Quartermaster Museum).

"cantonments" since there would be wooden buildings in which to house the troops. The National Guard training sites, in which tents would be used, would be known as camps. Each camp and cantonment was to be named after an American soldier or statesman of significance to either the camp's locality or to the geographic origin of the soldiers to be trained there. Regardless of the camp/cantonment distinction, all of the sites were named "Camp": Camp Devens, Camp Grant, Camp Sherman, etc. It was the home state or origin of the National Guard soldiers training at some of the camps in the South which led to such anomalies as having Camps Sheridan and McClellan in Alabama, Camp Wadsworth in South Carolina, and Camps MacArthur and Logan in Texas. With the American Civil War having ended only 52 years previously and thus still in living memory for many citizens, one might expect such "Yankee" names would have aroused some vigorous resentment or anger in the southern states. This doesn't appear to be the case, perhaps because the financial boom expected to be coming from the camps caused many areas to lobby vigorously to have the army camps, regardless of names, built in their area.

National Army soldiers arriving at their training sites usually found newly built two-story wooden barracks awaiting them. The upper floors were large dormitory-style rooms without partitions. The iron cots for the entire company were arranged side by side in long rows. There was a designated amount of floor space for each soldier. The lower floor in each of these buildings was divided into two long rooms. One served as a mess hall including long tables and benches with a serving counter at the far end. The other room served as an assembly room suitable for indoor training events or recreational activities. There was a problem, however, with the basic design of the standard barracks building. It was originally designed to accommodate 200 soldiers. A redesign of the basic infantry company had changed the size of the company to a new total of 250 men. As a result, for the convenience of command and control, often some 50 more men than were planned for were

A typical postcard sent home by soldiers training at Camp Devens, Massachusetts. Even a relatively small training camp such as Devens was impressive because of the sheer number of buildings and soldiers that quickly filled the camp (private collection).

2. What Is a Depot Brigade?

A typical scene inside the barracks building at one of the National Army camps. Originally designed to house 200 men, by the middle of 1918 most were filled with many more than that (U.S. Army Quartermaster Museum).

squeezed into a company barracks. This overcrowding became a problem and led to serious health issues, especially during the fall of 1918.

Yet, in spite of the overcrowding, "[the barracks] were by far the most comfortable army quarters any one had ever seen provided for men who were going into field service."[3] Outside of each barracks building was a latrine facility, containing shower stalls and the requisite toilets. The floor was made of cement, and in the center of each building was a large boiler to provide heat for the building and hot water for the showers and sinks. For some soldiers originating from more rural sections of the country, and even some from cities, this was the first time they would inhabit a building with electricity and running water. Others found the work of being a soldier in a training camp was a lot less tiring than the jobs they held before being inducted. One such Alabaman later recalled his brother Amos, who was serving in the same unit, saying, "Army work is shore foolish ... but it's a lot easier than sawmill work."[4]

In scope and size, the National Army camps were particularly impressive. Each was "capable of housing a population equal to the combined population of Arizona and New Mexico ... [with] stable room to care for as many horses as there are in the State of Oregon."[5] It was estimated that the amount of lumber used to build the camps could have created a four-foot-wide boardwalk which would stretch from Palm Beach to Baghdad. Indicative of the size and activity in these small cities, most camps were able to sell the food waste from the mess halls as pig's feed and the massive amounts of horse and mule manure as fertilizer to local farmers. Officials at Camp Lee, Virginia, went so far as to claim it was a farmer's civic and patriotic duty to buy U.S. Army manure.

It was decided by the Army leadership that each of the thirty-two divisional training sites would have in their organization a type of unit previously unknown in the Army: the Depot Brigade. It had also been previously determined that all camps should be set up in a giant horseshoe-shaped design to allow standardization of buildings, ranges, rail facilities etc. However, all of the camps differed somewhat in size based on local topography and the availability of land. Therefore, each camp was slightly different in layout than the prescribed horse-shoe model. Likewise, each of these new depot brigades would grow and develop in reaction to the local conditions and also to the number and type of men who were sent to them to be trained.

Almost immediately there were problems for these new brigades and their staffs. Overly enthusiastic, or possibly lazy, draft boards had judged some men fit for service that should have never been accepted. The reception center in the depot brigade at Camp Devens, Massachusetts, was shocked to receive "men who were actually cripples. One man had only one hand and some of the fingers were missing on that. Another had only one eye...."[6] Equally disheartening was the appearance at Camp Upton, New York, of Joseph Friedman, a young immigrant from Warsaw. Friedman had previously suffered an injury to his cheek and jaw which prevented him from eating solid food. He had requested exemption from the draft due to his disfigurement, but the local draft board sent him on to the camp anyway. Although the young Pole said he was willing to give the Army a try, the camp doctors quickly sent him home.

An equally strange case also occurred at Camp Upton when a burlesque show musician, Joseph Rigler, showed up at the depot brigade reception area. Rigler told the Upton staff that he not only had liver trouble, but he was under a doctor's care for a poisonous reaction to the theatrical face paint required for his civilian work. On a more personal note, he told the depot brigade clerk he really didn't want to leave his job and "had no idea who was fighting." The Army clerk filling out Rigler's information told him not worry; he would figure it out quickly enough when he got to France.[7]

One the most befuddling cases of all was seen at Camp Travis, Texas. A man from East Texas arrived at camp after being selected by his draft board. During his in-processing physical examination it was determined that he had a bad leg. He was sent home. A short while later his local draft board selected him again. He again appeared at Camp Travis where he once again failed the camp physical and was sent home. A few months later, his draft board once again sent him to Camp Travis. By this time, however, some development battalions had been organized to support Camp Travis's depot brigade, and he was placed into one designated to handle men with medical issues. The medical staff in the battalion determined that an operation could fix his problem. They performed the operation, and after three weeks in the hospital, he was returned to the development battalion for physical therapy. It was hoped that eventually he would be healthy enough to be transferred from the 165th Depot Brigade to another unit. There is no record of this happening and so it is most likely the war ended before he was ready for active or even limited service.[8]

The pensive look on Missouri-born Benjamin Henry Kinion's face is understandable. On his draft registration, Kinion requested exemption from military service due to his opposition to war. Nevertheless, he was selected and served in 61st Company, 12th Receiving Battalion, of the 162nd Depot Brigade at Camp Pike (private collection).

And so it went. Similar stories would be repeated at all of the camps. The usual excuse from the draft boards was that surely the Army could find some work for these men to do. Unfortunately, there was also a negative aspect to this which could not be measured but added to the overall appearance of confusion and Army incompetence. With each draft board being directed to send a certain number of inductees to a specific camp on a specific date, every time a man was rejected at the depot brigade reception station, another man had to quickly be notified by the draft board and dispatched to the camp in his place. As a result, instead of arriving as part of a contingent of men from the same area,

MEMBERS OF THE BOARD

L. F. HERRICK
E. F. CARD
J. E. GREENAN

REGISTRATION AND SELECTION
FOR MILITARY SERVICE
LOCAL BOARD FOR DIVISION NO. 4
ROOM 301, CITY HALL

OFFICERS OF THE BOARD

CHAIRMAN
L. F. HERRICK
SECRETARY
J. E. GREENAN

Oakland, Calif., March 25, 1918.

Mr. George F. Butler,
  801 -- 20th St.
    Oakland, Cal.

Dear Sir,

  You have been selected as alternate to take the place of any one of the men selected to go to Camp Lewis on March 30th, who may fail to report.

  You will therefore report at the office of this Board, Room 301, City Hall Oakland, at five P.M. on Friday March 29th.

    Yours truly,

    Local Board, Division No. 4,
    By J. E. Greenan
      Secretary.

Certainly a letter few were happy to receive. Although not yet drafted, the recipient has been instructed by his draft board to report just in case one of the men selected does not show up so he can go in their place (private collection).

many arrived in ones and twos, often creating further administrative nightmares. Adding to the muddle, there was a tendency among some draft boards in the South to select African American men disproportionately as a way to exempt local white men from service. Five Southern states, Florida, Georgia, Louisiana, Mississippi, and South Carolina, all inducted and sent to camp more blacks than whites. Even more insidious was the practice of local draft boards selecting for induction those blacks who owned their own farms before those that worked as sharecroppers or tenant farmers, thereby allowing local landowners to keep their hired hands to work on the farm.[9] Because of practices such as these, many men who should have failed the induction physical were sent to the camps only to fail the reception physical and be sent home again and replaced by other potentially equally unfit inductees.

2. What Is a Depot Brigade?

Another problem which was never solved was the negative effect caused by sending large numbers of men from one camp to another in order to fill up units scheduled for earlier deployment to France. Receiving orders to dispatch anywhere from five hundred to three thousand men to another training site, some camps used this as the opportunity to rid themselves of their problem soldiers. In many cases, these large levees of soldiers would include enemy aliens, recently arrived and untrained inductees, and men with physical, mental, or legal problems.

At Camp Lee in November 1917, the 318th Infantry Regiment received orders to ship a thousand soldiers away to other divisions. In addition to losing over a quarter of the regiment's strength, the 318th also lost their commander to a War Department staff position. It would be three months before another colonel was transferred from the 155th Depot Brigade to command the regiment. In the meantime, the 318th received a number of new soldiers, many of whom required the rudimentary training on basic soldier skills. In order not to hold back the men who were original to the regiment, it was wisely decided to put the new men into a separate unit and train them together on the basic soldier tasks. After they had completed this schooling, they were then assigned to their designated units.[10]

So with all of this going on in the background, what could the individual inductee expect on arrival

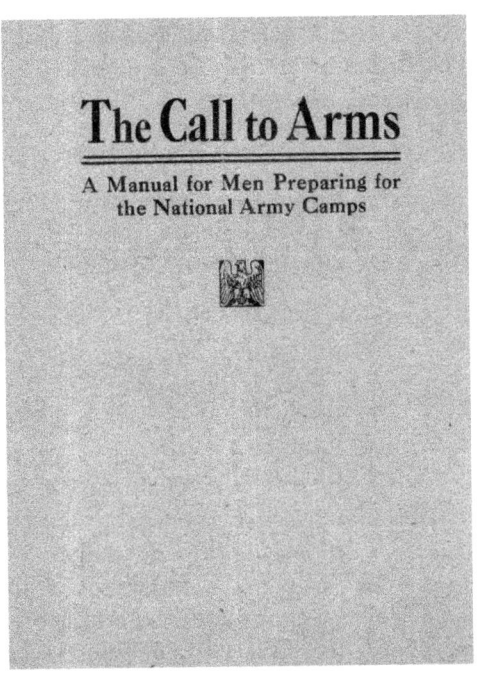

One of the pamphlets produced to help soldiers prepare for life in the training camps was *The Call to Arms*. Compiled by the authors from information gathered from camp chaplains and YMCA secretaries, the book gave guidance on everything from making friends to the books a soldier should read. Among the books recommended were *The Bible* and *The Modern Army in Action* by General John Francis O'Ryan, Commander of the 27th Division (private collection).

at his training camp? In most cases he had already received a letter from his draft board which included the following instructions:

> You should take only the following articles: A pair of strong comfortable shoes to relieve your feet from your new regulation marching shoes ... a comb, a brush, a toothbrush, soap, tooth powder, razor and shaving soap ... [a] woolen blanket, preferably of dark or neutral color. This blanket should be tightly rolled, the ends of the roll should be securely bound together and the loop of the blanket thus formed slung from your left shoulder to your right hip.
>
> You should wear rough strong clothing and a flannel shirt, preferably an olive drab shirt of the kind issued to soldiers.[11]

That last sentence should be taken as an indication that uniforms might be a little slow in making their way to Uncle Sam's newest soldiers.

In addition to this guidance, many had received a lot of great and not so great advice from the many books and pamphlets which were available. The pamphlets included "The Call to Arms: A Manual for Men Preparing for the National Army Camps" and "The Cantonment Manual" as well as several YMCA brochures and guides. From these books they received a number of helpful lists including one that was titled:

Ten "Be's" that will beat the Kaiser

1. Be clean.
2. Be properly clothed.
3. Be sure to eat nourishing food.
4. Be sure to sleep with lots of fresh air.
5. Be sure to get plenty of exercise daily.
6. Be sure to sleep eight hours every night, if possible.
7. Be sure to defecate daily.
8. Be ever busy, either with work or fun.
9. Be happy and look on the bright side of life.
10. Be ready with a smile to tackle any task set for you.[12]

There is little doubt that had the Kaiser and his generals known they would be facing an army of smiling, happy men who had eight hours sleep and defecated daily, they would have given up long before they did. Perhaps not. Nevertheless, most men did their best and tried to make the difficult transition from civilian to soldier as easily as possible.

To ensure that the camps were capable of receiving and processing the thousands of men who would be arriving at a National Army divisional training site, it was decided that only 5 percent of the selected men would be sent in the first wave. Using the first 5 percent as a test case, the camps were able to see where their internal systems worked or didn't work. It also meant that the camps now had an extra work force

2. What Is a Depot Brigade?

Nothing signifies the problems encountered in trying to quickly build a large army than this image of men using tree branches in place of rifles. These men are better off than others who had neither rifles nor uniforms and were required to wear their civilian clothes for the first few weeks in camp (private collection).

to help solve any of the problems which had been identified. With this early group now on site and hopefully the kinks worked out of the system, another 35 percent were then sent to camps. If this new influx of thousands of men didn't break the system, the rest of the men designated for training at the camp would then be sent in similar-sized increments. More often than not, even with this measured and systematic process, things could go horribly wrong.

Early in the war, most of the camps were sadly unprepared to issue the required uniforms and individual equipment for the arriving men. At Camp Funston, Kansas, camp officials found it was necessary to purchase large numbers of civilian denim overalls to give the men a semblance of a somewhat uniform appearance. At Funston and other camps, it was also necessary to make up for a shortage of rifles by issuing lumber or tree branches.[13] At many camps it was not unusual to see a wide mixture of uniforms and civilian clothes in a marching formation. Nor was it uncommon for field artillery soldiers to be seen practicing their crew drills using old Civil War or Spanish-American War cannons which had previous stood in front of small-town courthouses.

So, with all of the confusion flowing around the camps, what exactly was the mission of a depot brigade? The clearest explanation is this:

The purpose and function ... was to receive recruits sent by the various draft boards, clothe them, feed and house them and give them the various physical examinations and inoculations segregating the unfit ... and assigning the fit men to training battalions; to prepare all the preliminary records, make occupational and professional classification of men ... to organize development battalions for the purpose of rendering fit those men found temporarily unfit ... the assignment, distribution, and shipping of men to organizations and stations under orders from the War Department and to give such basic training to the recruit as time, circumstances, and exigencies of service permitted.[14]

With this wide spectrum of missions, it's no surprise that many depot brigades quickly ballooned in size, and most had several thousand men assigned. At most camps, the depot brigade was commanded by a brigadier general or a very senior colonel. Inside the brigade there would be a number of training battalions, each commanded by a colonel with a number of specialized training units and a staff of officers and enlisted men to function as instructors and administrative personnel.

Another common sight at all of the training camps: large numbers of men selected from the draft arriving by rail car and reporting for training. In this case the selectees are arriving at Camp Meade, Maryland, and soon will be processed by the 154th Depot Brigade (Library of Congress).

2. What Is a Depot Brigade?

Later a number of another new type of Army organization, the development battalion, would also be added to the depot brigade structure.

Taking each of the sub-missions of the depot brigade in turn, the complexity of the problem and the opportunity for confusion and chaos becomes obvious.

1. *Receive recruits sent by the various draft boards.* As noted earlier, the draft boards and the training camps were definitely not reading from the same playbook. From the previous examples, it is obvious that the tendency to send men who were unfit for service was an immediate problem at the camps. As a result, when men arrived at the camps in train carloads, it soon became the standard practice for medical staffs to perform an initial inspection before the men were allowed off the train. This allowed them to segregate any obviously sick or injured men and dispatch them immediately to the hospital. Later, with the arrival of Spanish flu, this preliminary check became doubly important as it would drive decisions about quarantining the men or allowing them to continue to the reception and administration sections in the camp.

2. *Clothe, feed, and house them.* If nothing else, the draftees (or soldiers being transferred from another camp) always came prepared with an appetite, expecting to be fed on arrival. At National Army training camps there were wooden barracks set aside for the newly arriving men. National Guard camps, for the most part, could only offer tents. Regardless, feeding and housing the new arrivals was a labor-intensive chore and required a number of staff just to make sure all arriving men were fed and given a place to bunk down. The YMCA representatives inside the depot brigade would assist in the clothing issue process. As each new soldier was being issued his uniform, he would be given a choice whether to have his civilian clothes sent home or turned over to a charity. Even this simple process created problems; the YMCA would have to retain the clothes on site for a while in case the man was rejected, injured, or failed during training. The rejected man in question would then have his clothes returned to him and his newly issued uniform taken away. Of course, all of this was predicated on the depot brigade having enough uniforms to issue. So many soldiers had been processed at Camp Lee by the 155th Depot Brigade in June 1918 that they simply had no uniforms to issue. A group of 500 selected men from the surrounding Virginia counties were being processed when they were told to remove their clothes, make a bundle secured with their belt, and place them in a large pile. After completing their physical examinations, they then had to dig back into the pile to find their own clothes. It proved to be quite a while before they would receive their uniforms.[15]

3. *Give them the various physical examinations and inoculations.* As noted earlier, a very rudimentary physical examination was often conducted before the men were in-processed. After the administrative process of checking them began, they would receive a more comprehensive physical. Among the diseases or conditions they were examined for included tuberculosis, syphilis, hernia, and hemorrhoids. Each depot brigade reception site was slightly different in arrangement, but the procedures were basically the same. The men were checked by a depot brigade dentist, and from there they were passed on to the "foot doctor, who made note of bunions, calluses, dislocated fetlocks, fallen arches, ingrowing nails, spavins, … and such other complications as came under his professional scrutiny."[16] They were fingerprinted and had their eyes, ears, noses, and throats examined. Taking into account that some selectees would not be able to read, the Army had prepared other vision charts beyond the standard alphabetic charts. Soldiers unable to identify letters were shown charts with drawings of different sized animals to prove their ability to see. Once the man had successfully identified a hen or a rooster, he was passed on to the next station.[17] Even something this simple became difficult and frustrating to the inductee and the administrator alike in many cases when foreign-born soldiers were given the animal chart to verify their vision. Few optometrists in the camps could speak enough Italian, Greek, Syrian, Latvian, Tagalog, or Pashtu to understand if the soldiers gave the right answer. And so on they went to the next station.

Those men who were found to have communicable or venereal diseases were immediately turned over to what were called "contact companies" for quarantine. Men fortunate not to have such medical issues were then moved on to the next station for inoculations. At this point they received a shot to protect them against typhus and a vaccination against smallpox. Many of the soldiers suffered very strong reactions to the shots and would be sick or have seepage flowing from the inoculation site for several days. One Elyria, Ohio, soldier wrote his mother:

> [W]e are under quarantine exspet [expect] to be able to go too different buildings in about 12 days and … they give us some dope in our supper Monday night that made us run all night to klean us out for the second shot. I am going over to the Hospital this afternoon to get a bandage around my arm where I got shot so the stuff oned [won't] stick to my shirt.[18]

4. *Prepare all the preliminary records.* The reception station in each depot brigade prepared a virtual paper storm of personnel forms to record the man's entrance into the Army. These included such important forms as the Form 88 S.G.O., which gave the soldier's tuberculosis status, venereal disease status, and the results of the physical examination,

the Form 637 Clothing Slip, and the Form 22–1 which records his date of entry into the service and his next of kin information. There were many more such forms, each requiring completion before the process could be completed and the man moved to the next station. Here again, the language problems with foreign-born soldiers are obvious. While having an Italian-born man list his uncle in Kenosha, Wisconsin, as his next of kin instead of his parents in Italy may not seem like much of a problem, if the soldier were killed in action or died of disease, it became an issue. As late as 1922, U.S. Army officials were still trying to determine the true next of kin and establish appropriate burial locations for some soldiers.[19]

5. *Make occupational and professional classification.* Each man would be questioned individually as to his education, marital status, civilian profession, or accomplishments as well as his possible preferences for a military assignment such as aviation, infantry, field artillery, etc. Obviously during this last part of the exam, the Army's needs would take precedence over the individual's desired job, but at times men were able to steer their path in a direction they preferred.

6. *Organize development battalions.* The conditions that drove the need for development battalions are so varied that they will be discussed

A unique portrait of three brothers serving together in the 151st Depot Brigade at Camp Devens. From left they are Private Harry W. Long, Sgt. Maj. Herman T. Long, and Sgt. Maj. Clifton A. Long. All three shared the same address in Springfield, Massachusetts, before the war and were sharing the same barracks at Devens. Herman, the eldest, was born in Canada before the family moved to the States and was a naturalized citizen (courtesy Library of Massachusetts).

later in great detail. For now, it is enough to say the longer the war went on, and the deeper the draft boards dove into the manpower pool, the greater was the need for the remedial services provided by these battalions.

7. *Assignment, distribution, and shipping of men to organizations and stations under orders from the War Department.* This simple requirement proved to be an incredible consumer of time and men as well as leading to much of the turmoil. The initial vision for building the U.S. Army was that each divisional training camp would receive enough men to build a 28,000-man division and then these units would deploy to France in an orderly fashion. That was the vision, but the reality came nowhere near it. Constant requests from the War Department to identify and transfer specialists such as linguists, carpenters, electricians, telephone linemen, automotive mechanics, heavy equipment operators, etc., reduced the number of men in camps. These were followed by orders to send five hundred men to this training camp or that transit camp, usually on short notice. It got worse. As some of the divisions began to deploy to France in early spring of 1918, the number of men being transferred was often in the thousands. The 82nd Division was training at Camp Gordon, Georgia, in late 1917 when almost all of the original troops were transferred out to support other divisions and left only a cadre around which the division had to be rebuilt. And where did these replacements come from? Although some were new draftees, others were transferred in from Camps Devens, Dix, Upton, Lee, and Meade. In March 1918 another five thousand men were transferred in from Camps Dodge, Travis, Devens, Gordon, and Upton. Among these replacements were 1,400 enemy aliens who had to be discharged.[20]

The 161st Depot Brigade at Camp Grant, Illinois, was tasked with raising and training the 86th Division. After three months of solid instruction, and just as the unit was beginning to work as a team, orders were received to transfer 5,400 soldiers to the 33rd Division. Three of the infantry regiments in the 86th were required to transfer 1,100 soldiers each. Shortly thereafter another 2,000 were transferred to Camp Pike, Arkansas. In February 1918 another 4,000 were transferred to the 4th Division, a Regular Army unit training at Camp Greene, North Carolina. The next month came with orders to send 8,000 more to fill up the 33rd Division still in training in Texas.[21] It was equally bad at Camp Meade, Maryland, and perhaps even worse. The 79th Division, supported by the 154th Depot Brigade, later reported that of the approximately 95,000 men who arrived for training at Camp Meade, only 27,000 would eventually be retained by the unit when it deployed. Of the soldiers who did eventually go to France with the division, some

2. What Is a Depot Brigade?

Not newly drafted men, these soldiers arriving at Camp Gordon, Georgia, have been transferred from another camp. For better or for worse they will now be the responsibility of the 157th Depot Brigade to examine, test, feed, clothe, and billet until they can be assigned to a unit (private collection).

15,000 had arrived at Camp Meade so shortly before the 79th departed they could be considered almost untrained. As the 79th's Division history later stated:

> The reasons lying behind the wholesale raids upon Camp Meade for men are much in dispute. Whether it was failure of the volunteer system, failure of the cantonment builders to meet contract time, failure of the War Department to call sufficient men to the colors in the beginning, or lack of vision....[22]

Regardless of the cause, the effect was obvious. Making it particularly distressing was that both the 79th and 82nd Divisions were destined to serve as combat divisions in the AEF. The 76th and 83rd Divisions suffered similar "raids" while in the States but were turned into depot divisions when they arrived in France. This negated some of the effect on these divisions since they were used to provide replacements for the front lines, but the cost to soldiers' morale and unit cohesion is obvious.

The overall effect of this constant movement between camps was chaos. A depot brigade would be handling large numbers of men coming into the camp at the same time large numbers were leaving. Gathering all of the appropriate paperwork per man, generated by the reception process as noted above, to accompany the transfer was impossible and men became lost in the system. With the already-noted tendency for camps to include their problem soldiers when they were ordered to transfer some men, these "problems" would sometimes be passed from camp to camp.

Unfortunately, there was an even worse result than chaos. When the most virulent wave of Spanish flu arrived in September 1918, the wholesale transfers of men from camp to camp carried with them the epidemic. Men who had appeared healthy while departing Camp Custer, Michigan, would be deathly ill when their train arrived at Camp Pike. Doctors and nurses working in the depot brigade hospitals would often find themselves as sick as their recently arrived patients.

8. *Give basic training to the recruit as time, circumstances, and exigencies of service permitted.* With all of the other mission requirements listed above, there often was little time to provide basic training to the new inductees. However, the brigades and their training battalions did as best they could. Obviously, the National Guard camps had a big advantage since so many of the soldiers in Guard units had already received some training in their home state as well as practical experience on the Mexican Border. It was because of this advantage that the first three divisions raised in the United States and deployed to France were all National Guard units: the 26th, 41st, and 42nd.

Emblematic of the National Guard units reporting to their training camps in the South, this group of New York Guardsmen from Tonawanda display a wide variety of hats, shirts, and coats as they pose for their unit picture (NYSDMNA).

2. What Is a Depot Brigade? 37

A typical sight early in the training phase for these depot brigade soldiers; while four of the soldiers have been issued uniforms, the fifth only has a hat. Although he knows how to salute, he hasn't learned yet where to hold his left arm while saluting (private collection).

So, what then was a depot brigade? In theory it was a facilitator of divisional training at the thirty-two main camps. In reality, it was everything listed above and so much more. It acted as the funnel through which men passed to be assigned to units and also the place they would be cared for if they were hurt in training or sick from the flu. It managed their records and retained their civilian clothing until they were either deployed or discharged. To the men who served as staff, instructors, or commanders of the units of the depot brigades, it was perdition. Anxious to get to France and show their military talents, many would instead spend the war teaching new recruits how to salute and march.

With the Armistice signed on 11 November 1918, the War Department, mainly in the person of the Army Chief of Staff, General Peyton March, flipped the switch and the funnel changed directions. Most inbound groups of inductees were halted, turned around, and sent home. Instead of trying to get men physically fit and ready to serve in the AEF, the camps now focused on getting them healthy so they could be demobilized and sent home. This meant discharging as many men as soon as possible to prepare the camps for the arrival of the victorious troops returning from France.

In the following chapter, we will visit all the depot brigades and all of the major training camps to understand the unique conditions at each. Some readers may question why there was such a rush to discharge

Barreled Beef

Mess Chuck Beef   Corned Beef   Rolled Boneless Beef

Soaps and Washing Powder

Wool Soap   Swift's Pride Soap   Swift's White Laundry Soap
Maxine Elliott Buttermilk Soap   Raven Tar Soap
Castile   Sunbrite Cleanser
Swift's Pride Washing Powder

What it takes to Feed an Army

This table shows the approximate quantity of the different food articles tabulated to feed 100 men.

Articles	Quantity per 100 Rations (1 meal per 100 men)
Boiled Ham	35 lbs.
Veal Loaf	30 lbs.
Corned Beef	40 lbs.
Dried Beef	30 lbs.
Sausage	35 lbs.
Bacon	25 lbs.
Eggs	17 doz.
Salmon	25 cans
Tomatoes	10 cans
Sauer Kraut	5 gallons
Corn	16 No. 2 cans
Peas	17 No. 2 cans
Asparagus	25 No. 2 cans
Peaches	12 cans
Strawberries	12 cans
Pineapple	12 cans
Apple Butter	7 lbs.
Peanut Butter	5 lbs.
Mince Meat (25 pies)	12 lbs.

The above furnishes an idea of the food requirements for one meal for 100 men. What it would require for 30 days to feed 40,000 men runs into stupendous and interesting figures. We are quoting the approximate requirements for this number of men:

Bacon	180,000 pounds
Flour	1,404,320 pounds
Hard Bread	60,000 pounds
Baking Powder	6,505 cans

One of the persuasive reasons for quickly demobilizing soldiers at the end of the war can be seen in this 1918 chart which shows the massive amount of food required to feed the American soldiers (private collection).

2. What Is a Depot Brigade?   39

the men in the camps so quickly and return the AEF to the States. Simply put, it was a financially driven consideration. A four-million-soldier army, such as the U.S. Army in November 1918, consumed twelve million meals a day. It wore four million coats and four million pairs of gloves and required at least eight million pairs of shoes. The amounts of ammunition, clothing, and equipment needed to support the AEF during the fighting in France from June to November 1918 are staggering. Staff members in the Services of Supply estimated it was handling some 51 pounds of supplies a day for each soldier serving in France.[23] It was further estimated that an enlisted soldier required a new overcoat every five months, a new blanket, shirt, and breeches every two months, a new service coat every 79 days, new shoes and woolen leggings every 51 days, new underwear every 34 days, and new socks every 23 days.[24]

Much of this materiel had to be transported across the Atlantic at another cost for ships, fuel, and sailors. Multiply these numbers by the two million men in France, and the need for speed in downsizing the Army is obvious. Even with the end of hostilities, the 250,000 soldiers who were sent to the German Rhineland for occupation duty kept the supply requirement high and required the transportation of most of their supplies from France to Germany. So added to the depot brigades' mission list was the requirement to demobilize units and discharge soldiers after the Armistice was signed. With all these tasks in mind, it is time to visit the brigades.

3

Depot Brigades by the Numbers

"There was at the outset some inevitable crossing of purposes and duplication of effort, and perhaps there may have been some disappointment that a more instantaneous use could not be made of all this wealth of willingness and patriotic spirit."[1]

When the War Department made the decision to establish thirty-two divisional training sites throughout the country, it had to take a number of factors into consideration. First and foremost was that some camp space was going to be required to assemble and train the regiments of the Regular Army divisions. Similarly, it was important to keep the training camps somewhat regionally based to minimize as much as possible any large-scale movement of soldiers around the country. Railroad capacity and assets were almost as jealously guarded as ocean shipping assets since much of the country depended on rail shipments for their food and coal. Unfortunately, while the camps were regionally based, the haphazard and seemingly random rail movement around the country of troops to fill gaps in deploying units continued right up until the end of the war. Finally, and perhaps most importantly, the War Department expected the National Army divisions would require a longer training period than the Regular Army or the National Guard divisions. The intuitively obvious reason for the longer National Army training period was that many of the Regular Army and National Guard divisions already had a number of trained soldiers in their ranks. Too, the time spent on the Mexican border had gone a long way to preparing those soldiers for arduous campaigning. Conversely, for the National Army divisions, the manpower pool was expected to come almost entirely from the draft which meant the men designated to serve in these units would show up to training camps with little or no prior military experience.

3. Depot Brigades by the Numbers

In addition to the soldiers who were to be trained at each division's training site, each camp had a depot brigade assigned. As we have seen, the depot brigade was designed to support the operation of the camp as well as serve as a reception station for arriving inductees and as a manpower pool for the divisional units in training. This ready source of replacements was important. Measured by today's standards, the number of soldiers killed or hurt in the stateside training camps was shocking. Even before the terrible waves of Spanish flu swept through the stateside training sites, the Army averaged a daily death rate of between fifteen and twenty soldiers from all manner of accidents, sicknesses, and even murder.[2]

Some of the accidental deaths were almost freakish in nature. Private Alfiero Olivelli, a 27-year-old butcher originally from Grosseto, Italy, died at Camp Devens after falling on ice and hitting his head. Another soldier at the same camp died from being accidentally bayonetted during training.[3] An unexpected fatal accident occurred at Camp Wadsworth where the New York National Guard units were training. A group of Wadsworth's soldiers were travelling to a nearby town in a

A typical scene at many of the training camps in the late summer/early autumn of 1917: long lines of recently inducted men arriving by train and making the trek to the receiving station. This is one of a series of photographs taken at Camp Custer, Michigan; the men in this photograph would have been introduced to the U.S. Army by the waiting staff of the 160th Depot Brigade (private collection).

military truck to put on a minstrel show. Unfortunately, the recent rains had softened the shoulder of the road, and the truck slid off, plummeting sixty feet down a hillside. Two of the soldiers were killed, and the other eighteen were hurt.[4] At Camp Bowie, Texas, nine soldiers were killed and another seven were wounded when a soldier attempted to load the wrong caliber shell into a mortar, causing it to explode.[5] Drownings, falls, barracks fires, airplane crashes, automobile accidents, and supposedly unloaded weapons also contributed to the daily death toll.

Among the many types of units assigned to the depot brigade were the communications detachments required to maintain the camp's telephone and telegraph system. Also in the brigade were the camp's firefighting units, the machine shops, provost guard company, ordnance depot, and some labor battalions. Most important, however, were the reception units which were organized to receive the incoming troops and prepare them for their eventual assignment. As we have seen, newly arrived draftees would be first assigned to a camp's depot brigade after their arrival for a check-in process, a physical exam, an initial issue of clothing and some rudimentary training before being forwarded to a unit in the division. Though often referred to as the "Spare Parts Brigade," the depot brigade served a critical mission. As each division in training was constantly losing men due to medical disqualification, sickness, or accident, the depot brigades were structured to quickly provide replacement soldiers.

These three well-dressed soldiers are assigned the 414th Engineer Depot Detachment in the 160th Depot Brigade at Camp Custer, Michigan. With winter hats and long overcoats, they appear to be prepared for duty in the worst of weather (courtesy John Adams-Graf).

3. Depot Brigades by the Numbers

By February 1918 an Army General Staff study determined that the current personnel methods were not keeping up with the manpower demands of the divisions in training and the AEF in France. A plan was developed to turn some of the National Army camps into combat arms

Private Constantino Diorazio of the 151st Depot Brigade at Camp Devens poses in front of what appears to be an elaborate three-dimensional studio prop representing a large railroad artillery piece (Connecticut War Service records via Ancestry.com).

training centers. The training at these camps would be restricted solely to basic field artillery and infantry tasks. The replacements needed in France would then be drawn from this pool of trained soldiers. The plan had to wait to be executed until the divisions already training at these sites had deployed overseas. As a result, it was never fully put into effect.

What follows is a synopsis of each of the depot brigades. Just like the divisions they supported, the depot brigades followed a strict numbering system. At the National Army camps, they started numbering at 151 in New England, working southward and westward until designating the 166th Depot Brigade at Camp Lewis, Washington. Clustered primarily in the South, the National Guard camps started with the 51st Depot Brigade at Camp Greene and ended with the 65th Depot Brigade at Camp Kearny, California. At some National Guard camps, the units performing the mission did not use the "depot brigade" designation and conducted their operations as camp staff. Nevertheless, on the Army Order of Battle and Table of Organization, the number and designation for each camp were assigned.

National Army Camps. For the most part the depot brigades assigned to the National Army training camps followed a fairly standard table of organization. As should be expected, the bigger camps had larger depot brigades with as many training and reception battalions as needed to meet the requirements. In most of the camps these units remained racially segregated; men serving in "colored" training battalions or development battalions would be transferred strictly to "colored" units. As time passed, most of the depot brigades at National Army camps continued to grow in size and function. This is, as

Posing for a portrait is Alexander McLea, who served in the 9th Battalion of the 151st Depot Brigade at Camp Devens. Before being drafted McLea worked as a bookkeeper at the International Purchasing Company in Boston (courtesy Library of Massachusetts).

Private Peter Grischuk, also a 151st Depot Brigade soldier, poses in front of another elaborately-painted backdrop. Grischuk's use of woolen-wrap leggings allows this portrait to be dated to the late-war or post-war period (Connecticut War Service records via Ancestry.com).

will be seen, in stark contrast to the depot brigades that were organized at National Guard training camps.

151st Depot Brigade—Camp Devens, Massachusetts

Camp Devens was established in 1917 on 5,000 acres of land near the towns of Ayer, Harvard, Lancaster, and Shirley. The camp was located only thirty miles from Boston and was noted for having the lowest average daily temperature of any of the National Army camps. Devens was the second smallest of the National Army camps, due more to scarcity of land in the congested New England countryside than any other factor. The construction of the camp began almost immediately with declaration of war. The building effort used the largest labor force ever assembled in Massachusetts at that time to hurriedly construct an entire city for the troops soon to arrive. The soldiers needed barracks, mess halls, post offices, administrative buildings, and classrooms as well as a complete water and sewer system. The construction crews built an average of ten buildings a day until the camp was completed.

The 151st was organized in August 1917 and remained active until May 1919. Almost immediately after it was organized, soldiers from the 76th Division, primarily draftees from the New England states, began to show up and needed accommodations. Very quickly six training battalions were established in the 151st Depot Brigade to handle the influx of trainees. The personnel for the 1st Training Battalion were from New York State while the 2nd and 3rd Training Battalions were filled with men from Connecticut. Massachusetts provided the men for the 4th, 5th, and 6th Training Battalions.[6] Later, six more training battalions and four development battalions were established. At this point, it was determined the initial mission of the depot brigade was to provide military training for the new arrivals. Only after the divisional units began to take shape would the depot brigade also focus on maintaining a manpower pool and providing replacements for those units.

Camp Devens was the first of the large National Army camps to complete its construction, and on the night of 30 August 1917 turned on the electrical grid which provided light to all of the buildings to signify the camp was ready. The newly electrified camp included 199 company-sized barracks, 74 officers' barracks, and hundreds of other buildings that would serve as regimental, brigade, and divisional headquarters, warehouses, hospital facilities, and recreational buildings. It was an amazing accomplishment.

There was some unsettling news in September 1917 when it was

3. Depot Brigades by the Numbers

announced that some conscientious objectors would soon be sent to Camp Devens and they would also have to be received and supported by the 151st. At the same time, just thirteen days after they had arrived, some 500 men were transferred from the camp to the 26th Division which was headed to France in a matter of days. That group was followed shortly by 75 more men who had not even been issued uniforms and had to join the 26th Division wearing civilian clothes. It was a sign of things to come where the depot brigades would transfer or receive large numbers of soldiers in order to respond to another unit's manpower requirements.[7] Later another 8,000 soldiers were transferred from Camp Devens to Camp Gordon, Georgia, to fill out the 82nd Division.

By mid–October there were over twenty thousand soldiers training at Camp Devens, and the 151st had set up the first six training courses. The classes, the first of many more to follow, were primarily for the men who would be caring for the draft animals of the division and the saddles and harnesses they would require. Yet the need to dispatch soldiers to support other divisions continued, outpacing the 151st's ability to provide replacements. In one large levy of 1,775 soldiers sent to Camp Greene, North Carolina, some 500 came directly from the 151st Depot Brigade. Of the first 40,000 men assigned to the 76th Division, 151st Depot Brigade, and the Camp Devens Headquarters, 15,000 were transferred elsewhere, many to units in the process of deploying to France. To

Another soldier in the 151st Depot Brigade, Ulysses Whitford was a farmer from Ticonderoga, New York. Whitford was serving in 1st Battalion of the Depot Brigade until February 1918 when he was sent to France to serve in the Headquarters Battalion of the General Headquarters at Chaumont. In this portrait he is wearing a USNA collar disk for the National Army (courtesy Library of Massachusetts).

replace them, more draftees were sent to Devens, and two thousand African American troops were assigned to serve in labor battalions in the camp.[8]

Another claimant on the soldiers of the 151st was an experimental training program designed to develop non-commissioned officers (NCOs) at a faster pace. Twenty of the best soldiers in each of the 52 companies in the 151st were selected to receive intensive leadership and unit management training. The program was deemed a success as the selected men were judged to have become high-quality NCOs. The downside was obvious; removing twenty of the best soldiers from each company in the brigade meant other soldiers' workloads increased significantly while quality of training and administration suffered.[9] Camp Devens' busiest three-month period, August through October 1918, also coincided with the worst period of the Spanish flu on post and was reflected in the sickness and death rates among the Doughboys there.[10]

The 76th Division started to deploy to France in July 1918 and was converted to a depot division on arrival. It became an in-theater source for providing replacements to other units. What remained of the division returned to the States in December 1918 and was demobilized on 14 January 1919 at Camp Devens. The three field artillery

Armed with a .45 caliber revolver, this unidentified lieutenant strikes a business-like pose in front of the door of 7th Company, 152nd Depot Brigade, at Camp Upton, New York. He appears to be wearing one of the M1907 cold weather caps, perhaps giving an indication of how cold it can get on Long Island during the winter months (courtesy John Adams-Graf).

3. Depot Brigades by the Numbers

units returned much later, during the summer of 1919. Camp Devens was a separation and demobilization center for over 150,000 troops on their return from France. In addition to the returning men, those men still in the 151st's development battalions were quickly demobilized and sent to their homes.

While that effort was underway, the 151st received orders to reduce its complement from thirteen battalions to four. The staff was allowed to retain the best soldiers from each unit as their skills would be needed to efficiently manage the 151st's new reception and demobilizing mission. Among the first to arrive from overseas were a large number of wounded men who would remain in the care of the 151st Depot Brigade until healthy enough to return to their homes. The initial arrivals were followed a short time later by thousands of others including the New England National Guardsmen of the 26th Division. The 151st took it all in stride and set the record by discharging

A group of hardworking NCOs from the 152nd Depot Brigade at Camp Upton take a break and pose for a group photograph. It is interesting to note that several of the men have work gloves while two of the men in front are wearing rubber overshoes, and the seated man in the center is cradling a bugle in his lap. Camp Upton had the reputation of being excessively muddy due to the rainy climate and intensive brush cutting and ground clearing was needed to build the site (NYSDMNA).

some 9,000 Guardsmen from the nearby states in a single day. The 151st did their best to work themselves out of a job, and the size of the camp continued to shrink. Before long, the stream of returning soldiers dwindled to a trickle. The African American labor battalions were demobilized and sent southward to their homes. These hard-working soldiers were replaced by a detachment of military prisoners who were transferred to Devens to provide labor support to the brigade until they too were unneeded and so returned to their military prison in New York.[11]

152nd Depot Brigade—Camp Upton, New York

Camp Upton was located near the town of Yaphank on Long Island in Suffolk County, New York. It was almost exactly halfway between Brooklyn and Montauk Point and was also near Camp Mills, a transit camp. The 152nd Depot Brigade was organized in August 1917 and remained active until May 1919. During the hectic and confusing early days after the declaration of war, the 152nd found itself not only supporting the organization of the 77th Division, but also serving as the transit camp for the early-deploying 42nd Division. This dual mission is reflected in the 152nd's unique structure. However, before they could focus on these missions, there were problems. Despite the many rules and precautions in place to prevent inducting enemy aliens into the Army, some draft boards insisted on sending German, Austro-Hungarian, Turkish, and Bulgarian men to the training camps. Although a large number of these men were quite willing to join the U.S. military and fight against their native countries, others were not; nevertheless, off to camp both groups went. Camp Upton quickly realized they had a problem in January 1918 when Federal agents showed up at the camp and arrested five Austrian-born men. Among the five were Josef Brien and Josef Stonitsch, both serving in the 152nd Depot Brigade. It appears all five of the men arrested had been "objects of suspicion for several weeks and some of them had been outspoken in their sympathies for the Central Powers." The five were removed from camp and taken to a detention center on Ellis Island.[12]

Almost immediately after the camp was opened, four training groups were established in the 152nd. These were followed in quick succession by two provisional training regiments and twenty training battalions. In June 1918, the 152nd added six development battalions to meet the need for specialized training or medical care for newly arrived

3. Depot Brigades by the Numbers

draftees. While most camps had to make do with mockup tanks to teach the soldiers about the use of armored vehicles, Upton was one of the few camps to receive a real British tank. The British tank crew used it to provide instruction in the tank's ability to cross trenches and defensive positions. By August 1918 there were some 18,000 soldiers assigned to the 152nd making it probably the largest depot brigade in the U.S. Army. One result of growing so large was that the 152nd was required to dispatch a number of its soldiers to other posts to fill out combat units getting ready to deploy.

Unfortunately, in the late summer and early fall the first waves of the Spanish flu were also riding the rails with the men. Among them was Antonio Destito, an Italian-born tailor who was living in Rochester, New York, when he was drafted. Shortly after being transferred from the 152nd to Camp Dix, New Jersey, Destito contracted the flu and died in September 1918, just four months after joining the Army. Even more poignant was the story of another Italian-born soldier, Antonio Nuccitelli. Born near Rome and a veteran of three years in the Italian Army, Private Nuccitelli was inducted into the U.S. Army in June 1918 and assigned to the 152nd Depot Brigade. He served in several of the 152nd's medical units until finally being assigned to Company G of the Medical Detachment in the Brigade. During December 1918 he contracted bronchial pneumonia and died the day after Christmas. On learning of Antonio's illness, his brother John travelled to Camp Upton to help care for him. While there he also contracted pneumonia

Italian-born Antonio Nuccitelli had already served three years in the Italian Army before coming to the United States and being drafted in June 1918. He was serving in the 152nd Depot Brigade's Medical Detachment when he became sick with bronchial pneumonia and died in December 1918 (*World War Service Record of Rochester*).

and died seven days after his brother. A third brother, Peter Nuccitelli, was still serving in France in the 335th Field Artillery Regiment, not returning to the United States until March 1919.[13]

153rd Depot Brigade–Camp Dix, New Jersey

Camp Dix was located approximately sixteen miles south of Trenton, New Jersey. The camp was designated as the training site for National Army soldiers from New York State (excluding those from the New York City metropolitan area who were assigned to Camp Upton) and Northern Pennsylvania. When construction was completed in June 1917 there were 1,414 buildings with a capacity of housing 42,806 soldiers. At times during the late summer of 1918, the camp had 54,000 soldiers crowded into its barracks. As a result, when the Spanish flu epidemic reached Camp Dix, it was passed quickly from unit to unit due to the overcrowding. It became necessary to convert eighteen barracks buildings into a hospital annex to care for the sick and dying Doughboys.[14]

The 153rd Depot Brigade was organized in August 1917 and was one of the first such brigades activated. Six training battalions were organized in September to handle the early influx of soldiers to the camp. Over the following months six more battalions and three provisional training regiments were organized and placed under the command of the 153rd. One of the soldiers serving in the 153rd was Canadian–born Charles Rose who had been working and living near Watertown, New York, when the draft was implemented. Reporting to Camp Dix in November 1917, he later wrote his mother to tell her that he had passed his physical exam while three of the other men from his group had failed and were "thrown out." He mentioned he had run into an old friend, Andrew Jackson Sipley, also serving in the 153rd who already had a uniform and appeared to like being at Camp Dix. In the letter, Rose also expressed his concern that because there were so many soldiers at the camp he didn't know where they were all going to stay.[15]

The 9th and 12th Training Battalions were converted to development battalions in June and August 1918, respectively. The 11th Training Battalion was transferred to Camp Wheeler, Georgia, in October 1918. After the Armistice, Camp Dix was designated as a demobilization station. The 153rd and the camp staff were responsible for demobilizing some 316,500 soldiers.

154th Depot Brigade—Camp Meade, Maryland

Although initially called Camp Annapolis Junction, the post was soon known by its permanent name: Camp Meade Cantonment and Field Signal School but was usually shortened to just Camp Meade. The camp was very big, covering some thirty square miles. The camp was nowhere near completion when the first soldiers—assigned to the 79th Division—began to arrive, but it soon took on the bustle and noise of all the other camps being built. By the time construction was completed and the first wave of trainees arrived, the camp was the second largest city in the state, surpassed only by Baltimore. After it expanded in size, it enveloped the nearby Signal Corps training site, Camp Franklin. Together the two camps had more than 2,000 buildings with a total troop capacity of 53,830.[16]

The 154th Depot Brigade was organized in September 1917 and continued to operate until May 1919. By the end of the war, it was comprised of twelve training battalions and six development battalions. Three of the training battalions were converted to development battalions in September to meet the specialized needs of many of the new arriving inductees. All of the other development battalions were also organized in September 1918.

On 28 August 1918, one of the newly arrived draftees wrote home to his sister in Succasunna, New Jersey, to tell her of his experience in the 154th Depot Brigade on arrival:

> I ate more for supper tonight than I have at any meal before. This morning I got my uniform and outfit which was as follows 2 uniforms (shirt and pants), 1 hat, 1 pr shoes Size 8½ ... 3 suits of underwear, 1 pr leggings, 1 coat blouse, 1 rain coat, 4 pr of socks, 1 pr overalls & jumper (Blue), 1 tooth brush ... 1 military brush, 1 cake of soap.[17]

This bounty of uniforms does give some evidence that the Army supply system was finally up to speed and providing much more to the incoming men than the first soldiers had received. Nevertheless, this same soldier still found something to complain about; his shoes were too big and he "can turn right round in them without touching the sides."

Another soldier, Sergeant W.S. Warren, assigned to the 154th Depot Brigade's 3rd Training Battalion, was more concerned with his chances of going to France. In September 1918, he wrote a friend asking if he had news of Charles, Frederick, and Joe:

> have they gone over[?] You know I am beginning to get ashamed for being here so long. I am anxious to get across. All my friends are over ... they [have] a song down here "Mother take down the service flag, I'm in the

Depot Brigade." Of course they need us [here] but they are going to get cripples to fill our place & give the old men [i.e., longer-serving men] a chance to get over [to France].[18]

155th Depot Brigade—Camp Lee, Virginia

The 155th Depot Brigade was organized in September 1917 and remained active until May 1919. During its peak operation period in late 1918 the 155th was comprised of 25 training battalions, five provisional training battalions, and four development battalions. Three of the development battalions were organized in the summer of 1918 and one in November of the same year.

Camp Lee was the second largest of the National Army sites. It was smaller in size and population only to Camp Lewis, Washington, and could accommodate 49,721 men. It contained 1,532 buildings. In population, Camp Lee was the third largest city in the state of Virginia. During July 1918, the camp's busiest month, more than 57,000 soldiers were on post, almost 8,000 more than were planned for or expected.[19]

Officers and enlisted men assigned to the 155th Depot Brigade

From the 155th Depot Brigade, by way of Wolf Glade, Virginia, is the service record of Thomas Hanks. Hanks, inducted into the Army in June 1918, was apparently hurt while in training and was discharged with a 20 percent disability on 7 November 1918 (Virginia National Guard).

3. Depot Brigades by the Numbers 55

came from varied backgrounds. Nathan R. Smith, for instance, actually started his military career in the Maryland National Guard as a member of Battery A, Maryland Light Artillery. After service on the Mexican border with that unit, he was assigned to the 313th Infantry Regiment, 79th Division, which was being organized and trained at Camp Meade, Maryland. Shortly thereafter he was promoted to sergeant. Smith was selected to attend the Officers Training Course at Meade and on completion was transferred to 9th Battalion of the 155th Depot Brigade at Camp Lee until June 1918. He was promoted to 1st Lieutenant in July and transferred to the 12th Battalion of the 155th. He remained there until he was demobilized in December 1918.[20]

After the 37th Division, comprised primarily of Ohio National Guardsmen, completed their training at Camp Hancock, Georgia, the

A section of a larger photograph showing the tent city occupied by soldiers of the 156th Depot Brigade at Camp Jackson, South Carolina. Since Camp Jackson was a National Army training site, the majority of soldiers assigned there lived in buildings, but as the size of the depot brigade and the soldier population grew, it became necessary to use tents for some of the troops (Library of Congress).

infantry and engineer regiments were transferred for a short training period to Camp Lee. On 14 June 1918, the 37th put on a divisional review with all of its soldiers taking part. Not to be outdone, many of the recently arrived draftees in the 155th Depot Brigade also marched in the review. As one participant later wrote:

> The Depot Brigade marched, too; not with the aplomb of the Ohioans, to be sure, but with just as much pride.... Many of the men were wearing the clothes in which they had come to camp.... In a column of platoons, the Depot Brigade, fifteen thousand strong, advanced on the level surface of the parade ground. The recruits carried no rifles ... no colors and no drums ... [but] they were determined to show that after only two weeks of drilling they could perform like the warriors they hoped to be.[21]

Presiding over the parade from the reviewing stand were Major General Charles Farnsworth, commander of the 37th Division, and Assistant Secretary of War Benedict Crowell, representing Secretary of War Newton Baker. Very shortly thereafter, the 155th Depot Brigade received a large influx of uniforms, hats, and boots, perhaps in response to the civilian clothes worn in the parade.

156th Depot Brigade—Camp Jackson, South Carolina

Although the 156th Depot Brigade was not officially organized at Camp Jackson until September 1917, four provisional regiments were formed at the camp in July to handle the earliest arriving soldiers. Ultimately there would be twelve training battalions serving in the 156th along with eight development battalions. Several of these would be dispatched to nearby Camp Sevier, South Carolina, in September 1918 to support operations there. At least two of the training battalions, the 11th and 12th, were designated specifically for African American soldiers.

After the 81st Division left the camp to deploy to France, the focus of training at Camp Jackson turned to field artillery instruction and even included a temporary airfield for aerial observation training.[22]

157th Depot Brigade—Camp Gordon, Georgia

The 157th was organized in September 1917 and remained active until May 1919. During its existence it was comprised of thirteen training battalions and two development battalions. The 82nd Division was organized at Camp Gordon in August 1917, and most of the original soldiers were inductees from southern states. After just six weeks of training, most of these men were transferred away to fill manpower gaps in National Guard divisions. Starting over, the 157th received 28,000 replacements from Camps Devens, Dix, Upton, Lee, and Meade. Of these men, it was noted that at least 20 percent were foreign-born, many of whom could not read, write, or speak English. While this percentage of foreign-born soldiers was actually the average across the Army, it appears that the other training camps had taken advantage of this opportunity to include a large number of enemy aliens in the transfer process. The 82nd Division's history recounted that after their arrival, this "confusion of races and speech was eventually modified by the elimination of confessed enemy aliens, the transfer to the Depot Brigade of suspicious cases," and the startup of language schools.[23]

The arrival of 5,000 more replacements from other camps and more draftees in March 1918 helped make up the manpower shortages. As it was, the 157th was responsible for discharging over 1,400 enemy aliens from the Army. By April the 82nd Division began the process of moving to the transit camps on the East Coast and then on to France.

By August 1918 Camp Gordon had been designated as an infantry replacement training camp. Two months later, in October, the training battalions were converted to receiving battalions but kept their original numerical designation. Some of the new renamed receiving battalions were transferred to Camp McClellan, Alabama, because many of the soldiers who had been assigned to the depot brigade there had been rolled back into their original National Guard units when the 29th Division departed for France. The 157th was designated as a reception site for treatment of medical, surgical, and venereal cases returning from overseas.[24] The 157th was also responsible for the demobilization of 116,228 soldiers after the Armistice.

158th Depot Brigade—Camp Sherman, Ohio

Camp Sherman was located three miles northwest of Chillicothe, Ohio. After completion, the camp was the third largest training camp in the nation. It was named after William Tecumseh Sherman, a native Ohioan and Civil War general. Construction began in July 1917. Over the next few months more than forty thousand soldiers received training at the 11,802-acre camp. Sherman was designated the initial training site and home to the 83rd Division.[25]

The 158th Depot Brigade was organized in August 1917 and remained in operation until May 1919. The first soldiers and instructors arrived on 5 September 1917. Almost immediately, the 158th established twelve training battalions to prepare for the expected large flood of draftees coming primarily from Ohio, Pennsylvania, and Tennessee. It was a wise move as very quickly the camp received more and more men to be trained. Construction was continuing even as the men arrived. Maintaining a standard barracks building design paid off when "it was reported that a barracks was completed every twenty minutes."[26] This amazing construction feat was made possible by having the construction workers divided into groups with each having a set function. This allowed one group to lay footers for a building and move to the next while a following group laid down the floor. These in turn were followed by the wall-building team and then the roofers. By the time construction was finished, there were some 1,528 buildings on the site. Adding a degree of difficulty, out of respect for some of the Native American burial mounds on the site, the builders deviated from the original building plan. By changing some of the locations or building orientations, it was possible to avoid damage to the mounds.[27]

What couldn't be avoided was the Spanish flu. With thousands of soldiers packed into overcrowded barracks, the flu and its associated diseases struck down thousands of soldiers at the camp in the autumn of 1918. When the final tally was made, over 1,200 had died, 689 of them in the week of 4 to 11 October alone.

Adding complexity to the mission of the 158th Depot Brigade, some one hundred German sailors whose ships had been interned at U.S. ports arrived at the camp in July 1917 and required housing in a secure compound. They were joined in November by another hundred

The only Germans many of the soldiers in Camp Sherman's 158th Depot Brigade ever saw were the captured sailors from submarines and interned ships. Here a guard detachment keeps a careful watch on the prisoners during a work detail (courtesy Brian Stewart).

also requiring housing and supervision. These prisoners remained at Camp Sherman until September 1919 when they were transferred to Georgia for repatriation to Germany.[28]

With the signing of the Armistice, Camp Sherman received notification to reorganize as a demobilization site. Almost immediately the 158th began to demobilize the soldiers still in training to make room for an influx of soldiers returning from France. The 158th Depot Brigade was also receiving injured and wounded men who required care beyond simple demobilization. The 158th kept some ten thousand men in four training battalions (primarily to continue camp functions and post security) and two development battalions. These development battalions had the mission of providing vocational training for the wounded or injured soldiers in the hospital facilities.[29]

159th Depot Brigade—Camp Taylor, Kentucky

The 159th was organized in August 1917 and remained active until May 1919. The first draftees began to arrive in early September 1917, and by November there were almost 25,000 men in the camp. By the summer of 1918 it had also received the missions to conduct field artillery training for officer candidates and to function as a replacement center. The camp was also unique in that it home to the school for Army chaplains; it was one of the very few integrated schools in the Army.

Some of the training battalions were reorganized several times, some keeping their original designation while others changed. There were three development battalions organized in June and August 1918. Two of these were shut down in October 1918 and the third transferred to Camp Beauregard, Louisiana.

With the signing of the Armistice, the 159th switched from training to demobilizing, but as late as mid–December 1918 some men drafted just before the Armistice were still showing up and requiring support from the 159th for food and lodging. From December 1918 to May 1919, the 159th Depot Brigade demobilized more than 150,000 soldiers.[30]

160th Depot Brigade—Camp Custer, Michigan

Camp Custer was located in Michigan's Kalamazoo and Calhoun counties. It was named after the Civil War Union Army's famous cavalry officer and Michigan native General George Armstrong Custer.

Although Camp Custer was the smallest of all of the National Army camps, it still numbered 1,282 buildings on 9,139 acres. The camp was built with a capacity for housing 35,458 soldiers, a total exceeded by more than five thousand soldiers in September and October 1918 as the need for replacements for the AEF continued to grow.[31]

The 160th was organized at Camp Custer in September 1917 and remained active until May 1919. During that period, it was comprised of twelve training battalions and four development battalions. Almost immediately the first groups of drafted men began to arrive. By December 1917 there were over 24,000 soldiers in the camp. Four of the training battalions were shut down in January 1918 as the number of soldiers arriving at camp tapered off. They hastily stood up again in June 1918 when large numbers of new draftees began to appear at the camp. In addition to providing support to the 85th "Custer" Division, the 160th was also responsible for conducting some medical corps training for non-divisional soldiers who would be assigned to either stateside hospitals or overseas medical facilities.

161st Depot Brigade—Camp Grant, Illinois

The 161st Depot Brigade was organized in August 1917 and remained active at Camp Grant until May 1919. Very soon after opening, large numbers of inducted men began to arrive at the camp and require logistical support. There were fifteen training battalions established, and four provisional training regiments were added in June 1918 to provide more training support; these units remained active until the Armistice. There were also seven development battalions established by the 161st.[32] Regardless of unit, the soldiers training at Camp Grant suffered miserably from the cold weather during the winter of 1917–1918. At one point the thermometer plunged to twenty-seven degrees below zero. Despite the frozen weather and snowdrifts reaching the barracks roofs, the soldiers of the division continued to train for war. After a number of transfers to other units, the 86th Division finally received orders to leave Camp Grant and deploy to France. Once there, the levy process was repeated, and again the 86th was forced to transfer most of its men to other units. The commander of one of the 86th's infantry brigades was Brigadier General Carl Reichman; a German–born officer whose promotion had been held up on account of some alleged pro–German statements. Exonerated finally by a military affairs committee in the U.S. Senate, Reichman arrived in France with his troops only to be sent back to Camp Grant to command the 161st Depot Brigade.[33]

3. Depot Brigades by the Numbers

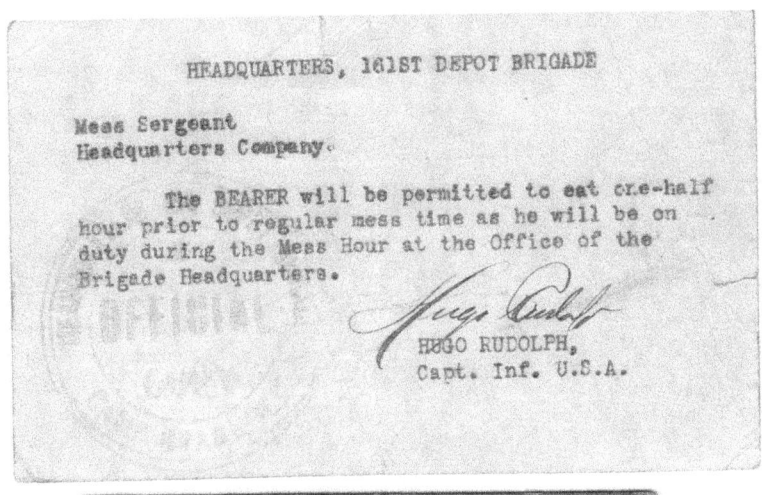

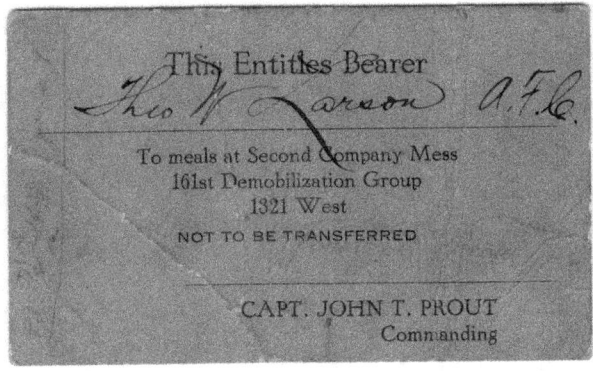

These two passes were issued to Theo Larsen serving at Camp Grant, Illinois, to allow him access to the mess halls there. The upper pass was issued by the 161st Depot Brigade and the lower pass was issued post–Armistice after the depot brigade was renamed to the 161st Demobilization Group (private collection).

In December 1918 the camp was designated as a demobilization center. Brigadier General Charles Gerhardt (father of the 29th Infantry Division commander in World War II, Major General Charles H. Gerhardt) was dispatched from France in February 1919 to take over the demobilization operation at Camp Grant. He found everything to be rather chaotic, as

> soldiers were marching everywhere for examination, supply, lectures, and motorcycles were carrying messages. The [demobilization organization] consisted of four battalions of four companies each (one battalion colored), each company orderly room working on the records. I had the colored

Striking a dramatic pose in front of a cactus while outfitted with outdated equipment, most likely provided by a photo studio, Russell C. Maple was a member of the 162nd Depot Brigade at Camp Pike, Arkansas. Maple enlisted at Jefferson Barracks, Missouri, and served in Hawaii before being transferred to Camp Pike as part of the medical staff. He met and married an Army nurse there and moved to St. Joseph, Missouri, after the war (courtesy John Adams-Graf).

soldiers [most likely men from the 370th Infantry Regiment, 93rd Division] discharged, gradually merged the companies on dull days, had all the activities concentrated in one row of five barracks, plus two extra buildings and reduced the time of discharge from six days to less than two.[34]

Gerhardt's success in streamlining the demobilization process was noticed, and he was transferred to Washington where he was assigned to inspect and assist the demobilization process at other camps across the country.

162nd Depot Brigade—Camp Pike Arkansas

The 162nd Depot Brigade was organized in August 1917 and remained active until May 1919. During this period the 162nd initially had fifteen training battalions. By early 1918 most of these kept their numerical designation but were converted to receiving battalions. In September and October another eight receiving battalions were organized as well as nine development battalions.

Throughout the war, Camp Pike remained one of the busiest training camps and was home to between 44,000 and 54,000 soldiers during the peak months of July to October 1918.[35] The large numbers of troops arriving in August caused the 162nd to move the 4,000 soldiers of 12 casual companies into a large tent city located on the Belmont baseball field. Almost immediately the soldiers began referring to their new home as Camp Belmont.

Pike drew most of its draftees from Alabama, Arkansas, Iowa, Louisiana, Mississippi, and Missouri. As a result, the number of black draftees appearing at camp reflected the drafted populations from those states. In July 1918, the Camp Pike version of the "Trench and Camp" soldiers'

Former teacher and citizen of Baltimore, infantry officer candidate Gobert Macbeth poses for a formal portrait during his time at the Central Officer Training School at Camp Pike, Arkansas (courtesy Marvin-Alonzo Greer).

newspaper announced there were more African American soldiers in camp than whites. Some of these men had completed their training and were to be transferred to Camp Bowie, Texas, as a temporary move. Camp Bowie was much less crowded than Camp Pike, and the men were held there until the shipping backlog at the Eastern transit camps seaports had cleared up.

In July 1918, after the 87th Division departed Camp Pike for France, it was reported that the 162nd Depot Brigade would be converted directly into a National Army or Regular Army division. After the first initial surprise at this potentially massive change in mission wore off, some of the brigade staff began to look at how the 162nd would have to reorganize itself. Ultimately, the plan was never put into place. When another influx of 17,000 draftees arrived, it became obvious that the camp would serve as a replacement training center, and the 162nd would be required to support and sustain it.[36] In October 1918 when the camp was at its fullest, the Spanish flu epidemic arrived with explosive force. Thirteen thousand soldiers, nearly 25 percent of the camp population, were hospitalized in a short span of

In a much more relaxed setting, Macbeth (standing in the center) and others from his training class pause for a smoke outside their barracks. After being discharged in January 1919, Macbeth went on to become a lawyer in Los Angeles until his death in 1943 (courtesy Marvin-Alonzo Greer).

time.[37] Fortunately, a fairly high percentage of the stricken men eventually recovered and were restored to duty. After the Armistice was signed, the 162nd turned its efforts to the demobilization process and discharged over 105,000 soldiers.

163rd Depot Brigade—Camp Dodge, Iowa

Camp Dodge today is still located near the city of Johnston, Iowa, and was the only one of the thirty-two divisional training sites actually in existence before 1917. Originally built in 1907 as a training site for the Iowa National Guard, the camp was named for Brigadier General Grenville M. Dodge, who organized Iowa's first National Guard unit in 1856. In 1917, the camp was turned over to the War Department and greatly expanded to become a National Army training camp. There were 1,409 buildings on the 5,209-acre camp. Camp Dodge was also the site for training some of the soldiers assigned to the African American 92nd Division[38]

The Army Surgeon General's January 1918 health report showed Camp Dodge as the third most disease-affected National Army training camp. It was much worse later in the year. Although the camp was designed to house a maximum of 42,227 soldiers, in July 1918 more than 46,400 soldiers were crammed into the camp's barracks. This made the camp a ripe target for the Spanish flu. As a result, Camp Dodge was one of the camps with the highest death tolls from the flu and pneumonia epidemic.[39]

The 163rd Depot Brigade was organized in August 1917 and remained in operation until May 1919. To receive the first drafted men, the 163rd set up two provisional regiments in September 1917. These were later superseded by fourteen training battalions. By July 1918, the large number of soldiers arriving at the camp required the establishment of six more provisional training battalions and three development battalions. One of the development battalions was transferred to Camp Cody, New Mexico, in November 1918. Its mission was to support the camp staff there while it organized the National Army 97th Division. After the war, Camp Dodge became a very busy demobilization site for soldiers from the Midwest. The 163rd received, processed, and discharged some 208,800 soldiers.[40]

164th Depot Brigade—Camp Funston, Kansas

The camp was named in honor of Kansas's adopted son General Frederick Funston who had established his reputation through combat

A magnified portion of one of the popular photographs of the period in which a Blue Star banner is created by thousands of soldiers at Camp Funston's 164th Depot Brigade. The Blue Star banner was developed during the First World War to indicate a family member was serving in the U.S. military (Library of Congress).

3. Depot Brigades by the Numbers

in Cuba and the Philippines. These exploits had earned him the Medal of Honor and a well-deserved reputation as a fighter and leader. Funston had succumbed to a heart attack in February 1917 in San Antonio, Texas, while commanding all the U.S. Army forces deployed against Pancho Villa in the United States and in Mexico. The site for Camp Funston was chosen originally for its proximity to Fort Riley,

> a long-established military post ... situated in the central part of Kansas.... The Military Reservation of the Fort comprises about 25,000 acres, shaped somewhat like a fan and lying on the north side of the Republican and Kaw Rivers.[41]

Camp Funston was unique because of this closeness to an already established Army post. This proximity led to some high-level friction as the commanders of the two posts vied for the overall command of both. A massive building program was required at the camp in preparation for the arrival of the draftees.

As stated above, the Camp Funston site "was selected on the Fort Riley Military Reservation near its eastern border and two or three miles from the Post."[42] After the location was selected, during "the months of June, July and August a vast wooden city was being built, capable of housing over 50,000 men. It was supplied with a system of waterworks and sewers, electric lights and steam heat."[43] When it was finished, Camp Funston had some 1,400 buildings spread across 2,000 acres. These buildings could accommodate 42,806 Doughboys, making it one of the largest cities in Kansas.[44] This capacity was exceeded in both September and October 1918 when there were more than 50,000 soldiers on post.

The 164th Depot Brigade was organized in September 1917 and remained active until May 1919. Over its lifespan it contained 24 training battalions and six development battalions. Of the development battalions, three were designated for "colored" soldiers and the remaining three for all others. Although the camp was designed to hold approximately 43,000 soldiers, there were more than 50,000 packed into its barracks during the months of September and October 1918.

During the war, Camp Funston also served as a detention camp for conscientious objectors (COs), many of whom were Mennonite. Since conscription was compulsory if no exemption was granted, some religious groups, such as the Hutterites, sent their young men to military camps, but restricted them from obeying any military commands or wearing a uniform. At Camp Funston, it was reported that these men were beaten and tortured, dragged by their hair, and even chased by men on motorcycles until they dropped from exhaustion.[45]

Perhaps a more typical account of life in one of the Fort Leavenworth/Camp Funston depot units can be seen in the letter written in June 1918 by Private John I. Walter to his mother in Indiana about his service to date:

> I am very busy now. I move most every other day. I have been in 4 different barracks since I came here.... I am in a depot battalion that is about the same as a service Co. [There are] men of all trades. When an order for men of certain trades comes in they will send some out to that camp.... I may stay here a week and I may stay here a year. I don't know how long. A big bunch of men [Authors' note: most likely part of the 89th Division] left here to-day for somewhere. They were singing and having a good time, seemed to be glad to go ... never can tell what I am going to do ... so we do not plan very far ahead of time.[46]

165th Depot Brigade—Camp Travis, Texas

The requirement to have a National Army camp in the Texas/Oklahoma region to accommodate the draftees from those states led the Army to look at the area around San Antonio. In 1917, San Antonio was the largest city in Texas and had a climate favorable for year-round training. It also had an abundance of open land. Adding to the appeal of the site was the nearness of Fort Sam Houston, a Regular Army post. Originally designed to house 42,809 soldiers, the highest occupancy rate for any one month at Travis was 37,681 in October 1918.[47]

Health issues appear to have been a constant cause for concern at Camp Travis. The January 1918 Surgeon General's health report identified Camp Travis as the most disease-afflicted of all National Army training camps. The report reflected a sickness rate of 6,153 per 1,000 soldiers. This meant, on the average, every soldier had been to sick call more than six times a year. This was a shocking four times the average of all of the other camps. Even more important statistically, 91 out of every 1,000 soldiers were reported as being physically unfit for service on any given day due to disease or accident. This, too, was well beyond the reported 47.6 average for all training camps. No other National Army or National Guard camp came close to these figures. In spite of these bad statistics, Travis actually was well below the average number of fatalities from disease. This anomaly may be an indication of either a successful camp medical treatment program or just good luck.[48]

The 165th Depot Brigade was organized in August 1917 and remained busy until it was shut down in May 1919. During its lifespan it was comprised of 23 training battalions and 6 development battalions. Four of the training battalions were inactivated in August

3. Depot Brigades by the Numbers

Pvt. Luciano Aguilar (center), a 21-year-old railroad worker from Roy, New Mexico, poses with two of his comrades from the 165th Depot Brigade at Camp Travis, Texas, c. 1918. Note that both of his comrades have chosen to pose with studio prop pistols and holsters and added to their Western image with bandannas (New Mexico War Service records via Ancestry.com).

1918 but quickly had to be re-activated due to another influx of soldiers. Three of the development battalions were designated for African American soldiers and the other three were for whites. Although originally designed to support 42,000 soldiers, the busiest month was October 1918 when 37,681 were present. It was designated as a demobilization site in December 1918 but due to its relatively remote location, the 165th demobilized only 62,500 soldiers, a much lower number than most other National Army posts and depot brigades. Of all of the National Army training camps, Camp Travis was the least expensive to construct.[49]

166th Depot Brigade—Camp Lewis, Washington

Camp Lewis was established in the area between Tacoma and Olympia, Washington. The camp was named in honor of Captain Meriwether Lewis, a leader of the Lewis and Clark expedition. The land chosen was ideal for a military post because of its open plains and excellent drainage. The camp was also well situated geographically with easy access to local railheads and seaports.

When it was completed, Camp Lewis was the largest National Army training site in area and was capable of housing 46,232 soldiers and 15,000 horses. The highest occupancy of the camp was in June 1918 when there were 44,015 soldiers present. Although Lewis was known for having the highest number of cloudy days annually of all the camps, it was redeemed by the fact that it also had the most comfortable annual temperature of the sixteen National Army sites. Along with the wide variation in terrain allowing different training scenarios, these features made it an excellent training site for the Army.[50] Construction of camp facilities began on 5 July 1917, and the camp was completed in ninety days, almost a month ahead of schedule and the shortest time period of any training base in the country. On completion there were 1,667 buildings in the 2,000-acre cantonment area.

The 166th Depot Brigade was organized at Camp Lewis in September 1917 and remained in operation until May 1919. During its period of operation, the 166th was comprised of nineteen training battalions and one development battalion. Five of the training battalions were shut down in early 1918 but had to be re-activated with arrival of a number of new soldiers. By the summer of 1918 five of the training battalions were also converted to development battalions but kept their original battalion number. The sole original development battalion was in operation from July to November 1918.

3. Depot Brigades by the Numbers

National Guard Camps. Things were different at the sixteen National Guard training camps. Beyond the obvious difference in living quarters, wherein the Guardsmen had tents and the National Army soldiers were billeted in wooden barracks, there was also the matter of geographic location. With the exception of Camp Fremont, California, the Guard training camps were located south of the Mason-Dixon Line. There were three sites in Texas and two each in Alabama, Georgia, and South Carolina. The others were located in Southern California, Louisiana, Mississippi, New Mexico, North Carolina, and Oklahoma.

Guard units arrived at their camps and were usually expected to set up their own tent cities. Kitchen, latrine, and training buildings were being built to support them, but they would have to do much of the work themselves. The command staffs at each of the Guard training camps organized the incoming units as best they could. Some units were immediately set aside to serve as the depot brigade at the camp. The remainder of the units were placed into training battalions.[51] One huge advantage the National Guard units had over the National Army divisions was that they arrived in their training camps as already existing military units. Although many of the units were eventually reorganized, the soldiers and officers knew each other and shared a common background. Later, when the units at each camp were being reorganized

One of the common complaints of Regular Army soldiers assigned to the depot brigades instead of duty with the AEF in France was the endless monotony of teaching new soldiers how to salute. Nevertheless, it was a basic skill, and therefore knowledge of military courtesies such as saluting was part of the often-difficult transition from civilian to soldier (private collection).

into the required divisional structure, there would be many complaints about the breaking up of the old state regimental organizations in order to make the new regiments and brigades. In the 29th Division, three old and very historic Virginia regiments disappeared into a new unit which became the 116th Infantry Regiment. Artillery batteries with names and lineages from the Revolutionary and Civil Wars suddenly became just Battery A or Battery C of a newly numbered field artillery regiment.

It was the same at all of the National Guard camps. Reorganizing these units was a necessary evil because regiments which previously would have been at full strength with 2,000 soldiers now needed 3,700 to reach war strength. Rifle companies that consisted of 150 men now needed to have 250 men to completely fill the ranks. Soldiers who had served and drilled together for decades suddenly found themselves in different units. At Camp Hancock, Georgia, the 8th Pennsylvania Infantry Regiment was consolidated with the 16th Pennsylvania Infantry Regiment to create the 112th Infantry Regiment of the 28th Division. The famous Richmond Light Infantry Blues of the Virginia National Guard had converted themselves to the 1st Virginia Cavalry Regiment (Provisional) to serve on the Mexican Border in 1916. Now they were converted again, this time to the 104th Ammunition Train. While most Guardsmen grew to accept their new numbers and organizational structure, there were many who mourned the disappearance of the historic names and numbers of their old units. What follows is the synopsis of the depot brigades at the National Guard camps.

51st Depot Brigade—Framingham, Massachusetts, and Camp Greene, North Carolina

The 51st Depot Brigade had unique history. It was originally established at a National Guard mobilization point in Massachusetts in August 1917 and then moved to Camp Greene, North Carolina, in November of the same year. The reason for this unusual transfer is due to the National Guard units of the 26th Division bypassing much of the stateside training program and deploying to France in early September. As a result, the 51st became the depot brigade for Camp Greene. This actually worked out better than expected because two Regular Army divisions, the 3rd and the 4th, used Camp Greene as their consolidation point and pre-deployment training camp. Another National Guard division, the 41st, also spent some time at Camp Greene before it started to deploy to France in November 1917. Somewhat ironically, the 41st, which struggled with the camp sewer line problems at Camp

Fremont, California, and was packed into Camp Greene with the two Regular Army divisions, was converted into a replacement division on arrival in France. It was later converted to serve as the 1st Depot Division at the St. Aignan training area.[52] A number of other New England National Guard units not assigned to the 26th Division also received support from the 51st Depot Brigade as did two African American units, the 802nd and the 804th Pioneer Infantry Regiments.

Like many of the southern camps, Camp Greene and the 51st Depot Brigade struggled mightily against the weather during the harsh winter of 1917–1918. Major General Joseph Dickman later wrote that, after having commanded the 85th Division at Camp Custer and then being transferred to command the 3rd Division at Camp Greene, a camp "in the wintery North, with comfortable barracks, and hard frozen ground for training, was considered in many respects preferable to a tent camp in the raw and rainy climate and deep red mud of the so called 'Sunny South.'"[53]

Dickman further noted that at times it was necessary to run pack trains on the icy roads to provide food to the soldiers in some of the outlying campsites. He also found it necessary to comment on the British and French instructors who were assigned to the camp's instructional staff. While much of their information was important and useful to the soldiers, Dickman believed that some of it was

> of so elementary a character that we could not help suspecting ... that their knowledge of the United States consisted principally of impressions gained from wild west shows, with their ponies, Indians and cowboys.[54]

Both the 3rd and 4th Divisions were gone by early summer of 1918 and the number of troops declined dramatically. In September 1918, the number of inbound draftees picked up and training at Camp Greene commenced again in full strength. Two development battalions were established, one in August 1918 and the other in September, to provide remedial training as needed. Both were inactivated by February 1919. Although the 51st was charged with the demobilization mission at Camp Greene in December 1918, the number of troops they processed through the camp was less than 12,000. By January 1919, the camp was ordered to be salvaged. The site was abandoned in June 1919.[55]

52nd Depot Brigade—Never Officially Organized at Camp Wadsworth, South Carolina

Camp Wadsworth was located in a rural area of South Carolina. Its terrain consisted of rolling hills bisected by small creeks and a heavily wooded area. The Piedmont & Northern Railroad ran through the northern section of the camp and served as the camp's primary rail line. Camp Wadsworth was the largest of the National Guard training sites. The camp had a housing capacity for 56,429 soldiers in its vast tent cities.[56]

Located near the Revolutionary War Cowpens Battlefield, Camp Wadsworth was also known for having the least amount of annual sunshine of all of the National Guard sites. Originally designated for training the white New York National Guardsmen of the 27th Division and the African American National Guardsmen of the 369th Infantry Regiment, the camp also trained a number of pioneer infantry regiments. After the New Yorkers deployed to France the camp became home to other units such as the Slavic Legion, comprised of Czechs, Slovaks, and Ukrainians.[57]

The 52nd Depot Brigade was never officially organized. Nevertheless, the camp support functions were performed by soldiers from the units in training, and the camp was extremely busy throughout its existence. It was designated a provisional depot for Corps and Army Troops and received soldiers from some 16 National Guard regiments and all excess National Guard officers from the entire country. These men were scheduled to be organized and trained for deployment to the AEF to serve at Corps and Army levels in France. Ultimately, many were converted instead to medical, signal, pioneer infantry, anti-aircraft machine gun, and labor units. Two development battalions were established at Camp Wadsworth, one in June and the other in September 1918. Both were shut down in February 1919. The camp was designated as a demobilization site after the Armistice and was responsible for discharging 11,431 soldiers.

53rd Depot Brigade—Camp Hancock, Georgia

The 53rd was assigned to support the training and organization of the 28th Division. Comprised primarily of Pennsylvania National Guard units, the 28th arrived at Camp Hancock in September 1917. These 27,000 soldiers were joined over the next few months by draftees and groups from other camps. Most of the cadre soldiers of the training units in the 53rd were from the 28th Division. By February 1918 there were 35,000 soldiers in camp. In May the 28th began to deploy to France and took with them their soldiers from the depot brigade. The 53rd was deactivated in November 1918, and whatever staff members remained were transferred to the camp staff.[58]

3. Depot Brigades by the Numbers

Under the watchful eyes of their marksmanship instructors and fellow guardsmen acting as score keepers, a group of soldiers at Camp McClellan, Alabama, practice sighting on the target. Note that all of the rifle bolts have been pulled open and to the rear, thereby giving the instructors a visual guarantee that there are no loaded weapons on the line at this point (Virginia National Guard).

After the 28th Division departed for France, Camp Hancock was designated as a machine gun training center. The camp staff supported training the machine gun battalions assigned to the 81st Division which was training at nearby Camp Jackson. Camp Hancock also established a development battalion in June 1918. Although designated as a demobilization site in December 1918, the camp was ordered to be salvaged less than a month later and was abandoned by March 1919.

54th Depot Brigade—Camp McClellan, Alabama

The site for Camp McClellan was chosen near the city of Anniston, Alabama. McClellan was unique among the camps because it had already been purchased for military use before war was declared. Originally intended to serve as the Army's artillery training center, with the declaration of war it was redesignated for use as a National Guard divisional training facility. Both the camp and the town of Anniston are surrounded by the foothills of the Blue Ridge Mountains.[59]

Camp McClellan was formally established on 18 July 1917, and like the other National Guard training camps, it was built quickly. It consisted of wooden buildings for headquarters, hospitals, mess halls, and latrine facilities. When complete, the camp had 1,551 buildings. The camp was designed to be capable of housing 57,748 soldiers, but it never reached that total. Its peak month was October 1918 when there were 27,977 soldiers present.[60] The 54th Depot Brigade was organized in September primarily from the inbound National Guardsmen from New Jersey, Maryland, Delaware and Virginia who were going to comprise the 29th Division. Nearly 25,000 of them arrived in the period between 1 September and 15 October 1917. At the same time a number of men who had just completed officers training at Camp Meade arrived in camp. Shortly thereafter a large number of recently inducted men also arrived to help bring the divisional units to full strength. All excess officers and enlisted men were assigned to the depot brigade. In this role they were able to conduct the support mission required by the 29th Division. Yet the 54th Depot Brigade remained a great topic of conversation and rumor. Perhaps unique among all the National Guard camps, the brigade had so many extra officers due to the consolidation of infantry regiments that there weren't enough jobs for them. As a result, men "who had several years of more or less valuable military training, were sitting on a hillside, doing absolutely nothing."[61] Undoubtedly these men would have been of great value at other camps where trained officers were in short supply. Unfortunately, it took a while before the dust cleared in all of the training camps and the excess officers could be transferred to appropriate organizations. Many of these men would later go on to become excellent officers who served their new units well, but quite a lot of valuable time was lost before this happened.

By the time the 29th completed training and was certified for deployment, many of the soldiers assigned to the 54th Depot Brigade were transferred to the 104th Motor Supply Train and the 104th Engineer Train. Some soldiers however remained with the 54th Depot Brigade. One of them, Thomas Barrett, a native of Norfolk, Virginia, had joined the Virginia National Guard in May 1917 before the draft was declared. He had served in the 4th Virginia Infantry Regiment and then in the 112th Machine Gun Battalion. In June 1918, as the 29th Division was preparing to depart for France, he was transferred to the 54th Depot Brigade and remained there for the rest of the war. In February 1919 he was transferred again, this time to the 155th Depot Brigade at Camp Lee, just sixty miles from his home. A few days later Barrett was discharged from the Army and returned to Norfolk.

In the early summer of 1918 as the 29th began to deploy to France,

3. Depot Brigades by the Numbers 77

Camp McClellan was designated as a field artillery brigade firing training center as had originally been planned. In conjunction with that designation an airfield, Henry J. Reilly Field, was built on the ground of the camp. Units of the Regular Army's 6th and 7th Divisions also trained at the camp before deploying to Europe, and elements of the 9th Division were training there when the Armistice put a halt to training. To carry on the support of the training at Camp McClellan, several receiving

A common sight in the National Guard training camps: troops armed with their rifles, bayonets, and pugil sticks make their way to one of the bayonet training sites. The pugil sticks were used as a method to simulate bayonet fighting without accidentally wounding a comrade (Virginia National Guard).

battalions were transferred from Camp Gordon. Two development battalions were organized, one in July and the other in November 1918. Both were deactivated in February 1919.

55th Depot Brigade—Camp Sevier, South Carolina

Camp Sevier, in Greenville County, South Carolina, was approved as a National Guard division training site on 21 May 1917. It was built to serve as the training site for the 30th Division which was comprised of North and South Carolina National Guardsmen. Among its important attributes was its proximity to four major railroad lines which gave it direct connection to Knoxville, Columbia, Charleston, Atlanta, and Washington, D.C.[62]

The 55th Depot Brigade was organized in September 1917 at Camp Sevier to support the training of the Tennessee, North Carolina, and South Carolina National Guard units which were to be consolidated in the 30th Division. Altogether these states provided almost 19,000 soldiers but were still quite a ways short of the required 28,000 needed for a complete division. Never one of the larger camps, Sevier's busiest month was April 1918 when there were 28,717 men in the camp. After the 30th Division departed for France in May of that year, the number of soldiers declined until August when a large number of African American soldiers arrived at the camp for training. Several receiving battalions from Camp Jackson were transferred to Camp Sevier in the autumn of 1918 to perform a depot brigade-like role. A development battalion was also organized at Sevier but was deactivated in September 1918. The Camp was designated as a demobilization site in December 1918 but just as with the other National Guard camps the number of soldiers demobilized was comparatively small, only 12,771. The camp was closed completely in April 1919.

56th Depot Brigade—Camp Wheeler, Georgia

Camp Wheeler was located seven miles southeast of the Macon, Georgia. The War Department designated Camp Wheeler as the mobilization and training center for National Guard units from Alabama, Florida, and Georgia. Together these units formed the 31st Division. The camp was officially organized on 18 July 1917 on 21,480 acres with 1,229 buildings in addition to the large tent cities for the soldiers. The camp was designed to hold a maximum capacity of 43,011 soldiers, but that figure was never reached. The highest monthly occupation for Camp Wheeler was 28,960 in July 1918.[63]

The 56th Depot Brigade was organized in October 1917. As at the other Guard training sites, inbound Guardsmen were used to build and staff the depot brigade. Later, as more troops arrived from other camps and from the draft, the 11th Training Battalion was transferred from Camp Dix to support the camp. After the 31st Division departed for France, Camp Wheeler continued to train other units and in the summer of 1918 organized the first two of four development battalions at the camp. All four of these battalions were inactivated in December 1918. The camp itself was salvaged and closed in April of the same year. Wheeler served for a short period as a demobilization site but only processed 12,534 soldiers before the camp was shut down.[64]

57th Depot Brigade—Camp MacArthur, Texas

The 57th was organized in September 1917 when 18,000 National Guardsmen from Michigan and Wisconsin reported to Camp MacArthur to form the 32nd Division. The camp was never one of the busier training camps, and the largest soldier population was reached in October 1917 when there were 27,274 men present. In two months the number dipped below the ten thousand mark. Soldiers needed to form the 57th Depot Brigade were drawn from the units arriving as well as from other camps and from drafted men. The 57th was inactivated in in November 1917 and the brigade's soldiers returned to their original units or became part of the camp staff.

After the 32nd Division deployed in early 1918 the camp appeared almost empty. Gradually the numbers of men arriving increased and the training mission continued. The camp was designated as an infantry replacement and training camp in August 1918. In this role it provided almost ten thousand officers and men for deployment to France. Performing a good portion of the now-inactivated 57th Depot Brigade's mission were five development battalions that were organized in August and September.[65]

58th Depot Brigade—Never Officially Organized at Camp Logan, Texas

Camp Logan was established near Houston, Texas, to train the Illinois National Guardsmen of the 33rd Division. The camp became a point of contention with the residents of Houston in September 1918 when the training camp was the scene of the first local outbreak of the deadly Spanish flu. The outbreak, most likely caused by the transfer of soldiers from other infected camps, soon resulted in some six hundred cases in the camp. At this point, the camp's military medical officials made an extremely poor and uninformed decision. They transferred the sick soldiers to local civilian facilities in an effort to keep the epidemic from infecting the rest of the soldier population. Within days, the flu had spread throughout the citizens of Houston with typically deadly results.

Few records remain from the camp staff which provided the services that would have been conducted by the 58th Depot Brigade. It appears the 33rd Division was blessed with several excellent officers, including the future Lieutenant General William H. Simpson, who developed and managed the training program for the 33rd Division while at Logan.[66] The 33rd struggled with receiving adequate replacements during the months preceding their deployment to France and had to spend an inordinate amount of time classifying inbound replacements coming from other camps. After the 33rd left Camp Logan during the period May–June 1918, the camp set up three development battalions to handle the subsequent influx of draftees. The battalions remained in operation until early 1919 when they were shut down. The camp itself was designated a demobilization site in December 1918 but discharged only about fifteen thousand soldiers which appears to have been just about the entire base population when the camp was closed.

59th Depot Brigade—Camp Cody, New Mexico

Camp Cody was located forty miles from the Mexican border and served as the training camp for the National Guard units from Iowa, Minnesota, Nebraska North Dakota and South Dakota. Together these units were designated the 34th Division. The camp was built during the summer of 1917 and used large tent cities for the troop's living quarters. The camp was originally designed to support a total capacity of 44,959 soldiers but never reached that amount.[67]

The 59th Depot Brigade was organized in September 1917 when the 12,000 National Guardsmen arrived at Camp Cody. The camp reached its largest soldier population in June 1918 when there were more than 27,000 soldiers in camp. The 34th Division started its long journey to the East Coast transit camps shortly thereafter, and the camp population dropped to less than ten thousand for the rest of its existence. When the 34th was still training in camp, the majority of the soldiers in the 59th Depot Brigade came from the National Guard units. Officially, the 59th was inactivated in November 1917 but a series of development battalions were organized to support the camp. For a short period, the 3rd Development Battalion from Camp Dodge served at Camp Cody until it was inactivated in December 1918. The camp was shut down in June 1919.

60th Depot Brigade—Camp Doniphan, Oklahoma

The 60th Depot Brigade was organized in September 1917 when the National Guard units from Kansas and Missouri arrived to form the 35th Division. Although both states had robust Guard units and together they totaled some 21,000 soldiers, more men would be required to meet the divisional quota of 28,000 men. A number of draftees arrived in October 1917 to fill in the units. The majority of the soldiers needed to staff the 60th Depot Brigade came from the National Guard units and were returned to them as the division neared its time to deploy.

The camp was located on the grounds of Fort Sill, at the time one of the Army's primary field artillery training sites and home today to the Army's Field Artillery School. As at most of the other National Guard training camps, the size of the soldier population remained small in comparison to the National Army camps. At its busiest, Camp Doniphan was home to only twenty-five thousand troops, and after the 35th Division departed in April–June 1918, the population remained below eight thousand for the rest of its existence. The numbers of men dropped so much that in July and September there were less than a thousand men on site. A development battalion was organized in July 1918, and it remained active until March 1919.[68]

61st Depot Brigade—Camp Bowie, Texas

Construction of Camp Bowie began on 18 July 1917 shortly after the site was announced as a National Guard training site. The camp, located about three miles west of downtown Fort Worth, was established to provide training for the 36th Division which was organized from the units of the Texas and Oklahoma National Guard. The site was a natural fit for a military training camp. The terrain consisted of gently rolling plains and open spaces. The camp was named for the famous defender of the Alamo, James "Jim" Bowie. Camp Bowie was opened officially on 24 August 1917, and the initial units that made up the 36th Division started to arrive. The first seventeen thousand Guardsmen from Texas and Oklahoma showed up in September 1917. Built to accommodate 41,879 soldiers, the highest number of soldiers training at Camp Bowie was 30,901 in October 1917. Altogether 1,316 buildings were constructed on the camp's 2,186 acres to support the large tent-city complexes inhabited by the units.[69]

The 61st Depot Brigade was organized in October 1917 and remained active until March 1918. A large number of drafted men, including 107 from the Panama Canal Zone, arrived over the next few months to bring the 36th Division up to required strength. Camp Bowie remained a fairly busy camp even after the departure of the 36th during mid-summer 1918. With that departure, Camp Bowie was designated an infantry replacement and training camp in July 1918. A number of diseases, such as measles, mumps, and meningitis, appeared at the camp while the 36th Division was training, but it was not until September 1918 that the situation became truly alarming. Appearing simultaneously with the arrival of a number of newly drafted men, were 4,439 cases of the flu. Fortunately, most of these were in the depot brigade's arrival/detention camps where the new men were isolated before joining the rest of the camp population. These patients were put under a strict regimen of twice daily examinations with their noses and throats being sprayed. After they were released from the hospital, they remained under observation for five more days to ensure they wouldn't infect anyone else. A great deal of sanitary work was also done in the detention camp's tents and buildings where all of the woodwork was sprayed with a chlorinated lime solution, and the canvas was also disinfected.[70]

By December of that year the camp was redesignated a demobilization site but very few men, approximately 3,500, were actually discharged from Camp Bowie. This number is so low that it is possible it reflects the demobilization of the camp staff, the 117th Supply Train (the Texas National Guard contribution to the 42nd Division), and the soldiers of the two development battalions which had been formed. The camp was designated for salvage in April 1919 and was completely shut down in August.[71]

62nd Depot Brigade—Camp Sheridan, Alabama

Shortly after the declaration of war in April 1917, groups of businessmen in Alabama, recognizing the potential business boom in having military installations in their region, successfully lobbied for the establishment of two National Guard training camps, Camp McClellan near

3. Depot Brigades by the Numbers

Anniston and Camp Sheridan near Montgomery. The site chosen for Camp Sheridan was located on the bluffs overlooking the Alabama River and close to the state capitol. Although Alabama is in the heart of the South, the camp near Montgomery was named after a Civil War Union general, Phillip Henry Sheridan, in recognition of the Ohio National Guard soldiers of the 37th Division who would train there.[72]

To prepare the camp for its mission, more than five miles of railroad track had to be laid. Equally important, a water system capable of providing 350,000 gallons a day was built to support the camp. The 62nd Depot Brigade was organized in September 1917 from the 18,992 Ohio National Guardsmen who arrived at Camp Sheridan in September with the 37th Division. The 62nd Depot Brigade was inactivated in October 1917, and most of the staff returned to the 37th Division to prepare for deployment and other specialized training. The 62nd Depot Brigade functions were then passed to the camp staff. In the months that followed the camp received a number of draftees including groups from the University of Arizona and the University of Texas. Even after the 37th began to deploy to France in June 1918, the camp remained a busy place. A development brigade was organized at Camp Sheridan in

Perhaps unconsciously mimicking the overseas hats worn by the U.S. soldiers in France, these depot brigade soldiers have folded their winter-weather hats in an unusual manner and achieve a uniform look (private collection).

July 1918 and remained active until January 1919. The camp was designated a demobilization site in in December 1918 and was responsible for discharging some 8,265 soldiers from the Army before the camp was closed in March 1919.[73]

63rd Depot Brigade—Camp Shelby, Mississippi

Camp Shelby was established in May 1917 and was named in honor of Isaac Shelby, a Revolutionary War hero. Located ten miles southeast of the city of Hattiesburg, the camp has served as a training site almost continuously since it was established. The first division to train at Camp Shelby was the 38th Division, a National Guard unit originally organized with soldiers from Indiana and Kentucky. The soldiers at Camp Shelby lived in regimental tent-cities and were supported by 1,206 buildings. The total capacity for housing soldiers was set at 36,010.

The 63rd Depot Brigade was organized in September 1917 using the National Guard soldiers from Indiana and Kentucky who arrived to form the 38th Division. By October there were more than 22,000 soldiers in camp, and this number would rise until it reached 36,000 by September 1918. With the departure that month of the 38th Division for France, the numbers dropped significantly. While the 38th was actively training at Camp Shelby, much of the 63rd Depot Brigade's staff consisted of Guardsmen and a number of recently inducted soldiers. A development battalion was organized in July 1918 and remained active until March 1919. Camp Shelby was designated a demobilization center in December 1918 and processed over 60,000 soldiers before it was shut down and all the camp materials salvaged.[74]

64th Depot Brigade—Never Officially Organized at Camp Beauregard, Louisiana

Located near Alexandria, Camp Beauregard's 21,600 acres had 1,068 buildings supporting the vast tent cities occupied by the units in training. The camp's maximum troop capacity was 29,212. This capacity was never reached, and the highest number of soldiers training at any one time was 24,294 in July 1918.[75] Designated as the depot brigade for Beauregard, the 64th was never officially organized. The National Guard soldiers from Louisiana, Arkansas, and Mississippi began to arrive in camp in early September to form the 39th Division. After completing training, the 39th deployed to France in August 1918 where it was reorganized as the 5th Depot Division for the AEF. After the 39th departed, Camp Beauregard established three development battalions. One was inactivated in December but the other two remained active until May 1919, even though the camp began shutting down in March 1919.

65th Depot Brigade—Never Officially Organized at Camp Kearny, California

Camp Kearny was established a few miles north of San Diego on 18 July 1917. The camp was named in honor of Brigadier General Stephen Watts Kearny who led the U.S. Army of the West to San Diego in 1846. As one of the National Guard sites, the camp was originally designed to house and train 32,066 troops. This number was never reached, and the highest occupancy of the camp was in November 1917 when 24,132 soldiers were on site. On completion, Camp Kearny had 848 buildings and hundreds of eight-man squad tents spread across its 12,721 acres.[76] Few records remain of the depot brigade functions at Kearny, but the camp was established to provide training for the National Guard soldiers from Arizona, California, Colorado, New Mexico, and Utah who were to comprise the 40th Division. A large number of draftees began to arrive at Camp Kearny in October and November 1917. During the summer of 1918, as the 40th Division began to deploy to France, a development battalion was established. It remained active until February 1919. Camp Kearny was designated a demobilization site in December 1918. It was credited with discharging over sixteen thousand soldiers which appears to have been the population of the camp and the 102nd Division, a draftee division which was just beginning to form. By the end of the war, more than 65,000 soldiers had been trained at the camp.

From the information provided in this chapter, it should be clear that the organization of development battalions to provide remedial training, medical support and even disciplinary control for the training camps' depot brigades was crucial to the formation of the U.S. Army in World War I. In the following chapter, these development battalions will be discussed in detail.

4

Lame, Halt and Blind

The Development Battalions

"The percentage of illiteracy in this country is small, so that the greatest need ... is among our foreign–born soldiers.... Some of the men who come from the remote mountain districts of this country are also unable to read or to write. Among them were draftees who, when they reached the cantonment, thought they had arrived in France!"[1]

Even before the United States entered the war on 6 April 1917, most military and many civilian officials knew that the U.S. Army was not ready to fight the kind of war being waged in Europe. As of June 1917, the Regular Army stood at about 6,000 officers and 238,000 men while the National Guard mustered about 3,000 officers and 107,000 men in Federal service, mostly returned from duty on the Mexican border.[2] Clearly, many more men would be needed. In addition to infantry, artillery, and engineer troops, the army required a bewildering variety of other units. Men were needed to fill the units involved with all types of supply, administration, transportation, and medical duties. Special units performed railroad construction and operation, forestry, water supply and treatment, butchery, bakery, and other types of duties. To build an army capable of making a difference in the world war, it was obvious the United States would have to resort to a national draft.

Congress passed and President Woodrow Wilson signed the Selective Service Act in May 1917. By war's end, after three national registration days, approximately 24 million men aged eighteen to forty-five registered for the draft.[3] Between September 1917 and November 1918, some 2.8 million men were inducted into the Army while voluntary enlistments totaled about two million.[4]

4. Lame, Halt and Blind

The draft registration, conducted at a local board and administered by local residents, provided the first opportunity for a cursory physical review of the registrant. The registration clerk answered the following question for each registrant: "Has person lost arm, leg, hand, foot, or both eyes, or is he otherwise disabled (specify)?" Also, the registrant himself was given the opportunity to claim exemption from the draft (for a variety of reasons) at this time.

Shortly after registration, a man would be notified to report to his local draft board for examination to determine his fitness to serve in the U.S. Army. There, the prospective draftee would answer some general questions about his health, and a doctor would give him a physical examination which covered his weight, height, and other physical measurements, as well as a hearing and a vision test. The thorough exam also covered the man's nose, throat, heart, lungs, feet, genito-urinary organs, and teeth. The doctor also checked to see if the man had a hernia or hemorrhoids. Finally, the examining doctor would indicate whether the man was: physically qualified for general military service; physically qualified for special or limited military service; or physically deficient and not physically qualified for military service (and a reason then given). Later, after the man had returned to his home, the local draft board would meet to ratify the doctor's findings. If a man were found fit, he was notified get his affairs in order and be ready to be called at any time.

With so many men entering military service, it was inevitable that some men would be below acceptable physical or mental standards to be a soldier. Such men, ideally, would be screened and "weeded out" during the draft registration or induction process. But some men slipped through the cracks. Thousands of other men were marginally physically unfit and many more could not speak or understand English well enough to function as an American soldier. With this in mind, the War Department, somewhat belatedly, devised military units, called development battalions, to accommodate such men. The first development battalions were formed at training camps across the U.S. in May 1918. Many of the men assigned to a development battalion had trouble with the English language; although perhaps willing to serve in combat, their lack of understanding hampered their ability to perform well enough to function in a combat unit. These men spent their term of service in these development battalions drilling, reading, learning English, and attending lectures, all in an effort to make them better soldiers. Over time, more and more development battalions were organized in order to deal directly with the many medical or educational issues.

At Camp Bowie, Texas, in the 61st Depot Brigade, a development battalion was organized in June 1918. Quickly it grew to having four companies. The companies were each designated for a certain developmental category. The categories were: orthopedic cases, venereal cases, medical convalescents (other than orthopedic, venereal, or lung cases), and those men unable to read, write, or speak English. There were two Army Medical Corps officers assigned to the battalion, and they were assisted by an orthopedic surgeon who made daily rounds to check on the soldiers in the companies.

Each man in the battalion was examined weekly and the results of the examinations were noted on both the personnel files and the medical files. While the men with serious medical problems were not required to perform any duties, the others were expected to perform some drills as well as moderate physical fitness training. Those incapable of such activities were reported to the camp disability board for discharge. The Camp Bowie disability board met daily to consider the cases and track progress.[5]

Camp Wadsworth, located near Spartanburg, South Carolina, had been the training site for the white soldiers of the 27th Division and 16 pioneer infantry regiments as well as the black soldiers of the 369th Infantry Regiment. After most of these soldiers left for France, the camp became an overall training facility and included the Army School for Nurses and the Army School for Cooks and Bakers. At the same time two development battalions were established and focused on teaching English. Development Battalion No. 1 had 21 officers and 809 enlisted men assigned, and Development Battalion No. 2 was just slightly smaller with 13 officers and 708 men.[6]

The formal portrait of Pvt. Arthur Keefer, who served in Company H, 5th Limited Service Regiment, in the 161st Depot Brigade at Camp Grant in 1918. The growth of the U.S. Army supply system late in the war is evident here by the high-quality woolen uniform and "Montana Peak" campaign hat with appropriate branch of service cord (courtesy Greg Jacobs).

4. Lame, Halt and Blind

At Camp Devens, Massachusetts, with a much larger soldier population, a separate development battalion was needed for each of the developmental categories. It was noted however, that while a number of men were upset to be assigned to a development battalion at Devens, perhaps an equal number were quite content to sit out the war in one. As some officers noted, "the development battalions provided a safe hiding place for a considerable number of shirkers who were willing to do almost anything rather than go across to France."[7] Eventually some men were deemed cured or educated enough and were sent to Europe, but others managed to stay until the war was ended. The same author also noted that when the fighting ended and the rules for demobilization were published which required men to be healthy before they could be discharged, "there were more remarkable and swift cures in the Development Battalions than in any other outfits."

Just who were the men who were assigned to development battalions? Professor Ralph V.D. Magoffin, former Army morale officer, remembered:

> Everybody who was sent to [a development battalion] considered himself a derelict, stranded more eternally and to be buffeted more rudely than even a soldier relegated to the Depot Brigade. In our camp was a Development Battalion of 10,000 men, 3,000 of whom could not even speak English. ... Many men were lame, halt, and blind, and I speak advisedly, because the feet of several pointed backwards, hundreds carried canes and went to their daily exercise so slowly that they were called the Caterpillar Brigade.... Many were dropped a class or two in physical qualifications because of venereal disease. Some were white pacifists, some were yellow, and 3,000 were Italians, Poles, Yids, Russians, Armenians, and other foreigners, who could not speak English, and seemed not to have the faintest idea of what it was all about. All of them wanted to go home.[8]

Even allowing for hyperbole we get the impression that these men presented a serious challenge to the Army's training program.

Despite Magoffin's assertion, there were plenty of men in development battalions who had their own thoughts about the causes of the war. Samuel Adelo, a New Mexico merchant drafted in May 1918, was one such man. Adelo, born Asaad Abdallah in 1892 in Syria, began his service assigned to Company C, 12th Infantry Regiment, 8th Division, at Camp Fremont, California. In July, Adelo was transferred to the development battalion at Camp Fremont, likely due to physical reasons. Adelo stated that "personally I did not like the Army for the first few weeks but later on, the more I was in it the more I liked it." At the time of his registering for the draft he was working as a dry goods merchant and had requested exemption from service based on being the sole financial

Private Samuel Adelo, born Asaad Abdallah in Syria in 1892, was serving in the 12th Infantry Regiment, 8th Division, at Camp Fremont, California, before he was transferred to a development battalion. Throughout his military service Adelo maintained strong opinions about the war being primarily Germany's fault (New Mexico War Service records via Ancestry.com).

support for his mother and brother. Nevertheless, he appeared to have adjusted to military life and felt the Army promoted "good character in young men." Adelo thoughtfully summed up his ideas on the causes of, culpability for, the war as well as the desired outcome of the peace process:

> Although the assassination of the Archduke was the excuse for the general conflagration but I believe the real cause was the European ambitions and political intricacies that had been going on for years and the real blame falls on Germany because she was aspiring to things the spirit of the age does not permit. It should be an end to all wars and should bring into existence the principle of arbitration instead of settling disputes with the force of arms. The lessons our country should draw out of this war is that we must in the future be prepared for emergencies and that we shall have a reasonable standing army.[9]

Adelo was discharged on 16 September 1918 for physical disability from being "overworked." He returned to New Mexico to recover, married, had seven children, and operated a general store.

Before the creation of development battalions these men suffered through training in combat units or languished in depot brigades performing menial chores if they were able to do even that much. Certainly, many thousands were discharged on a surgeon's certificate of disability (SCD). And even after the battalions were created not everyone who was considered unfit was sent to one. Despite close scrutiny, the sheer volume of men proceeding through induction centers meant some men who should have been immediately rejected for service would fall through the cracks and be inducted. Even if men initially escaped detection, it didn't take long for their difficulties or disabilities to reveal themselves. A cursory examination of the records of some of these men reveals several reasons for early discharge. One man who served only twelve days at Camp Sherman, Ohio, suffered from "flaccid flat feet with abduction and eversion which existed prior to induction and was not incurred in the line of duty." A man who served eight days at Camp Taylor, Kentucky, was discharged for being under weight. Another Camp Taylor draftee served only four days before his discharge due to a hernia. Other reasons ranged from general physical disability to general inaptitude. Obviously, many of the physical defects in these men should have been caught before their induction and shipment to a training camp.[10]

With the signing of the Armistice on 11 November 1918, and notwithstanding the necessity for providing an Army of Occupation to serve in Germany, the U.S. Army began to demobilize. Such a huge task had to be accomplished systematically; the first men to leave the service were of necessity the recent inductees who were undergoing training, along with men in development battalions. It would be necessary, of course, to retain a cadre of men in stateside camps to allow for the reception and processing of the roughly two million men from overseas who would soon be returning and awaiting discharge.

To understand the typical foreign-born soldier assigned to a development battalion, we may look at a sample of thirty-nine such men, drawn from the neighboring Wisconsin cities of Kenosha and Racine. These two cities can be considered typical mid-western industrial cities of that time, with a good mix of native born and immigrant men. Men who hailed from old immigrant stock mixed with African Americans and immigrants from Southern and Eastern Europe who were in their draft pool. The cities had factories, tanneries, and rail yards; they were about seventy-five to eighty miles north of Chicago making them an important link between Chicago and the Northwestern prairies.

Private Jose Garcia poses for a portrait while serving in a development battalion at Fort Sill/Camp Doniphan in Oklahoma. That Garcia has only one collar disk is probably a sign of the uneven performance of the Army's supply chain, especially in low priority units such as development battalions (New Mexico War Service records via Ancestry.com).

The following table shows the native country of the men in the sample. The results reflect the overall complexion of the tide of immigrants to the United States in general, and to this area in particular.

Origin Country	Number of Men
Italy	17
Armenia/Turkey	8
Russia	5

4. Lame, Halt and Blind

Greece	3
Poland	2
Denmark	2
Belgium	1
Sweden	1

Since most men were sent to one of the large training camps upon their induction, their camp of assignment reflects, in general, their mid-western geographic location. Of course, men were transferred among the various camps, and an immigrant soldier could be assigned to a development battalion anywhere along the way. In the case of these men, most were sent to Camp Taylor, Kentucky, with others going to Camp McClellan, Alabama, and Camp Grant, Illinois. The citizenship status of the men at induction breaks down as follows:

Status	Number of Men
Naturalized	1
Declarant	10
Alien	18
Unknown	10[11]

The occupation followed by the men in this sample is, again, typical of the overall U.S. immigration pattern, with more men in unskilled or semi-skilled positions than in skilled or professional positions. By their very nature, of course, development battalions drew immigrant men who tended to be illiterate or semi-literate in the English language; many of these men were laborers.

Typically, drafted men were transferred from a depot brigade to a unit preparing for deployment to France. If it was determined instead that the man needed extra training or was unfit for active service, he might then be transferred to a development battalion. A good example of this is Yervant Chakmakian, who was born in 1888 in Armenia. He was a baker living in Kent, Connecticut, when he was drafted into the Army on 24 July 1918. He was initially assigned to the 38th Company, 10th Training Battalion, 151st Depot Brigade, at Camp Devens, Massachusetts. On 17 August Chakmakian was transferred to the 36th Machine Gun Battalion, 12th Division, also at Camp Devens. On 9 November, just two days before the Armistice and while the 12th Division was awaiting orders for shipment to France, Chakmakian was transferred to Company M, 3rd Development Battalion, at Camp Devens. He spent the next ten days in the Base Hospital. Chakmakian was discharged on 30 November 1918.¹²

Other men weren't so lucky. Russell E Perrine, a Pennsylvania-born soldier, was inducted into the Army in May of 1918 and began his training at Camp Dix, New Jersey. Shortly thereafter, and most likely due to some physical issues, he was transferred to the 13th U.S. Guards Battalion and from there to the 152nd Depot Brigade at Camp Upton on Long Island. On arrival he was assigned to Company D, 1st Development Battalion. He died of "Broncho [Bronchial] Pneumonia" a month later. Sadly, the book which was written and published by the city of Rochester to honor its soldiers who died in service misspelled his name. Another soldier credited to Rochester, George A. Robbins, also died in service from bronchial pneumonia. He had joined the army in June 1918 and went to Camp Upton for training in the 152nd Depot Brigade. By October, Robbins had been promoted to corporal and assigned as part of the staff of Company M in the 3rd Development Battalion. In December he was transferred to Company M of the Venereal Department in the 152nd, and less than a month later on 11 January 1919, he was dead. While the *Rochester War Service Record* book managed to spell Robbins' name correctly, it made no mention of the fact that his final unit was a venereal unit.¹³

Armenian-born Yervant Chakmakian fixes the photographer with an intense stare while posing at a studio near Camp Devens. Although he was listed as the sole support for his sister, Chakmakian, a pre-war baker in Connecticut, did not request an exemption, and he was drafted in July 1918. He served in the 36th Machine Gun Battalion, 12th Division, and then in the 3rd Development Battalion (Connecticut War Service records via Ancestry.com).

4. Lame, Halt and Blind

The War Service Record AGO Form 724–8 for Russell E. Perrine from Monroe County, New York. Perrine was inducted into the Army in May 1918 and served in a U.S. Guards Battalion and the 1st Development Battalion at Camp Dix, New Jersey, until his death on 17 October 1918 (New York War Service Records via Ancestry.com).

In spite of these rather sad stories, most men accepted their assignments to the development battalions and did their best. Wasil Phillipchuck, a native of Russia, was assigned to the 4th Development Battalion at Camp Sheridan. Phillipchuck "did not want to be a soldier but when I was drafted I took what came my way." Remarking about his thoughts on his service, Phillipchuck stated: "Germany [was] entitled to her whipping."[14]

Antonio Antonopulo was born in Smyrna, Turkey, in June 1890. He was a barber living in Bridgeport, Connecticut, when he was drafted into the Army on 12 November 1917. Antonopulo was assigned to various development battalions within the 151st Depot Brigade at Camp Devens until his honorable discharge as an enemy alien on 15 January 1919. It's unusual that Antonopulo served for more than a year before his discharge as an enemy alien and that the discharge came after the Armistice.[15]

It is important to note here the War Department had recognized early on that "even the United States has not such a vast supply of physically fit men that its army can be restricted to such men." It also realized "that many duties in the army can be performed just as well by men with

Turkish-born Antonio Antonopoulo poses in front of a snowy background with a Model-1917 Enfield at Camp Devens. Somewhat surprisingly, Antonopoulo, a declared candidate for U.S. citizenship who had not requested exemption from service, was discharged as an "enemy alien" after a year in the Army (Connecticut War Service records via Ancestry.com).

certain physical defects." Accordingly, the War Department established a "limited service" classification to encompass such men.¹⁶

Thus we can see that assignment of men to development battalions was not done capriciously or without some regard to the men themselves. Nevertheless, Stanley Lane claimed to have been assigned to a development battalion based solely on his lack of United States citizenship. Lane, an immigrant from Poland, enlisted in the Army at the age of sixteen. After initial assignments to cavalry regiments in Texas, he was sent to Camp McClellan, Alabama, for artillery training as part of a division going to France. Lane tried to become a U.S. citizen prior to shipping out, but for some reason his application was denied. Instead, Lane was sent to a development battalion where he was promoted to corporal and then acting supply sergeant in relatively short order. At one point, Lane was given a weekend pass and with two friends went to Birmingham, Alabama, for some fun. During their return trip to Camp McClellan, their car became stuck in the mud. After being towed free, the men returned to camp on Monday afternoon. Lane was charged with being absent without leave for one day, much to his chagrin. This blemish in his record didn't seem to affect Lane; after the war he reenlisted, became an American citizen, and served in the Army until his discharge as a lieutenant colonel in 1955.¹⁷

In November 1918, preliminary statistics showed that "at least 68 per cent

Private Luciano Segura, from Three Rivers, New Mexico, poses for a studio portrait near Camp Travis, Texas, where he was serving in the 32nd Development Battalion in 1918 (New Mexico War Service records via Ancestry.com).

(152,807) of the men transferred to development battalions were reclaimed and assigned to some duty in the Army, thus releasing an equal number of able-bodied soldiers for combat service. Without development battalions the majority of these men would have been immediately discharged."[18]

By December 1918 the Army had organized a total of seventy-three development battalions. These were assigned to the depot brigades that were located at the various training camps. In addition, there were thirty-two separate development battalions, not assigned to a depot brigade, at sixteen other camps. Most of the battalions were organized in the summer and fall of 1918 with the earliest in June and the latest in December. Most of the battalions were disbanded by the end of 1918, but a few of them continued until early spring 1919. Most camps and depot brigades seem to have had between four to six development

Private Jose Abeyta was assigned to the 1st Development Battalion at Camp Cody, New Mexico, in 1918. Under magnification it is clear that Abeyta is wearing a brand-new wool M-1917 service coat; to prevent the standing collar from chafing his neck, he has pulled out the collar of his shirt and affixed his collar disks to the shirt. Unfortunately, he didn't notice that his infantry disk is affixed upside down (New Mexico War Service records via Ancestry.com).

Another New Mexico soldier, Petriconio Gonzales, was a farmer before the war. Inducted into the Army in May 1918, Gonzales was assigned to the 3rd Development Battalion in the 165th Depot Brigade at Camp Travis. When he was discharged in December 1918, he returned to farming near Albuquerque (New Mexico War Service records via Ancestry.com).

Also assigned to a development battalion at Camp Cody, Salomon Gonzales noted on his draft registration form that he was the Sheriff of Precinct Number 40 and he suffered from two broken ribs. Nevertheless, he was inducted and then chose this unique pose for his portrait (New Mexico War Service records via Ancestry.com).

battalions. The 153rd Depot Brigade (Camp Dix, New Jersey) had none, and the 166th Depot Brigade (Camp Lewis, Washington) had one. The 156th Depot Brigade (Camp Jackson, South Carolina) and the 162nd Depot Brigade (Camp Pike, Arkansas) had the most development battalions with eight each. Many camps had separate "white" and "colored" development battalions.[19]

Some of the men who served in development battalions took pride in their service. Juan Sedillo, a farmer from Encinosa, New Mexico, who served in the 1st Development Battalion at Camp MacArthur, Texas, remembered his first day as a solder. Sedillo was "given the honor of being appointed Special Police Officer of the contingent of drafted men of Local Board of Lincoln County, New Mexico" as those men reported to their training camp. Sedillo summed up his feelings about his service:

> I have a good word to speak for the army. I was at all times satisfied with my work. I have nothing to say about the army that would tend to cause anyone to believe that I was dissatisfied. The army or my company was under excellent supervision.[20]

The War Service Record AGO Form 724–6 for Oney Curtis Simmons, a Pulaski, Virginia, soldier who was serving in the 2nd Development Battalion of the 155th Depot Brigade at Camp Lee, Virginia, when he died on 4 October 1918 of acute bilateral Bronchopneumonia. Simmons first reported as being sick on 29 September and was dead just six days later (courtesy Library of Virginia).

4. Lame, Halt and Blind

Without more complete service records, it is difficult to evaluate the efficacy of development battalions for these men. Certainly, some men moved from development battalions to other units during their service. For example, Giuseppe Salvatore Loizzo went from a development battalion to an infantry replacement regiment at Camp Logan, Texas; Clemente Morrone served in a development battalion before being sent to a quartermaster unit at Camp Knox, Kentucky, where he was promoted to corporal; and Beniamino Chiappetta served in a United States Guards battalion after a stint in a development battalion.[21] There were many others, and it is not known how many development battalion *alumni* were able to serve overseas in any capacity. Since the development battalions were formed only in early 1918 and given the challenge of training vast numbers of foreign language-speaking men, it is not surprising that more men did not make the transition from development battalion to overseas service.

It is worth noting that these battalions served an important function in the wartime Army. True to the Progressive Era ethos, the battalions tried to Americanize foreign-born men and to help others who needed assistance mentally or physically. The development battalions enabled the Army to train men and retain them, if only for a few

The portrait submitted by Krikor Kevork Jivanian, an Armenian-born soldier who was inducted into the Army in April 1918 and assigned to Company C of a development battalion at Camp McClellan, Alabama. Some mystery remains about this portrait because Jivanian's collar disk reflects United States National Guard (USNG), which is appropriate for Camp McClellan, but the disk on his hat reflects membership in Company I, 1st Infantry Regiment, a Regular Army unit. The medal on his chest is the War Service Medal awarded by New Haven, Connecticut (Connecticut War Service records via Ancestry.com).

months, with the hope that they might be able to serve in some capacity. Many of the men in these battalions became U.S. citizens during their service; there is no telling what impact the battalions had on the men and, in turn, on their families and communities after their discharge.

We turn now to another unique feature of the soldiers serving in the "hilt of the sword," the divisions that trained for combat but never left the United States. Many of these men and their officers had prepared diligently and with enthusiasm only to find the big game was over before they got off the bench.

5

Silver Chevrons Instead of Gold

The Stateside Divisions

> The most unfortunate man today
> Is the man who jumped at the chance
> To fight like hell from the tap of the bell,
> But who'll never see service in France.[1]

As strange as it may sound, for many of the soldiers training in the United States the war ended too quickly. The strategic plan developed by the Allied commanders was for a massive Allied offensive in the spring of 1919. America's contribution would be the four-million-man AEF which would be available in France by then. Among the influx of new troops to the Western Front would be the new Regular Army and National Army divisions still training diligently in the United States when the Armistice was signed. These divisions, like their predecessors, would have 28,000 men and reflect the Army doctrinal and organizational structure which was constantly evolving and based on intensive study of combat conditions on the Western Front from 1914 to 1917.

But before that massive American force can be understood, it is important to return to the period before the United States declared war. By 1916, the Army had already started building towards a new structure and away from its regimental focus. In this new design, the "Division" would be the basic building block for combat operations. Within its structure would be all of the combat arms and logistics support units needed to fight. There would later be some adjustments to this structure as the very size—some 28,000 soldiers—would prove to be difficult to support with the supply and transportation units assigned to the division.

When war was declared, it became necessary to impose a logical numbering system on the emerging divisions, brigades, and regiments.

A surprisingly simple scheme was developed. The 1st through 25th divisions would be considered Regular Army divisions and be filled with volunteers. The 26th through 50th were to be National Guard divisions and manned by the troops from the forty-eight states and the U.S. territories. The 51st through 75th were set aside for future use, and the National Army divisions would start at 76 and be filled with men selected through the draft. It was a good plan and worked fairly well in practice. The 1st through 7th Divisions were deployed to France prior to the Armistice. Likewise, the 26th through 42nd Divisions, comprised originally of National Guardsmen, were deployed to Europe. For the draftee-based National Army Divisions, the 76th through 92nd also made the long voyage to France. The 93rd Division was an anomaly because it was made up of some "colored" National Guard units and some units comprised of drafted African Americans. It was never constituted as a full division and really only consisted of four infantry regiments.[2]

Ultimately, the AEF in France consisted of a mix of 42 divisions from all three sources: Regular Army, National Guard, and National Army. More importantly, however, by mid–1918 it was recognized by many senior leaders that maintaining the exact kind of soldiers in each type of division (volunteers in the Regular Army, Guardsmen in the

Camp Lewis in Washington State was noted for having the most conducive climate for training of all the main camps, a fact that is in evidence in this picture of Company K, 76th Infantry Regiment, 13th Division, taken at the camp's rifle range in October 1918. Most of the soldiers appear to be comfortably dressed as they pose with their Enfield rifles and a football (private collection).

5. Silver Chevrons Instead of Gold

National Guard, and draftees in the National Army units) was just too difficult with very little payback to the war effort. Army Chief of Staff General Peyton March finally put an end to the differences by declaring there was now only one Army. Thereafter officers and enlisted men—volunteers, Guardsmen, or draftees—could be assigned to any unit.[3] In spite of this mixing of types of soldiers, the Army still continued to segregate black soldiers into separate units from whites, Hispanics, and Asians.

What, then, of the divisions still training in the States when the Armistice was signed? Prior to March's logical decision to consolidate into the single "Army," the stateside units had already been designated as Regular or National Army units and received their divisional numbers accordingly. Some of these units had been training for months, had dispatched advanced detachments to France and were actually moving towards the transit camps located near the seaports when they were redirected to other locations for demobilization. Others had barely begun to fill in their ranks and prepare for training. In either case, it appears as many men were disappointed at not making it to France as were happy at not having to face the Germans on the Western Front. In addition to their final pay before demobilization, those men who had served in the States were entitled to wear a silver, downward-pointing chevron on their left sleeve near the cuff for every six-month increment in uniform. In contrast, men who had actually served in France were entitled to similar but

Most likely a pre-war Regular Army soldier assigned as cadre to one of the divisions training in the U.S. late in the war, this unidentified corporal still has his rank chevrons on both sleeves as opposed to the wartime change to wearing them only on the right sleeve. Under magnification it can be seen that he is wearing a collar disk for Company G, 2nd Infantry Regiment that was assigned to the 19th Division (private collection).

blue or gold-colored chevrons; blue for less than 6 months service in France or gold for every six months increment spent overseas. As will be shown later, even this simple system to recognize soldiers' service would become a source of aggravation.

What follows is a short history of these Regular Army and National Army divisions which were assembling and training in the States when the Armistice put an end to their efforts. This second wave of divisions presented a new set of problems for the men charged with organizing and training them. The Army decided to build the new divisions around cadres of Regular Army soldiers. The cadres were usually comprised of some forty Regular Army sergeants, corporals, and privates who would form the nucleus of the new regiments. In building these divisions there was, at times, a thoughtful, guiding hand behind some of the confusion. As will be seen shortly, a number of cavalry units were converted and redesignated as field artillery units. The logic for this was actually common sense—the field artillery units were to be horse-drawn and the cavalry units were filled with men who knew how to ride horses and care for them, thus simplifying and shortening the training required for those units.[4] Other decisions regarding these units would prove to be much less logically based.

Newly selected draftees would then be added to these new units' cadres to make up the rest of the strength required. By the time these later divisions were forming, most of the men aged twenty-one to thirty-one and registered in the first draft and second draft, were already serving in uniform or exempted from service. This meant that a great number of the new inductees came from the third draft which was comprised of men aged eighteen to twenty-one and thirty-one to forty-five. Obviously there were maturity problems with some of the younger men and some physical problems with the older men that had to be taken into consideration in the training camps.

Undoubtedly, an even greater problem stemmed from the fact these new divisions had the great misfortune to be organizing and training as the most widespread and deadly wave of Spanish flu swept through almost all of the military training and transit camps. The earlier wave of flu which had struck in January 1918 had made thousands of soldiers in the camps extremely sick but almost all survived and recovered well enough to go to France and join the AEF. The second wave was deadly, and nearly all of the training camps on the East Coast had to suspend training. The new focus then became keeping their soldiers alive long enough for the epidemic to complete its devastation and move on to other locations. It also important to remember that, by this point, all of the National Guard divisions (26 through 42) and most National Guard soldiers were in France. Therefore, the only types of divisions in training

5. Silver Chevrons Instead of Gold

in the States were those originally designated as either Regular Army or National Army.

The Stateside Divisions

8th Division (Regular Army— Camp Fremont, California)

The 8th Division was truly a unit with one foot in America and the other in Europe. Part of the 8th Division, including the Divisional Headquarters, the 8th Infantry Regiment, the 2nd, 81st and 83rd Field Artillery Regiments, the 8th Trench Mortar Battery, and the 319th Engineer Regiment with their logistics train, actually reached France before the

Not enough to go around

An interesting cartoon which shows the situation in the 8th Division when the Armistice was signed; the soldier with the full plate of "War Pudding" is from another division in France while the 8th Infantry Regiment soldier receives only a small portion by arriving so late in the war. Meanwhile another 8th Division soldier from the 12th Infantry Regiment, still in the States, is crying because he receives none (*Twelfth U.S. Infantry, 1798–1919*).

Armistice. But just barely; the Brigade Headquarters for the field artillery units arrived on 9 November 1918. Other divisional units had in fact boarded ships in Hoboken harbor when word was received not to sail. Shortly thereafter, the troops on these ships received orders to disembark and head for a demobilization station. Of the 8th Division units

Private Leonardo Gonzales (seated in the center) from New Mexico was one of the soldiers assigned to the 62nd Infantry Regiment, 8th Division, who arrived at the port of embarkation on 11 November 1918. The unit was sent back to Camp Devens and demobilized. In Leonardo's case, it may have been for the best since he had already suffered an accident in training when he shot himself in the hand (New Mexico War Service records via Ancestry.com).

that did make it to France, they very quickly were absorbed into other units or sent to transit camps to wait to return to the States. The sole exception was the 8th Infantry Regiment which was soon set aside and designated for service in the Army of Occupation in the German Rhineland.[5] As a result, the 8th Infantry Regiment, the last of its kind to arrive in France, would remain in Europe until February 1923 when the very last component of the American Forces in Germany (AFG) furled its flag and returned home. Ironically, while the 8th Infantry Regiment was the last complete combat unit to arrive in France in late October 1918, it would be among the very first to return to France in World War II by landing on Utah Beach on the morning of 6 June 1944.

9th Division (Regular Army— Camp Sheridan, Alabama)

The 9th Division was organized at Camp Sheridan in August 1918 after the 37th Division, composed of Ohio National Guardsmen, departed. Consisting of a full complement of units, including the two brigades of infantry (45th, 46th, 67th, and 68th Infantry Regiments) and one of field artillery (25th, 26th, and 27th Field Artillery Regiments and the 9th Trench Mortar Battery), the 9th continued to train through the heat of the Alabama summer. Receiving large drafts of men from Camps Hancock, Meade, Taylor, Travis, and Upton as well as from Fort Slocum and Columbus Barracks, the 9th Division was brought up to a strength of twenty-five thousand soldiers. By November, the 9th was preparing to move to the East Coast for deployment to France. The 9th Division was so close to deploying it sent an advanced detachment to the port of embarkation

Born in Constantinople, Turkey, James Soterios Mellas was a chef and the owner of the Hallett Restaurant in Bridgeport, Connecticut, when he was drafted. He was serving in the 9th Division which was training at Camp Sheridan, Alabama, when the Armistice was signed (Connecticut War Service records via Ancestry.com).

on 28 October. The signing of the Armistice a few days later put an end to further deployments. Although the division was officially trained and declared ready for combat, at least one man had definite opinions about some aspects of his unit's training and readiness. Reese B. Fullerton was a federal law enforcement officer in Santa Fe, New Mexico, when he was drafted on July 30, 1918. Fullerton was eventually promoted to sergeant and sent to Camp Sheridan, Alabama, where the 209th Engineer Regiment, 9th Division, was training. After the war, Fullerton gave his opinion on his regiment's training:

> Regiment crippled by incompetency and bad judgment of young Major Elliott (only 24 years old), who force marched regiment in hot sun under full pack eleven miles and sent an average of 65 men out of each company to the hospital. Regiment never got on its feet in time to get across [to France].[6]

After 11 November, the 9th received orders to begin the demobilization process. By February 1919, with the exception of Regular Army soldiers assigned to the 45th and 46th Infantry Regiments, all of the soldiers were demobilized and returned to their homes.

10th Division (Regular Army—Camp Funston, Kansas)

The 10th Division was organized at Camp Funston in August 1918 after the 89th Division had completed their training and departed. The 10th Division began its short life under the guiding hand of Major General Leonard Wood who had also trained its predecessor division at Funston. Wood had expected to command the 89th in France but after a short pre-deployment visit there with other divisional commanders, he received the word that he was assigned instead to organize, train, and command another division, the 10th. The division was comprised of the 20th, 41st, 69th, and 70th Infantry Regiments and the 28th, 29th, and 30th Field Artillery Regiments, plus other support units. It reached peak strength of 24,829 soldiers and an advance detachment was sent to Camp Mills, an East Coast transit camp, and sailed to France on 2 November 1918. The detachment arrived at Brest on 9 November. With the Armistice declared just two days later, the detachment was sent back to the States. Other units of the 10th were actually at Camp Mills awaiting transportation to Europe when the Armistice was declared.[7]

Among the more unusual and more travelled members of the 10th Division was Captain Joseph A.W. Iglehart of the 28th Field Artillery Regiment. Iglehart had originally joined the Maryland National Guard in

5. Silver Chevrons Instead of Gold

December 1915 as an enlisted soldier in Battery A of the Maryland Light Artillery. By December 1916 he was a lieutenant. He graduated from the Officers Training Course at Fort McPherson, Georgia, in August 1917 and was promoted to captain. After serving as an instructor at Camp Gordon, Georgia, and Fort Sill, Oklahoma, Iglehart was selected to be the commander of Battery F, 321st Field Artillery, 82nd Division. He sailed with the 82nd to France in June 1918 and, now promoted to major, commanded Battery F in the St. Mihiel sector. Two days before the American St. Mihiel Offensive started, Iglehart received orders to turn over his command and return to the United States to serve as a field artillery instructor at Camp Funston. With the organizing of the 10th Division started, Iglehart was assigned to the 28th Field Artillery Regiment and remained with them until he was demobilized in December 1918.[8]

Even with the war having ended six weeks earlier, there was still a significant number of soldiers in the stateside camps for Christmas 1918. From Camp Funston, Kansas, comes this Christmas menu for Headquarters Company of the 69th Infantry Regiment, 10th Division. Along with an impressive holiday meal menu the pamphlet contains a complete unit roster (private collection).

11th Division (Regular Army—Camp Meade, Maryland)

A Regular Army division, the 11th, nicknamed the "Lafayette" Division, was being organized and trained at Camp Meade when the war ended. Among the units designated to be part of the 11th Division were the 17th, 63rd, 71st, and 72nd Infantry Regiments and the 31st, 32nd, and 33rd Field Artillery Regiments. Camp Meade had the misfortune

Pennsylvania-born James Boyd Kleckner was working as a machinist in Berwick, Pennsylvania, when he was drafted. Already married and with a child when he registered on 5 June 1917, his request for exemption from the draft was denied. Kleckner served in the 154th Depot Brigade at Camp Meade from May until September 1918 when he was transferred to the 72nd Infantry Regiment, 11th Division (private collection).

5. Silver Chevrons Instead of Gold

to be one of the hardest hit camps by the Spanish flu and so little training progress was made during September and October 1918. By early November, the division was at its peak strength of twenty-five thousand soldiers and an advance detachment had reached Liverpool, England, on 8 November 1918 to prepare for the division's arrival in Europe.[9] Shortly thereafter the Armistice was signed and the 11th was quickly marked for demobilization rather than deployment. By February 1919 the demobilization of the 11th Division was completed and Camp Meade began to receive returning AEF units to begin their demobilization process. Among those returning from France were Maryland National Guard units from the 29th and 42nd Divisions as well as the 79th Division and a regiment of the 92nd Division.

The draft registration card for another 11th Division soldier, Reece B. Gardner, a draftee in the 17th Infantry Regiment from Roy, New Mexico. As can be seen in the responses on the card, Gardner seemed to take a simple view of the world; claiming employment as a farmer, he listed the location of his work as being "on farm near Roy." On his New Mexico war service questionnaire, when asked about his parents, he mistakenly listed "Kentucky" and "Tennessee" in place of their names (New Mexico War Service records via Ancestry.com).

12th Division (Regular Army— Camp Devens, Massachusetts)

The first division to train at Camp Devens—the 76th Division—deployed to France during July and August 1918. The 76th was quickly replaced at Devens by a new Regular Army division, the 12th, which was nicknamed the "Plymouth Division." Assigned to the division were two Regular Army regiments, the 36th Infantry which had been in training at

Camp Snelling, Minnesota, and the 42nd Infantry which had been parceled out to guard seaports and critical infrastructure. The regiments were shipped to Devens to become part of the 12th Division. Also assigned to the 12th Division were the 73rd and 74th Infantry Regiments and the 34th, 35th, and 36th Field Artillery Regiments, plus the normal support units. The artillery units did not train with the rest of the 12th Division but instead were organized and trained at the field artillery training center at Camp McClellan, Alabama. The bulk of the manpower for the 73rd and 74th Regiments was drawn from the 151st Depot Brigade. Most unit personnel shortages were made up from draftees from New England.

Commanding the 12th Division was Major General Henry P. McCain, a very determined and enthusiastic soldier from Mississippi. Perhaps indicative of McCain's personality was his establishment of several new tactical-weapons training courses on his very first day as commander. A number of French and British instructors were also brought in to train the division's soldiers in the latest tactics and techniques of trench warfare.

Many of the soldiers shared General McCain's enthusiasm. Private Lewis G. Wells was numbered among them. He had first tried to get accepted into officer training and then into the Army

Attilio Fiore, an Italian-born woolworker in Stannisville, Rhode Island, was 23 when he registered for the draft on 5 June 1917. After he was inducted, Attilio served in the 33rd Field Artillery Regiment in the 12th Division, training at Camp Devens. In this portrait this crossed cannons of the field artillery are visible on his left collar disk (Connecticut War Service records via Ancestry.com).

5. Silver Chevrons Instead of Gold

Air Service but had been unable to pass their physicals. Drafted in September 1918, he reported gladly for duty and was assigned to the Headquarters Company of the 12th Division's 212th Engineer Regiment with duty assignment in the Topographical Office. Military service suited Wells:

> I gained 10 pounds in weight and even after having lived a sedentary life for three months since my discharge, I am stronger than I ever was before. ... I have a much greater tolerance for men in general and for what are commonly known as their vices.[10]

Still, Wells' experience left him with a definite impression of some of the men with whom he served:

> From my experience of the boundless egotism and brainless arrogance of all young West Point graduates I saw, I am firmly convinced that West Point needs a reform.... I have a very much lower opinion of the intelligence of the average man.[11]

An interesting photograph of Lt. Col. Frank B. Edwards, the Chief of Staff for the 12th Division at Camp Devens, July 1918. By the time the 12th Division completed its training and was ready for deployment to France, it was considered one of the best trained units in the United States (courtesy Library of Massachusetts).

Another enthusiastic 12th Division soldier was Private Bedros Hachodoorian (sometimes spelled Hockodoorian), of Company H, 74th Infantry Regiment. Hachodoorian, an Armenian immigrant from Cesaria, Turkey, had been working in a Bridgeport, Connecticut, boarding house before he was drafted. According to him, the Army was "a fine training for a young man. I derived great benefits both mental and physical while in the service. I can say that the training that Uncle Sam gives his men is thorough, and treatment the best."[12]

Also serving in the 74th Infantry Regiment was Private Felexforo Gomez, a native of Spain. Gomez believed felt his training had been beneficial: "I think that military service is the best thin a man can do for mental and physical. I know that was a great think for me."[13]

In agreement with both Gomez and Hachodoorian was another 74th Infantry Regiment soldier, Leonard W. Smith, who had first attempted to volunteer but was rejected because of a problem with an ear. He was, however, drafted later and entered service on 25 July 1918. Assigned to the Headquarters Company of the regiment, Smith remained, in his words, a "Buck Private to the last." Asked about any engagement he might have participated in, Smith stated he fought "sham battles only." He managed to survive the flu, no small accomplishment at Camp Devens in late 1918, spending three days in the hospital. He was discharged in January

Private Guerino Pierro was another Italian-born soldier in the 12th Division. He was working as a velvet weaver in the Cheney Brothers Mill in Manchester, Connecticut, when he was inducted into the 74th Infantry Regiment. The mill complex where Private Pierro worked is still standing today as part of the Cheney Brothers Historic District. Pierro was lucky to survive the Spanish flu after spending 24 days in the Camp Devens hospital (Connecticut War Service records via Ancestry.com).

5. Silver Chevrons Instead of Gold

1919. During his service Smith benefited both mentally and physically and he thought "most soldiers feel, as they return to civil life, that they have established themselves in better relations with each other and with their fellow man."[14]

Sadly, the only enemy the 12th faced was the Spanish flu which arrived at the camp with a deadly effect. Over eight hundred soldiers died there, including eighty-one on 27 September 1918, the single worst day of the epidemic at the camp. Among the dead were five nurses and two doctors.

An advance detachment was sent to Europe and arrived in England on 8 November, just three days before the Armistice. The 12th received orders to demobilize in January 1919 and by the end of February, the division had been dispersed.[15]

Felexforo Gomez was born in Spain and inducted into the 12th Division. In this portrait, it appears that he is wearing the light-blue hat cords of an infantryman on his campaign hat. He later filled out a post-war questionnaire and extolled the benefits of military service as being constructive both mentally and physically (Connecticut War Service records via Ancestry.com).

Balthasar J. Lies, a farmer from Minneola, Kansas, poses for a highly detailed portrait. Lies registered for the draft on 5 June 1917 and was later inducted into Company H, 44th Infantry Regiment, 13th Division, which was training at Camp Lewis, Washington. He reached the rank of corporal before being demobilized with the rest of the inductees in the division (private collection).

13th Division (Regular Army—Camp Lewis, Washington)

A Regular Army division, the 13th (nicknamed "the Lucky Thirteenth Division," it used a black cat and a horseshoe on its shoulder patch) was being organized at Camp Lewis when the war ended. It was comprised of the 1st, 44th, 75th, and 76th Infantry Regiments and the 37th, 38th, and

U.S. Government poster announcing that there would be a 31 July 1917 draft registration day for men between the ages of 21 and 31 who were living in the Territory of Hawaii. Note that all of the information is presented in English and in the local native language (Library of Congress).

5. Silver Chevrons Instead of Gold

39th Field Artillery Regiments, and support units. The division began training in August 1918 and reached a total strength of 21,700 soldiers. It was declared ready for overseas service in early November but never deployed due to the Armistice.

The 13th Division was demobilized in March 1919.[16] Some of the Regular Army units, the 1st and 44th Infantry Regiments, were reassigned to other posts. Part of the 1st Infantry Regiment was ordered to Tacoma and Seattle in February 1919 for riot duty.[17]

14th Division (Regular Army— Camp Custer, Michigan)

A Regular Army division, the 14th, nicknamed "the Wolverine Division" as a tribute to the animal which was native to Michigan with a well-earned reputation as a fierce fighter. It was comprised of the 10th, 40th, 77th, and 78th Infantry Regiments and the 40th, 41st, and 42nd Field Artillery Regiments. The 14th was organized at Camp Custer in July 1918 when the 85th Division left for France but did not deploy before the war ended.[18]

Joseph Halulu Amos had to cross the Pacific Ocean before he could report to Camp Lewis. Born in Honolulu and working as a mechanic's helper, Amos registered in the special 31 July 1917 draft which was specifically for men living in the Territory of Hawaii. Unlike most draftees, Amos had already served three years in the Hawaiian National Guard. Here he poses for a portrait and proudly shows his 13th Division patch and his silver-colored stateside service chevron (courtesy James Miller).

15th Division (Regular Army— Camp Logan, Texas)

Camp Logan was established near Houston, Texas, to train the Illinois National Guardsmen of the 33rd Division. As noted earlier, the camp, although welcomed at first by the local population, became a

Despite the damage and fingerprint smudges on the original, this portrait of Abraham Avesian provides an interesting image for study. Avesian enlisted in April 1917 before the draft started and served with the 6th Cavalry Regiment in Texas where this photograph was most likely made. He was then transferred to the 10th Infantry Regiment, 14th Division, training at Camp Custer. In the image, Avesian is armed with the .03 Springfield rifle and a .45 caliber automatic pistol, and is wearing the leather leggings associated with cavalry units (New Mexico War Service records via Ancestry.com).

major problem when the Spanish flu appeared among the soldiers training there. The subsequent decision to transfer the sick men to local hospital facilities only served to make the problem worse by spreading the disease throughout the city.

When the 33rd deployed to France a Regular Army division, the 15th, was organized at Camp Logan in August 1918. The 15th was comprised of the 43rd, 57th, 79th, and 80th Infantry Regiments and the 43rd, 44th, and 45th Field Artillery Regiments, along with support units. Divisional training began in October 1918. The 215th Engineer Regiment was organized and trained in Virginia at Camp Humphreys and joined the division in Texas in November 1918.[19]

By 3 December 1918 the division was already starting to demobilize. In February, except for two Regular Army units, the 43rd and the 57th Infantry Regiments, the division completed demobilization and the drafted soldiers returned to their homes. Remnants of the camp can still be seen today as chunks of concrete, building foundations, and portions of the trench complex used by the soldiers remain.

16th Division (Regular Army— Camp Kearny, California)

The 16th Division was organized at Camp Kearny in August 1918. It was comprised of the 21st, 31st, 32nd, and 82nd Infantry Regiments and

Two individual portraits of unidentified soldiers serving in Company H, 32nd Infantry Regiment, at Camp Kearny, California. The 32nd was originally assigned to duty in the Hawaiian Islands but was transferred to California to serve in the 16th Division in July 1918 (private collection).

the 46th, 47th, and 48th Field Artillery Regiments, plus support units. Several cavalry units were sent to Kearny to provide manpower for the 48th Field Artillery and 16th Trench Mortar Battery. A number of draftees from western states were also brought to the camp to provide necessary manpower for the division. Training began in September 1918, but the unit strength never got above 12,000. The 16th Division did not deploy to France before the war ended and was demobilized in March 1918.[20]

17th Division (Regular Army—Camp Beauregard, Louisiana)

After completing the training of the National Guard 39th Division in August and September 1918, Camp Beauregard was designated as the site for training the Regular Army's 17th Division. The 39th was designated as a Depot/Replacement Division for the AEF shortly after it arrived in France, and so the Division Commander, Major General Henry Clay Hodges, returned to Camp Beauregard in November to command the newly forming 17th Division. Two cavalry units were inactivated to provide manpower for the field artillery units. Some of the men forming the division came from U.S. Army units in the Panama Canal Zone. There were also a number of draftees from Louisiana. Nevertheless, in spite of these additions to the manpower, the total number of troops in the 17th Division never exceeded nine thousand. Hodges arrived back at Camp Beauregard just in time to receive orders to demobilize the division and its assigned 5th, 29th, 83rd, and 84th Infantry and 49th, 50th, and 51st Field Artillery Regiments, and support units.[21]

Henry Clay Hodges, an 1881 West Point graduate, was selected to train and command the 39th Division at Camp Beauregard, Louisiana. On arrival in France the 39th was converted to a depot division and Hodges returned to Camp Beauregard to train the 17th Division (U.S. Army).

18th Division (Regular Army—Camp Travis, Texas)

After the 90th Division departed Travis in June and July 1918, the camp was converted to serve as an induction and replacement center. During this period the average soldier population at the camp was 34,000 with a mix of white and black troops. The Army decided to organize and train a Regular Army division there starting in August 1918. This new division, the 18th, was given the nickname of

The shoulder patch designed for the 18th Division was certainly appropriate for a combat unit raised and trained in Texas: a prickly looking cactus plant with the motto in Latin: *Noli Me Tangere* meaning "Don't Touch Me" (private collection).

New Mexico–born Servando Gonzales (on left) was a farmer before being selected in the draft. Seen here with some of his also musically inclined comrades, Gonzales served in the 19th Infantry Regiment, 18th Division, while training at Camp Travis in 1918 (New Mexico War Service records via Ancestry.com).

Listing his pre-war occupation as a laborer at the American Smelting and Mining Company in Durango, Colorado, Severiano Garcia (left) registered for the draft on 5 June 1917. Selected in July 1918, the New Mexico–born soldier was assigned to Company L, 86th Infantry Regiment, 18th Division. Garcia and his comrades pose for their portrait while wearing various shades of clothing and styles of canvas leggings, a sign that the Army supply system was focused on the AEF in France and not on the soldiers training in remote Camp Travis (New Mexico War Service records via Ancestry.com).

5. Silver Chevrons Instead of Gold

"the Cactus Division" and the motto "Noli Me Tangere" which is Latin for "Don't Touch Me." The 18th's Field Artillery Brigade was trained at nearby Camp Stanley while the divisional engineer regiment was trained at Camp Humphrey in Virginia. The Infantry and Field Artillery Brigades were comprised of the 19th, 35th, 85th, and 86th Infantry and the 52nd, 53rd, and 54th Field Artillery Regiments. Two cavalry units were inactivated to provide manpower for the field artillery units. With a soldier strength of fourteen thousand men the 18th began their divisional training and had reached the advanced level of tactical operations just as the war ended.[22]

The 18th was quickly demobilized starting in January 1919, and the 19th Infantry Regiment, a Regular Army unit, was dispatched for service on the Mexican border. Shortly thereafter Camp Travis was designated as a demobilization center and its depot brigade processed over 60,000 soldiers for discharge in about eight months.

19th Division (Regular Army— Camp Dodge, Iowa)

A Regular Army division, the 19th, began organizing at Camp

Before the U.S. military placed restrictions on family members serving in the same unit, it was a fairly common occurrence. Here the Corley brothers, John and Aaron, pose for a portrait, and their collar disks show that they are serving in Company I, 14th Infantry Regiment, 19th Division. The 19th Division was organized at Camp Dodge, Iowa, but the 14th Infantry Regiment served at Vancouver Barracks, Fort George Wright, and Fort Lawton, all in Washington State (private collection).

Dodge in August 1918 but did not deploy to France before the war ended. The main units in the 19th Division were the 2nd, 14th, 37th, and 38th Infantry Regiments and the 55th, 56th, and 57th Field Artillery Regiments. By October 1918 there were 12,000 soldiers assigned to the division. Serious combat training had begun when news of the Armistice reached the camp. Demobilization began in December and most draftees were discharged by February 1919.[23]

With the end of the war Camp Dodge was downsized and returned to state authorities for Iowa National Guard use. Today Camp Dodge remains a National Guard training site and is fortunate to have three original World War I training camp buildings remaining: two warehouses and an ammunition storage building.

20th Division (Regular Army— Camp Sevier, South Carolina)

After the 30th Division departed for France, the Regular Army's 20th Division was organized at Camp Sevier starting in August 1918. The main divisional units were the 48th, 50th, 89th, and 90th Infantry Regiments and the 58th, 59th, and 60th Field Artillery Regiments. The 310th Cavalry Regiment at Fort Ethan Allen, Vermont, and 312th Cavalry Regiment at Fort Russell, Wyoming, were inactivated to provide soldiers for the

A damaged but still interesting image of Thomas Bryant, a drafted soldier originally from Mahanoy City, Pennsylvania. Bryant was a shipping clerk at a biscuit company in New Haven, Connecticut, when he was selected for service in the 20th Division. The 20th was trained at Camp Sevier, South Carolina, formerly a National Guard training site, which may explain why he is standing in front of a squad tent rather than a wooden barracks. About his military service, Bryant stated: "Thought it was a great cause. I was perfectly satisfied." After the war, Bryant returned to the bakery industry and lived in New Haven until his death (Connecticut War Service records via Ancestry.com).

field artillery units. The 20th was augmented with the 220th Engineer Regiment which had trained at Camp Humphreys. The division selected a unique insignia—a skull and crossbones with the number 20 at the top. Although the Division reached a total strength of 15,400 men and underwent extensive training, it never deployed to France. It was demobilized at Camp Sevier on 25 February 1919 and all assigned draftees were discharged.[24]

94th Division (National Army— Puerto Rico)

The 94th Division was authorized in June 1918 and most of the soldiers were to come from men drafted in Puerto Rico. Although initial plans called for it to be a full-sized division, the 94th was later redesignated as a provisional brigade. The original design included four complete infantry regiments: the 373rd, 374th, 375th, and 376th. The four infantry regiments were reduced to three when the 94th was downgraded to a brigade with three full regiments and a number of separate infantry companies. Interestingly, one of the regiments, the 375th, was designated as "colored," perhaps indicating that the 94th Division/Brigade would have been an integrated unit. Only the 94th's field artillery brigade, comprised of the 355th, 356th, and 357th Field Artillery Regiments, would have been comprised of English-speaking personnel, all others were Spanish-speaking. By October 1918 there were 10,600 men assigned but with the Armistice, the regiments were demobilized in January 1919 and all of the soldiers discharged.[25]

95th Division (National Army— Camp Sherman, Ohio)

After the 83rd Division completed its training and deployed to France in June 1918, another National Army division, the 95th, was organized and began training at Camp Sherman. Two of the regiments which were to comprise the 95th's 191st Infantry Brigade were already in France and serving as the 1st and 2nd Pioneer Infantry Regiments. The other two infantry regiments, the 379th and 380th were organized at Camp Sherman and augmented by a large number of men transferred from Camp Lee, Virginia. The 95th's 170th Field Artillery Brigade was comprised of the 67th, 68th, and 69th Field Artillery Regiments. Much of the manpower for these units came from inactivating the 311th and 313th Cavalry Regiments. The 95th only had some 6,400 men assigned and was still in its initial phase of training when the war

Another unique document: the honorable discharge for Private 1st Class Domingo Paradis, a 23-year-old teacher in Puerto Rico who was drafted into the 94th Division's 374th Infantry Regiment. The 94th Division was formed primarily from drafted men living in Puerto Rico (private collection).

ended. The division was demobilized in December 1918.[26] With the war over, Camp Sherman also temporarily functioned as a trades and vocational school to educate returning veterans and prepare them for civilian employment.

96th Division (National Army— Camp Wadsworth, South Carolina)

A National Army division, the 96th, was organized in September 1918 at Camp Wadsworth. Two of the infantry regiments which were to be part of the division were already serving in France as the 3rd and 4th Pioneer Infantry Regiments; these would have been reflagged and assigned to the 96th when it arrived in France. The other infantry brigade of the division was comprised of the 383rd and 384th Infantry Regiments. These units were formed primarily from soldiers already at Wadsworth and undergoing training to serve as corps-level troops in the AEF. The 96th's 371st Field Artillery Brigade was organized at Camp Kearny, California, and was comprised of the 64th, 65th, and 66th Field Artillery Regiments. Two cavalry regiments, the 302nd and 308th, were inactivated to

Above: This photograph accompanied a story in an upstate New York newspaper detailing the military adventures of a local man, Harold E. Burton, from the city of Rome. The short clipping describes Burton's transfer in November 1917 from the 153d Depot Brigade at Camp Dix to the 157th Depot Brigade at Camp Gordon. What the newspaper did not know was that Burton would be transferred again, in September 1918, to Camp Wadsworth where he would be assigned to the 62nd Pioneer Infantry Battalion, and then the 384th Infantry Regiment in the 96th Division. Burton, promoted to sergeant, was demobilized in December 1918 (private collection).

Private Ignacio Gonzales, assigned to the 388th Infantry Regiment, 97th Division, at Camp Cody poses for his portrait in front of an American flag backdrop. Many of the men serving in the 387th and 388th Infantry Regiments were drafted from the American Southwest while the other two infantry regiments of the 97th Division were to be formed from pioneer infantry units already serving in France (New Mexico War Service records via Ancestry.com).

provide some of the manpower for these units. By October 1918 there were still only 3,100 soldiers in camp for the 96th, and training was still in the initial phase.[27]

The 96th appears to have been one of the first stateside divisions to be demobilized, starting on 30 November 1918 and finishing on 7 January 1919.

97th Division (National Army— Camp Cody, New Mexico)

When the 34th Division deployed to France starting in September 1918, a National Army division, the 97th, was directed to organize at Camp Cody. The Field Artillery Brigade for the 97th Division was comprised of the 61st, 62nd and 63rd Field Artillery Regiments being organized at various camps. These units were augmented with personnel from inactivated cavalry units at Fort Bliss and Fort Russell. The division was ordered to form at the Artillery Training Center at Camp Jackson, South Carolina, and completed that action on 4 November 1918. The division's infantry regiments were to be the 5th and 51st Pioneer Infantry Regiments already serving in France and the 387th and 388th Infantry Regiments which were to be formed from draftees. An engineer regiment in training at Camp Humphrey, Virginia, was designated for the 97th Division but never joined it. The war ended before all the units could be gathered together, and the 97th Division, like the 96th, was among the first to be demobilized starting in late November and completing at Camp Cody by the end of December. The divisional field artillery brigade, still at Camp Jackson, was demobilized by mid–January 1919.[28]

98th Division (National Army— Camp McClellan, Alabama)

After the departure of the 29th Division from Camp McClellan, a number of other units were organized and/or trained there, including the 1st Separate Negro Company of Maryland, the 6th Division (Regular Army), and the 98th Division. Organized in October 1918, the 98th Division was supposed to be formed from personnel drawn from two of the 52nd and 53rd Pioneer Infantry Regiments already serving in France. The other infantry regiments, the 391st and 392nd, never formed, nor were the field artillery regiments. The 26th Trench Mortar Battery was organized at Del Rio, Texas, and assigned to the 98th but never joined the division at Camp McClellan. With the signing of the Armistice, the

Another 97th Division infantryman, Juan Garcia, poses for his portrait outside the Company C building. Perhaps another sign of the problems in the Army's supply system: while Garcia has an M1917 Enfield rifle and bayonet scabbard, he has no bayonet or collar disks. From the wear on his boots, it is apparent that he has been in camp for a while (New Mexico War Service records via Ancestry.com).

division was no longer needed and the few troops, primarily headquarters staff and reception staff, who had been gathered, were quickly demobilized on 30 November 1918.²⁹

99th Division (National Army— Camp Wheeler, Georgia)

After the 31st Division departed from Camp Wheeler and deployed to France, a Regular Army division, the 7th, was organized and trained there until they also deployed to France. The National Army 99th Division was organized at Camp Wheeler in October 1918, and the 54th and 55th Pioneer Infantry Regiments, already serving in France, were designated to be reflagged and serve in the 99th's 197th Infantry Brigade. The 198th Infantry Brigade, comprised of the 395th and 396th Infantry Regiments and the 372nd Machine Gun battalion, was never organized. Of the designated field artillery or divisional support units, none were organized except for the 28th Trench Mortar Battery. The 28th was organized at Fort Sheridan, Illinois, but never joined the division. The 99th was demobilized in November 1918.³⁰

Frank Burro was not a typical draftee for several reasons. Born in Italy, Burro had served 28 months in the Italian Army and was a veteran of the Italian-Tripoli war of 1911–1912, one of the violent precursor wars to the First World War. He was also an aircraft mechanic in New Haven, Connecticut. Assigned to the 98th Division's field artillery school, Burro died from the Spanish flu on 19 October 1918 while training at Camp McClellan, Alabama (Connecticut War Service records via Ancestry.com).

100th Division (National Army— Camp Bowie, Texas)

Camp Bowie continued to function for five months as an infantry replacement and training facility after the 36th Division, a National Guard division comprised of Texas and Oklahoma soldiers, deployed to France in July 1918. Including the totals from the 36th Division, more than 100,000 men trained at the camp. A National Army division, the

100th, was organized at Camp Bowie in October 1918, and one of its infantry brigades was supposed to be made up of the 56th and 57th Pioneer Infantry Regiments which were already serving in France. The other units assigned to the division were never organized except for the 25th Trench Mortar Battery which was organized at Camp Stanley but never moved to Camp Bowie. The few soldiers actually assigned to the division were ordered to be demobilized on 30 November 1918.[31]

101st Division (National Army— Camp Shelby, Mississippi)

In July 1918 Camp Shelby was designated training site for the 101st Division. The 58th Pioneer Infantry Regiment in training at Camp Wadsworth, and the 59th Pioneer Infantry Regiment already in France, were to form the 101st's 201st Infantry Brigade. The infantry units for the other infantry brigade were never organized, nor were the field artillery units with the exception of the 27th Trench Mortar Battery. The 27th was organized at Camp Bowie in August 1918 but never joined the 101st at Camp Shelby. Although a divisional Chief of Staff and some staff officers were selected for the 101st, no division or brigade commanders were appointed. The 101st was ordered to demobilize in November 1918 and all men were quickly discharged or reassigned.[32]

102nd Division (National Army— Camp Dix, New Jersey)

After the 79th Division completed its training cycle and departed for France, another National Army Division, the 102nd, was assigned to train at Camp Dix. Just as in the other high number divisions, one infantry brigade was to be formed from two of the white pioneer infantry regiments, in this case the 60th and 61st which were training at Camp Wadsworth. The only 102nd Divisional unit actually organized was the 29th Trench Mortar Battery which was formed at Camp Kearny, California. The war ended before any of the senior officers were appointed, and only a few 102nd Division soldiers arrived at Camp Dix. The division was ordered demobilized in late November 1918.[33]

15th Cavalry Division (Regular Army—Texas and Arizona)

The 15th Cavalry Division began to organize in November 1917, partly in response to General Pershing's request for a cavalry division to serve in France with the AEF and partly to provide coverage of the Mexican Border. Apparently, it was decided to organize the division first and then decide where and how to deploy it later. It was to consist of three cavalry brigades; one each headquartered at Fort Sam Houston, Fort Bliss, and Fort Douglas. The 1st Brigade, at Fort Sam Houston, consisted of the 6th, 14th, and 16th Cavalry Regiments. The 2nd Brigade, at Fort Bliss, consisted of the 5th, 7th, and 8th Cavalry. The 3rd Brigade was located in Arizona and consisted of the 1st, 15th, and 17th Cavalry.

There were also a field artillery and an engineer regiment as well as extensive divisional trains and support troops. The training regimen was both practical and unique in the Army at the time; two thirds of each brigade would train while the remaining regiment would conduct Mexican-border patrolling operations. The regiments would then rotate through this system to ensure that both the training mission and the real-world mission were accomplished.[34]

By May 1918 the commander of the Southern Department recommended that the border patrolling part of the mission would be improved if the divisional/brigade structure was done away with and the units reverted to regimental operations. This recommendation fit nicely with Army Chief of Staff Peyton March's thoughts. He had no intention of filling Pershing's request for the 15th Cavalry Division to join the AEF. March's previous experience in France led him to believe that cavalry units were wasted on the Western Front. As he wrote in *Nation at War*, the British and French had maintained strong cavalry forces in their armies and had nothing to show for it.[35] Accordingly, the 15th Cavalry Division was broken up, and its units remained in their current locations patrolling the border. The 6th and the 15th Cavalry Regiments later deployed to France as separate, independent regiments.[36]

Regular Army Units in Hawaii, Alaska, the Panama Canal Zone, the Philippines and China

Even with the obvious need to dispatch the Army to France, there were still some other global missions which required U.S. soldiers. When war was declared there were almost 11,000 Regular Army soldiers stationed in the Hawaiian Islands. These men were primarily at Fort Shafter and Schofield Barracks in the Hawaiian Division. The units included the 1st, 2nd, and 32nd Infantry Regiments, several field artillery units as well as cavalry and some support units. There were also a number of Coast Artillery Corps units manning key harbor defense sites and forts throughout the islands. There was a Hawaiian Brigade at

Schofield Barracks which consisted of the Hawaiian National Guard 1st Infantry Regiment and the 25th Infantry Regiment comprised of African American soldiers.

In February 1917, even before the U.S. had entered the war, the authorities in Hawaii seized the German raiding ship *Geier* while it was anchored in Honolulu. The crew and other suspected enemy aliens in the Islands were later transferred to an internment camp at Fort Douglas, Utah. By the summer of 1918 the great majority of soldiers in the Regular Army units had been transferred to the mainland and assigned to some of the newly forming divisions. Their places in the Hawaiian Islands' defenses were taken by newly formed National Guard units.[37]

In contrast to Hawaii, there were very few soldiers in Alaska. For military purposes Alaska fell under the command and control of the Western Department headquarters in San Francisco. The 30th U.S. Guards Battalion was sent to Alaska in 1918 with Company A assigned to Fort William H. Seward, Company B to Fort Liscum, Company C to Fort St. Michael, and Company D to Fort Gibbons. All were demobilized by November 1919.[38]

From Fort Shafter, Territory of Hawaii, comes this unique view of a guard detachment. There were more than 10,000 soldiers serving in the Hawaiian Islands when war was declared. It's important to note that, although some of the soldiers appear to be playing around with their weapons, most are wearing a marksmanship badge on their service coats implying some high level of expertise with their weapons (courtesy Pineapple Army photograph archive of Craig Alexander Rothhammer).

5. Silver Chevrons Instead of Gold

The Panama Canal Department had 11,200 Regular Army soldiers assigned when the United States declared war. Most of these were assigned to the four Regular Army infantry regiments: the 5th, 10th, 29th, and 33rd. Of these, only the 33rd would remain on site to guard the Canal while the others were transferred to the mainland to be part of the new Regular Army divisions forming in the summer of 1918. The 5th Infantry Regiment was later sent to Germany to serve in the occupation of the Rhineland and remained there until April 1922.

In February 1917, working with Panamanian officials, the U.S. military forces in the Canal Zone interned five German ships and their crews. They also arrested over a hundred German or Austrian citizens living in the Canal Zone. The prisoners were kept initially at a camp on Taboga Island and later transported to internment facilities in the United States.[39]

There were also some Regular Army infantry regiments stationed in the Philippine Department. In April 1917, when war was declared, almost twenty thousand Regular Army soldiers were serving in the Philippine Islands. These included the 8th, 13th, 27th, and 31st Infantry Regiments and the 2nd Field Artillery Regiment. The latter two infantry regiments were the unlucky ones chosen to go to Russia as the U.S. contingent to Allied forces gathered in Siberia and would not return until March and April 1920. The 8th and 13th Infantry Regiments and the 2nd Field Artillery Regiment headed in the other direction and were assigned to the 8th Division which was training at Camp Fremont, California. Ultimately, the 13th Infantry Regiment would remain in the U.S. and the 8th would be the last infantry regiment to arrive in France as the Armistice was signed. The 2nd Field Artillery reached Europe just in time to turn around and return to the United States. After serving for a few months in France, the 8th Infantry Regiment was sent to Germany to replace the original combat units sent there in November and December 1918. As noted previously, the rifle battalions of the 8th served as the nucleus of the American Forces in Germany in the occupation of the Rhineland until January 1923.[40]

Also assigned to the Philippine Department were all U.S. Army forces in China. The 15th Infantry Regiment made up the greatest part of this force, and it was stationed primarily in Tientsin at Liscum Barracks in Northeast China. At times, detachments from this force would be used to guard critical locations on the railroads. The 15th remained in China throughout the war.[41]

6

The Students' Army Training Corps (SATC)

> "Success in battle is the ultimate object of all military training; success may be looked for only when the training is intelligent and thorough."[1]

In addition to the many training camps across the country, in the spring and summer of 1918 the War Department established a completely new training program, the Students' Army Training Corps (SATC). The program was designed to augment the ongoing work of the Reserve Officers Training Corps (ROTC) and prevent the massive war mobilization effort from emptying the country's colleges while simultaneously providing some military training on existing college campuses. Another goal was to provide a pool of enlisted soldiers with technical and mechanical skills that were crucial in supporting the infantry and artillery soldiers being trained at the divisional camps.

In August the War Department formed the SATC. Manned by voluntary induction, SATC units were created at institutions of higher learning in order "to utilize effectively the plant, equipment, and organization of the colleges for selecting and training officer candidates and technical experts for service in the existing emergency."[2]

Under the provisions of this program, more than five hundred colleges and universities trained officer candidates while instructors also provided specialized and technical training in fields such as auto mechanics and radio operation for enlisted men. By the end of the war, almost 158,000 men had enrolled in SATC programs, and approximately 11,000 of these students were assigned as candidates to officer training schools.[3]

The colleges that participated in SATC became full-time military posts and were placed under the command of U.S. Army officers. That most college and university administrators willingly agreed to this action underscores the strong patriotism of the period. The War

6. The Students' Army Training Corps (SATC) 139

Department provided an Army officer, either active or retired, to serve as the commanding officer at each college participating in the program. From this point on, the commanding officer was responsible for enforcing military discipline and administering the training program for the SATC students. At a higher level, the War Department administered the SATC through the Committee on Education and Special Training of the Training and Instruction Branch in the War Plans Division.

Each SATC unit could be divided into two sections: a Collegiate section and a Vocational section. The Collegiate section trained men for a commission, while the Vocational section trained technical experts. There were different requirements for admission into each section. On admission to the SATC, the student became a soldier in the Army, "subject to military law and to military discipline at all times."[4] The members were considered to be on active duty in the rank of private with all commensurate pay, allowances, subsistence, uniform, and equipment. Men were normally allowed to select their branch of service within each unit, subject to the needs of the military. Thus in any given SATC unit there were companies of men in the Infantry, Artillery, Signal Corps, etc. For men in the Collegiate sections, the training consisted of military subjects (drill, military theory, physical training, etc.) for eleven hours per week and allied subjects (standard college courses and others prescribed for specialized training) for forty-two hours per week. Men in the Vocational sections had fifteen-and-a-half hours per week of military training plus thirty-three hours of instruction in "auto-driving, auto-repair,

Even late in the war (note the date on the United War Work campaign) people were still being exhorted to do more. This poster appealed directly to college and high school students (Library of Congress).

bench wood work, sheet metal work and electrical work, etc."[5] Members of both sections were also required to attend special "War Issues" classes.

There were about 157 SATC units in the collegiate category in 48 states plus the District of Columbia, the Territory of Hawaii, and Puerto Rico. There were sixteen segregated "colored" units, some in traditionally black colleges. The vocational SATC units numbered about 134 in 45 states plus the District of Columbia; seven of these units were for black students. About ninety-five Navy units were located in thirty-seven states plus the District of Columbia, and there were twelve Marine Corps units located in twelve states.[6] As an example of the type of technical training provided by the nation's colleges and universities, the University of Michigan's programs included training for telephone electronics, auto mechanics, machinists, carpenters, gunsmiths, blacksmiths, surveyors, and draftsmen.[7]

Colleges and universities, by the autumn 1918 semester, had already been training enlisted men in such technical specialties as motor mechanics, telegraphy, driving, etc. These men had the opportunity to apply for admission to the Vocational section of the SATC upon the activation of such units. Furthermore, once the semester got underway qualified men could apply for transfer from the Vocational to the Collegiate sections.

Although born in Illinois, Ralph Pitman Rudesill enrolled in the SATC at the University of Nebraska. Seen here posing on the Nebraska campus in September 1918, Rudesill served in Company B of the Training Detachment and was assigned to the Army Signal Corps (private collection).

6. The Students' Army Training Corps (SATC)

In one illustrative case of the close ties of the Army to these educational institutions, the Kansas State Agricultural College assisted the 342nd Field Artillery Regiment training as part of the 89th Division at nearby Camp Funston. Since there was little chance of them receiving the motorized vehicles required to haul their equipment in time for the unit to train before deploying, thirty men per week from the unit were sent to the Agricultural College for instruction in driving and maintaining large trucks and tractors.[8]

The War Department required instructors to instill military bearing even in non-military classes. Regarding SATC students at Berkeley, the War Department stated:

> Instructors are urged to require that members of the S.A.T.C., when reciting in the class-room, shall stand at attention and shall speak with clearness and decision. Instructors should require that enunciation be distinct and the pronunciation of words correct. The possession of these qualities of speech is regarded as of military importance.[9]

The War Department and schools made every effort to ensure adequate housing was available for the SATC students. Mirroring the rapid construction of thirty-two divisional training camps and cantonments a year earlier, barracks for SATC soldier-students sprung up on fields on and near colleges throughout the country in August and September 1918. As the regents of the University of Colorado stated in August, "The University is making every effort to provide quarters and mess in suitable barracks by October 1. The time is very short and the emergency has arisen without warning, so that there will doubtless be a period of inconvenience during the first weeks of the session."[10] Many SATC men ended up housed in temporary makeshift barracks in gymnasiums, fraternity houses, and other available spaces.

The SATC was set to begin on 1 October 1918; eighteen-year-old college students, however, had to register for the draft on 12 September 1918. If their draft number was called before 1 October the student was required to report to their draft board for induction. If they enlisted in SATC after 1 October and their number was subsequently called, the War Department would decide whether each man would remain at his university for continued training or whether he would report for duty elsewhere.

The daily schedule for SATC students at the University of Colorado gives some idea of the military basis of the program: "Reveille 6:45, mess 7:00, drill 7:30 to 9:30, classes 9:30 to 12:00, mess 12:00 to 1:30, classes 1:30 to 4:30, athletics and exercise 4:30 to 5:30, retreat and mess 6:00, freedom 6:30 to 7:30, supervised study 7:30 to 9:30, taps 10:00."[11] It is not known how closely the University of Colorado, or, indeed, any other school, adhered to this schedule.

The influenza epidemic in 1918 impacted colleges just as it did the rest of the country. All university activity at the University of Kansas was suspended between 8 October and 11 November 1918; by the time the epidemic there had subsided, ten SATC men had died.[12] Approximately twenty-seven members of the University of North Dakota SATC died from influenza.[13] On the other hand, Westminster College suffered no fatalities among its SATC students. This was largely due to the proactive attention given by Lieutenant (Dr.) A.J. Courshon, the medical officer at Westminster's unit. At the first indication of an epidemic, Courshon, at his own expense, inoculated soldiers and used fraternity houses as hospitals. As a result, Westminster's unit was the only Missouri SATC unit not to undergo quarantine and the only one not to have any new cases after the first two weeks of the outbreak.[14]

According to J.H. Wigmore, Dean of Northwestern University, the SATC succeeded in two main areas. First, it succeeded in providing a cadre of "trained officer-material" vital to the growth of the Army during the war. And second, the program rescued "the country's universities and colleges from disastrous disruption."[15] Wigmore's second point reflects the fact that the nation's universities would have suffered disorganization and financial hardship had the draft, which in September 1918 encompassed men as young as eighteen years of age, continued into 1919. This assertion is perhaps valid, although by no means would all eighteen to twenty-year-old men have been drafted in late 1918 and early 1919. His first point, however, must remain unproven. Most of the men in the SATC, especially those in the collegiate sections, had no other military service during

Pvt. Walter B. Freeburg, Section A, SATC, University of New Mexico, poses in his heavy Model-1917 overcoat. Freeburg appears to have started his college studies at Clarendon College in Texas and later transferred to the University of New Mexico (New Mexico questionnaire via Ancestry.com).

6. The Students' Army Training Corps (SATC)

the war, thus their contribution to victory must be viewed as a potential contribution, or at most as a real pool of upcoming manpower.

Because these units consisted of college students, most of the men were from eighteen to twenty years old in October 1918. There were a few who were older, but most fell into the eighteen to twenty-year-old range. The academic requirements for entry into the SATC meant that the student-soldiers had greater educational attainment and a higher intelligence level than the average soldier during the war. How did these men feel about their brief military service? Certainly their opinion of their service varied, but Humbert Cofrancesco, a student at Yale in 1918, left a brief contemporary record of his opinion.

Cofrancesco was born in New Haven, Connecticut, on 25 January 1900, the son of Italian immigrants. He entered Yale on 26 September 1918, and then enlisted in the Yale SATC unit on 3 October; although he served in the field artillery branch, he had special duty in the Quartermaster office at Yale until his discharge on 19 December 1918.

As a son of immigrants, Cofrancesco's thoughts about his service bear examination. Overall he was pleased with his service and impressed by the military. He admired the Army which "functions from the standpoint of a maximum of work-accomplishments; efficiency, speed, satisfaction, and admiration with a minimum of discomfort for the personnel." But Cofrancesco noted exceptions:

> Time and time again, I saw grumblers—those who always complained when detailed for

Looking studious and proudly displaying his field artillery collar disk, Humbert Cofrancesco was a member of the Yale SATC. Reflecting on his time in the SATC, Cofrancesco was quite complimentary about the mental and physical benefits provided by his service in the SATC (Connecticut War Service records via Ancestry.com).

policing or fatigue duty; those who were repeatedly reprimanded for slight infractions of discipline, due to apparent carelessness and inattentiveness. No discrimination or preference was evident in the attitude taken toward the members of the Students' Army Training Corps at Yale University. It was, indeed, curious to see the workings of democracy—for such it was.[16]

According to Cofrancesco:

> The most pronounced effect on me was physical. The human body was a living engine in the army. With painstaking care, every precaution was taken to safeguard the men's health, especially during the influenza epidemic. In fact, every man was, upon his discharge, healthier—stronger and stouter. All weaknesses and feebleness were eliminated. Backs were straightened; round shoulders disappeared. One of the losses of military training most seriously felt by the ex-soldier will be that of good, helpful physical exercises and drills.[17]

Men enlisted for a variety of reasons, with serving one's country in a time of need being a very commonly cited reason. Reflected in this duty could be a feeling of pressure if one did not enlist. Arthur Stenberg, who served in the Infantry unit at Storrs Agricultural College from 31 October to 17 December 1918, wrote, "I felt that I had to enlist, so I did. I felt that when the war was over, my mind would certainly feel a lot better if I enlisted."[18]

Despite the short duration of the SATC, some men did actually move from their enlisted SATC status to various officers' training camps. For example, five men from St. Olaf College, Northfield, Minnesota, went to officers' training camps, and ten men from Westminster College, Fulton, Missouri, did likewise. After a rousing send-off the ten men departed from Westminster for officers' training at Camp Pike, Arkansas; they got as far as St. Louis when the Armistice put an end to their military career.[19]

The disappointment must have been keen for such men as Merton Strickland, a member of the Infantry SATC at Wesleyan University, who reported: "Received appointment to Infantry O.T.C. [Officers' Training Camp] at Camp Freemont, Palo Alto, Cal. Ordered to leave Springfield, Mass. Nov. 12, 1918. Held back because of Armistice."[20] Strickland had been anxious to join the military at age seventeen, but he had to wait until he could enlist in the SATC at age eighteen. Four members of the SATC at Illinois College were called to active duty, but "they never left campus, since the Armistice was declared on the day before they were ordered to report to Camp Grant."[21]

One may form an idea of the training emphasis in at least the Yale unit by Cofrancesco's observation regarding his training: "The drills in particular demanded a steady, concentrated mental effort. Military topography taught the man to be keen, observant, appreciative of details under unusual, and sometimes, discomforting circumstances."[22]

So impressed was Cofrancesco by his military service that he observed,

> if ever there was a time for introducing a light system of military training—e.g., the Swiss system—it will now meet with hearty approval on the part of a very large majority of the people; for now is the psychological moment.[23]

This was an astute observation which went unheeded. Indeed, it remains to be seen what long-term impact service in the SATC had upon the future college graduates who were members.

Lest one suspect Cofrancesco's views were colored by any pre-war fascination with things military, his statement regarding his state of mind prior to the war is included in its entirety:

> My idea, or state of mind before the war—and I feel certain I am voicing the sentiments of others who have seen service elsewhere—was very dissimilar to my actual experience. I used to think that army life was very dull and monotonous; lacking that stimulative, creative force, which we call spirit. But I found the army to be as human as—if not more so than—any other organization, institution, or association of people. By its heterogeneous character, it lacked no worldly element. It contained every variety of people—from the point of view of race, nationality, religion, political views, domestic and financial conditions, manners, thoughts, ambitions. Its diversity made it an attraction—a lovableness in itself. Its morale was high; it was enthusiastic, looking forward to some great accomplishment. This is, indeed, an amazingly novel thing to one who had rather radically different pre-war conception of military life and experience.[24]

The idea that service in the SATC, and, by extension the military in general, fostered a democratic spirit among the men seems to have been a common idea. William Seltzer, a member of the Signal Corps section of the SATC at New York University, stated, "military service was beneficial to make all democratic." He also felt that his brief service made him stronger and his nerves steadier.[25]

As befits a program consisting of volunteers, the young men were eager to enlist. According to Leon Thorp of Company D (Infantry) of the Amherst College SATC unit: "As it was apparent that the War Dept. wanted college men for officers I was ready to do my part in the most efficient way possible."[26] Walter Harrigan served in the SATC unit at Holy Cross College, Massachusetts, from 21 October to 14 December 1918. According to Harrigan,

> I am and was a strong believer in military preparedness. I was very willing and exceedingly anxious to join some form of service. When the formation

of the SATC branch was affected I decided to enlist at once. ... I was benefited physically by the gaining of 10 lbs of much-needed weight. ... [I gained] a full appreciation of the value of Army life in both advantages and handicaps.[27]

Harrigan wasn't alone in his appreciation of Army food. Samuel Hyman, a native of Russia and member of the infantry SATC unit at New York University, declared: "The physical side of me improved

Another SATC soldier from Yale, Maurice B. Ullman poses in his uniform. Ullman noted that during his time in the SATC program he had gained 10 pounds; this may be reflected in his portrait as the lower buttons on his service coat are clearly stretched, an indication of weight gain since earlier uniform issue (Connecticut War Service records via Ancestry.com).

Like many of his contemporaries, Leon A. Thorp (seen here in his army uniform at Amherst College), found service in the SATC to be extremely beneficial in improving his physical condition and his overall mental abilities. Prior to joining the SATC, Thorp had served in the Connecticut State Guard (Connecticut War Service records via Ancestry.com).

6. The Students' Army Training Corps (SATC)

wonderfully. I gained 10 pounds in one month."[28] Maurice Bernhard Ullman of the Yale unit also gained ten pounds. Apparently the men thrived during their two and a half months of military training. Leon Thorp reported, "before entering the army my physical condition was poor but it was rapidly built up. Through physical fitness my mental ability was proportionately increased."[29]

Some men joined the SATC directly from the ranks of the Army. Arthur Price entered the Army in June 1918 and served as a private in the 51st Pioneer Infantry Regiment until he was transferred to the Princeton Aviation School in September. The next month Price was transferred to Yale where he became part of the SATC. Price actually received a commission in the field artillery in December, and he was discharged as a second lieutenant in January 1919. According to Price, his experience "more strongly impressed the principles of Americanism on me and made me less tolerant of such things as radicals and bolshevists."[30]

Even in the short time the men spent in the SATC there could be advancement in rank, at least of a sort. Fermor Church, in the Coast Artillery section of Harvard's SATC, noted his promotions to brevet corporal and brevet sergeant, while other men noted promotions to acting corporal and acting sergeant. On the other hand, Hyman Rothstein enlisted in the Chemical Warfare branch of Yale's SATC on 3 October four days later he was promoted to corporal, and the day before the Armistice he was promoted to acting sergeant. Rothstein was discharged on 14 December; on 1 August 1919, he was given a warrant as an Army Field Clerk, a rank roughly equivalent to a warrant officer. He worked at the demobilization center at Camp Dix, New Jersey, for five weeks, engaged in tackling the mountains of paperwork associated with processing soldiers for discharge. When asked about the effects of his two months in the SATC, Rothstein wrote: "Twelve pounds and $60 [roughly two months' pay]."[31]

Of course not everyone was gung-ho. Harold Sanford of the Pratt Institute (Brooklyn, New York) SATC "was neither greatly in favor or opposed to military service." His experience as the "best possible under the conditions." John Barrs of the Harvard SATC was eager to enter the service. After his brief stint he stated: "I am still glad the opportunity came although I should not wish to repeat the experience if it could be avoided.... I no longer have any desire to enter the Service unless it is a case of great necessity."[32]

John Conroy, a member of an unidentified SATC unit in Brooklyn, New York, disagreed. Stating the army life was "very satisfactory," Conroy declared that he "liked the physical and mental training very well." Anthony Corsello, a member of the Fordham University SATC, agreed,

Striking a dramatic pose is Fermor S. Church, a member of Harvard's Coast Artillery SATC unit. A sign of the times and the shortage of equipment due to the rapidly expanding army, his bayonet is the kind that was used with the obsolete Krag-Jorgensen rifle. Prior to his SATC service, Church had some military training in the Harvard Regiment of the ROTC (Connecticut War Service records via Ancestry.com).

declaring his experience was "the best as to building a young man into manhood." After the war, Corsello reenlisted in the National Guard. Even comparative late-comers like Emerson Quaile, who served in Battery C of the artillery section of the Yale SATC from 1 November to 19 December

6. The Students' Army Training Corps (SATC)   149

1918, wrote: "I liked the artillery immensely, and I should not for a moment hesitate to reenlist in case of another war." Daniel Quigg who served in the Syracuse University SATC from 2 October to 9 December stated that his service "improved me mentally and physically."[33]

William Fulton Quigg, Jr., was born in Hartford, Connecticut, in 1899. Shown in his uniform on the campus of Connecticut Agricultural College in Storrs, Connecticut, he served in the SATC from 28 October to his discharge on 17 December 1918 (Connecticut War Service Records via Ancestry.com).

Service in the SATC prompted Thomas Congdon, in the Amherst unit, to strive for an appointment to the U.S. Naval Academy after the war. Congdon, who felt his SATC service was a "great help—physically, morally, and mentally," passed his Academy examination and was sworn in on 16 July 1919. Francis Biddy, a native of the British West Indies and a member of the Connecticut Agricultural College SATC, echoed the notion of duty: "[My service] awoke me mentally to the fact that one's duty is not always pleasant, but that it is much pleasanter to do it than leave it undone." His service gave him "a better understanding of the responsibilities of a citizen."[34]

A different, perhaps more pragmatic, view was expressed by Wilbur Jay Dowd, who was a member of the SATC unit at Trinity College in Hartford: "I was willing though not anxious to go." Another view was held by Chester Haberlin of Company E of the New York University Unit: "I was against military service before we declared war but after the declaration of war I believed everyone who could possibly do so should enter the service and put a quick end to the war."[35]

Not all soldiers in the SATC were aspiring college students. Among the vocational category was twenty-year-old Maurice Bryant Rector from the appropriately named Rectortown, Virginia. He had been too young for the first draft, but when the age limits were extended to include all men from ages eighteen to forty-five, Rector became eligible and was selected. His draft registration card reflects that at the time of registration, he was nineteen and employed in his father's store as a clerk. His AGO Form 724–1 (War Service Record) reflects that he was inducted on 23 October 1918. The short period of Rector's actual service is reason for the minimal information on his card. Looking at Rector's Form 724–1, we can determine he was twenty when inducted and assigned to the SATC. Rector was assigned to the Bliss Electrical School in Takoma Park, Maryland. The Fort Bliss School was a long-established training facility for electrical engineers. Under Army supervision and as part of the SATC, the school was responsible for training some 700 soldiers in three detachments in 1918. Rector was in the third detachment which was disbanded on 6 December 1918. He was discharged after just six weeks in uniform and returned home to work in the family general store and gas station.[36]

Given the short duration of the SATC's existence, it's understandable that many men felt dissatisfied with the degree of their contribution to the Allies' victory. Joseph Hawley served in Company G of the Yale unit from 28 October to 19 December 1918. Hawley stated: "Glad to offer my services and very sorry I did not go over to do some real fighting." Hawley "felt [he] had rendered very little service." So disappointed was Hawley that he enlisted in the Marine Corps for special

6. The Students' Army Training Corps (SATC)

Another Amherst College SATC soldier: Thomas Congdon was so enthusiastic about military education that after the war he applied to the United States Naval Academy and was accepted (Connecticut War Service records via Ancestry.com).

duty in France in July 1919, hoping for overseas service with the Army of Occupation of Germany. After training, however, he was discharged in September of that year. Hawley reenlisted in the Marines in 1921 and served as part of the Marine Corps contingent present for the interment of the Unknown Soldier in Washington, D.C. In 1922 he was discharged for disability. Ralph Chaffee, Connecticut Agricultural College SATC, said he "would have preferred more active branch than Students Army Training Corps had home conditions been different."[37]

As we have seen in earlier chapters, there were many soldiers training in the States when the Armistice was declared who felt let down by not getting a chance to go to France and fight. There appears to have been an equal number who were quite content not to have to make that trip. Among them was Lloyd Lamb, a Collins, New York, farmer who had just turned nineteen when the draft age was extended to include all men eighteen to forty-five years of age. He wrote to a friend who was serving in the 156th Depot Brigade at Camp Jackson that "I was drafted but did not have to go. I was going down to Cornell SATC University and take up the radio electrician army course, was going the 25th of November, but peace was declared and that put me out from taking it up." He went on to say that he had just gone to the movies to see the latest Harold Lloyd film, and in it Lloyd was "knocking the Germ out of Germany." He also described for his friend the celebration that took place when they heard about the Armistice and how "everybody made all the racket they could.... I am glad it is over with anyway, [my cousin] Ralph got as far as England but I guess he is on his way back."[38] Lamb was misinformed. Ralph actually made it to France in October 1918 and was assigned to the 83rd Division. He did not return to Collins until May 1919. Having missed his own chance to escape the farm by going to the Great War, Lamb went on to marry, run the dairy farm, and have six children and twenty-six grandchildren by the time he passed away in 1974.

Pertaining to the recruitment of African American soldiers in segregated SATC units, there were racial issues involved at some schools. Still, many blacks did enlist and serve honorably in the SATC. Regarding their service, many felt much the same as white student-soldiers. Emmason Dickerman Fuller, a member of the SATC unit at Howard University, declared that military service "is of great value to the physical and mental development of American manhood. I received valuable training in discipline, physical training, and contact with real men." He, too, believed the SATC "proved the advisability of universal military training throughout this country."[39]

Members of the Students' Naval Training Corps also felt much the same as their Army brothers. Lewis Renshaw, a member of the Rensselaer Polytechnic unit from 4 October to 20 December 1918, stated: "I am strongly in favor of Universal Service and I believe that the Navy is as important to the United States as that of England is to that nation." Lester Midas, a member of the Naval unit at Yale, stated that he was

6. The Students' Army Training Corps (SATC) 153

The AGO Form 724–1 for Harry Timothy Manponyane, a student at Atlanta's Morehouse College. Because he was 36, Manponyane wasn't required to register in the first Selective Service draft. When the age range was expanded in September 1918, the British citizen from Kentani, South Africa, registered and was inducted into the SATC at Morehouse College on 1 October 1918 (Georgia World War I War Service Records via Ancestry.com).

"perfectly satisfied," and that "the training put me in fine physical condition." Kenneth Redick, a member of the Naval unit at Yale, declared he was glad he was "old enough and fit to join." Unfortunately, "influenza pulled me down physically while I was in the service...." Meredith Gillette felt his naval SATC experience at Cornell University enabled him to "realize the meaning of (and appreciate) co-operation, sacrifice, and the brotherhood of my fellow men."[40]

But not everyone agreed with the utility or efficacy of the SATC. Kenneth Andem served in the SATC unit at the Massachusetts Institute of Technology; after the war, Andem stated: "I enjoyed the military service but the combination of military and academic work seemed to me to be a failure as it was worked out." Charles Strant, of Tufts College, agreed, stating about the effects of his experience: "Cannot say as school work was intermingled with training." Calvin Parks, who served in the infantry unit of the SATC at Brown University, felt that the program didn't have time to develop enough to prove its worth: "I feel the SATC did not have time to accomplish much. Camp experiences had practically no effect on me."[41]

In the end, it's difficult to judge the efficacy of the SATC. At the most, a student soldier would have served from 1 October to about 18 December 1918, just over two and a half months; men who enlisted later in October or in November served even fewer days. The creation of the SATC nearly coincided with the outbreak of the Spanish influenza which ravaged training camps in the United States. The SATC men, housed in dormitories just like other soldiers, were also susceptible to the sickness; in many cases training was curtailed, and men were placed under quarantine further shortening effective training time. Too, supplies were slow in getting to the men. For example, at Illinois College "the uniforms did not arrive until the war was over, and it is stated that the guns did not come much earlier."42 Furthermore, some men at Illinois College were quarantined for the whole period of their enlistment.

A nice studio portrait of Kevin S. Andem, a member of the Massachusetts Institute of Technology. Andem later wrote that he enjoyed the military service aspect but didn't believe the combination of the military service and academia was very useful or successful (Connecticut War Service records via Ancestry.com).

So what can be determined about this very large program which began too late to have much effect on the war effort? No doubt had the war continued into the summer of 1919 as was predicted, many of the men in the SATC would have been in France doing their part. As it was, the short duration of the program gave many men a chance to serve their country in uniform while enhancing their education at the same time. Moving into the next chapter we will find other parts of the stateside war effort in General March's hilt of the sword which are much harder to define or even understand.

7

The "Spare Parts" Brigades
Unique and Unusual Events

"It is better to make a mistake than to remain inactive in any emergency. Action counts. Do something even if it is wrong...."[1]

Military forces throughout history have always had unexpected or unusual episodes which fail to fit the mold of the rigidly disciplined martial ethos most people expect. This is due to the human nature of the soldiers who, when viewed in large formations, appear to be similar in every way, yet, in fact, are uniquely individual. This chapter presents some of the stories of the depot brigades, and other United States places, people, and events from the "hilt of the sword" that break the mold. While some may be hard to believe, it is their anomaly or absurdity which makes them so interesting. To paraphrase the quote which opens this chapter and is taken directly from *The Cantonment Manual*, mistakes made in haste are often better than good decisions made slowly; after reading the following episodes and events, you can decide whether this was good advice or bad.

How Do You Draft Four Million Men? (July 1917)

As relations with the Germans continued to worsen, President Wilson and the War Department planners met to discuss the practicality of designing and operating a national conscription system. With only the poorly run Civil War draft to serve as an example, many worried that an unfair, inefficient, or ineffective draft might provoke a similar riots and violent response among the population. This time, however, Major General Enoch Crowder and his Provost Marshal staff had a far better idea. Rather than having the Army organize, operate, and enforce the draft, as the North had done in the Civil War, they decided to rely on city and state governments, overseen by civilian officials, to manage the total draft operation in each locality. Draft boards were established in local communities, each representing a region or a population of up to thirty thousand people. Under this method, the members of the draft board were known and, hopefully, well respected in their communities.

Working quietly Crowder's staff prepared instruction sheets in twenty-seven languages and also began the process of secretly printing the necessary notification and registration cards. This undercover approach was required because Congress had not yet voted on or approved a national conscription. Therefore Crowder's staff swore the printers and all appropriate post office personnel to secrecy. Planning ahead, the staff also wrote letters to each governor, draft board official, mayor, and sheriff explaining to them their specific duties in the event the draft legislation was approved. The printers producing the registration cards quickly used up almost the entire country's supply of the appropriate-sized card stock. As the cards were turned over to them, Crowder's men and women began to address the cards and pack every available mailbag with the forms. It was a huge endeavor which quickly filled all of the unused storage space at the Washington Post Office and the Government Printing Office. Crowder's staff then wrote letters to some four thousand mayors and city administrators explaining their storage space problem. This time the letters asked the recipients to accept shipment of the mailbags and draft registration forms for their districts and to store them in local bank vaults and safes until notified to distribute them. This huge task had to be done in utmost secrecy. It is characteristic of the patriotism of the period that these local government officials complied and maintained operational security through the entire period leading up to the U.S. Congress voting to execute the program. When Secretary of War Baker was finally briefed on what had transpired without his knowledge, instead of being angry, as Crowder's team expected, he was quite pleased with the entire operation.

When Congress approved the conscription act which included all men from ages twenty-one to thirty-one, the forms were distributed throughout each local community. As one of the organizers later wrote, it "was one of the most spectacular developments of the war. It was completed in a single day—nearly ten million men [were notified] ... within twenty-four hours afterward we had almost complete national returns of the result."[2]

The next step was to set up the actual drawing of the lottery numbers to call the men to camp. At first a very simple solution was designed, using only numbers 1 through 10. In this system, should the number 3 be drawn, every man who had a draft registration number ending in 3, such as 13, 143, 2073, etc., would be called to report. However, for a variety of reasons, including the fact that whichever number was selected 10 percent of the selectees would be dispatched at the same time, this method was ruled impractical. This was far too many for the camps to handle, especially in the early days. Instead, a new system where the numbers 1 to 10,500 would be used to select draft registration numbers was devised. The number 10,500 was chosen as the upper limit because this would be the maximum number of men a draft board would register.

Even the fairness of this newer system was almost negated on the night before Secretary Baker was to pick the first number out of the glass bowl; one of the capsules containing a number fell on the floor. Unnoticed, a female staff member stepped on it and it stuck to her shoe. When she arrived at home and realized what was trapped on her heel, she immediately returned to work and ensured the capsule was returned to the rest of the numbers.

On 20 July 1917, Newton Baker was blindfolded, escorted to the bowl and drew out a capsule. It was the number 258. With that simple selection, every man who had been issued the number 258 at his draft board was considered selected. The remaining capsules were then drawn until the bowl was empty and the order of draft had been established. The next year, with the age range expanded to include all men from eighteen to forty-five, the process was repeated with Baker again drawing first and this time selecting number 246. Army Chief of Staff Peyton March then drew the next number. He was followed by other dignitaries and Draft Information Bureau staff members until all numbers were selected. Because of the carefully guarded processes used to establish the selections, there were few questions or complaints about the fairness or integrity of the draft. More importantly, there was no repeat of the Civil War protests and riots.[3]

A New Vocabulary Emerges

In every army a unique vocabulary is developed and used by the soldiers. This is often a mix of mangled local phrases and newly minted words. The Doughboy wordsmiths were no different. Keeping some of the words and phrases they learned on the Mexican border, in the training camps, and later in France, they developed their own colorful language. Among the more common words were: *AWOL*, the abbreviated form of "absent without leave"; *Buck Private* which was defined as "someone who is always wanting to be where he is not" and when the "buck" is passed, it always ends on his back; *Camion*, the French word for truck, was quickly adopted by the American soldiers for any motorized vehicle; *Chow* was (and is) the Doughboy word for food and was also used as a descriptor (chow time, chow line, and chow hall); *Cootie* was the unlovable name for the body lice which seemed to be everywhere, all the time; *MP* was short for Military Police, the tormenter of buck privates seeking a little fun; *SOL* was short for "shit out of luck," and used commonly as in the phrase "We were SOL because the chow hall was closed"; *Slum*, a holdover from the Mexican border campaign and meant to signify any form of the watery stew or meat they were served; *Straight Dope* meant the unvarnished truth as in "I got the straight dope from the corporal, we are the next unit to sail for France"; and *Toot Sweet* (adapted from the French *tout de suite*) meaning "right now" or "right away," used as "If we don't go toot sweet, we will be SOL when the chow hall closes." Canned salmon became *gold fish* or *sea turkey* and corned beef was renamed *corn willy*. All other forms of canned meat became *bully beef* or *monkey meat*.[4] Their sons, serving in the Second World War, would expand greatly on this vocabulary.

The Unusual Case of George Zador (June 1917–March 1918)

Certainly falling in at the top of the "you can't make this stuff up" category is the story of George T. Zador. Zador was born in Hungary in 1888 and was educated in Vienna and Paris. He graduated from the Hungarian Officer's Training School and served as an infantry officer for a few years. He finished his service requirement and then went to work at the New York City branch of the Bank of Vienna in 1914. His idyllic life in America came quickly to an end with the start of World War I. Zador reported to the Austro-Hungarian consulate general for guidance because he still held a reserve officer's commission in the Hungarian Army. He was told to return to Hungary and join the army. With the British naval blockade of the Atlantic this was no longer possible and so he remained in neutral America. Neutral, that is, until April 1917, when the U.S. entered the war. Zador dutifully registered for the draft in June 1917 and noted on his form he was an alien with former military service. A short while later in August 1917 he married Anna Batsch, the American-born daughter of Austrian parents.

7. The "Spare Parts" Brigades

Zador was surprised when the local draft board notified him he had been selected for service with the U.S. Army and that he needed to report to Camp Upton, New York. After again pointing out his unique status as an enemy alien, Zador was told that since he was Hungarian, it

The draft registration form filled out by George Zador clearly showing his prior service in the Hungarian Army. Zador's misadventures with the U.S. Army and the Enemy Aliens Bureau of New York illustrate some of the pitfalls that could beset a man living in the United States but originating from an "enemy" country (National Archives Draft Registration records via Ancstry.com).

was not a valid excuse. He would be exempt, he was told, only if he had been a German. So leaving Anna, he dutifully reported to the reception station at Camp Upton and began the process of becoming an American soldier. With his former military training obvious, he passed quickly through the 152nd Depot Brigade reception station and was assigned to Company E of the 307th Infantry Regiment. Being persistent, even while performing at a high level as an enlisted soldier, Zador told his story every chance he had. Finally he was summoned by the Camp Upton and 77th Division Commander, Major General J. Franklin Bell, and told his story yet again. Bell was impressed by the forthrightness and honesty in Zador's plea. After confirming with Zador's company commander that he had been an excellent soldier, Bell ordered him discharged from the U.S. Army as an enemy alien on 26 November 1917. George gathered his belongings and before heading home to Anna, he addressed the men of his company, saying, "You boys have every reason to be proud of your service. No other country in the world treats its men so well as the United States."

But that's not the end of the story. In January 1918, Zador was arrested by the newly formed Enemy Aliens Bureau of New York. He was transported to Ellis Island and registered as an enemy prisoner of war, accused of having entered the United States to spy. Once again, he demanded a hearing and although it took a while, he was finally brought before Assistant United States Attorney General William Wallace, Jr. Zador told his story. Wallace confirmed the facts with the Army and granted him a parole, saying "in my opinion, this young man's trouble has been due to a misapprehension for which he was in no ways responsible." And with that, Zador was free to return to Anna. Once again, however, he insisted on having the last word and told a reporter: "I have no feeling against America ... for I admire American freedom and fair play. But please don't call me an Austrian. I am a Hungarian and there is all the difference in the world between an Austrian and a Hungarian." One can only wonder how that sentiment went over with Anna, the child of Austrian parents.

And that's not the end of the story either. It appears Zador never returned home to Hungary, and by 1925 he was living in the Bronx with Anna and their two children. In 1926 Anna, perhaps remembering the "Austrian" comment, filed for a divorce and took the children with her. Later records show Zador made his living as a salesman and passed away in December 1953. His remains are in a columbarium in the Middle Village, Queens County cemetery. And Anna? She met and married a gentleman from the motion picture industry. Together they had a child, and her new husband was hopefully smart enough not to insult Austrians.[5]

7. The "Spare Parts" Brigades

Another Homeland Defense Force?

With the federalization and mobilization of the National Guard units shortly after war was declared, it quickly became apparent that

A soldier of Company C, 3rd Regiment, Washington State Guard, poses for a portrait while equipped with a caliber .45–70, Model 1888 Springfield Trapdoor carbine. Organized to perform state military duties after the National Guard units were federalized and deployed to France, the state guard units usually were comprised of men who were exempted from the draft due to age, physical issues, or working in in a critical war-related occupation (courtesy John Adams-Graf).

other groups or organizations would have to step in to replace them and perform their state-duties. These new units were filled primarily with men either too old or too young to be drafted as well as men whose civilian occupations exempted them from active service. With the original draft limited to men between twenty-one to thirty-one years of age, there were many candidates outside that age group who still wished to serve. In late 1918, when the age bracket was extended to eighteen to forty-five, some of these men became draft eligible and were thus added to the Army.

Perhaps representative of the country as a whole, Virginia raised and equipped over sixty companies of state guards and used them frequently to perform military services such as guarding key infrastructure such as rail yards, bridges, and industrial complexes and providing aid to civil authorities by serving as prisoner escorts or riot control during disturbances.[6] Many of the officers were Spanish-American War veterans or had been educated at the Virginia Military Institute. Enthusiasm for serving in the state guard units was surprisingly high. In November 1917, after inspecting all of the State Guard units in the state, the Virginia Inspector General reported his findings and included the following about the Blue Ridge Rifles of Montvale: "Although Montvale is not more than a village, this company has enlisted 75 men ... and 3 officers.... This company has already been drilled and disciplined and has

The age and physique of some of the soldiers in this formation indicate that this is a State Guard unit. This unit has been equipped with Spanish-American War era Krag-Jorgensen rifles and the appropriate ammo belts (courtesy Brian Stewart).

7. The "Spare Parts" Brigades 163

Although equipped with the more modern Springfield 03 rifle as opposed to the Washington State Guardsmen in the previous photograph, this State Guardsman, possibly from Massachusetts, has been issued a Spanish-American War caped overcoat (courtesy Brian Stewart).

received constant attention from its officers, all of whom are thoroughly interested in perfecting the company."⁷

One common feature of the State Guards across the nation was their dependence on weapons considered too obsolete to be issued to the soldiers bound for France. As a result many photographs show State Guard soldiers equipped with weapons from the Indian Wars or Spanish-American War. Likewise their uniforms were often salvaged from previous eras; indeed, some units didn't have enough uniforms to go around. One Virginia State Guard unit, known as the Richmond Greys, reported that it had 68 men but only 63 coats and trousers to issue. While the obsolete weapons and mismatched uniforms tend to give a slightly comic-opera appearance, there were some who truly appreciated the service of these men. In 1920, Westmoreland Davis, the Governor of Virginia, noted that the State Guard "rendered the state a

The State Guardsman from the previous photograph is now teamed up with a comrade in a motorcycle equipped with a sidecar. Under magnification it appears the sidecar is marked with "M.S.G." to indicate it is a State Guard vehicle (courtesy Brian Stewart).

signal service in affording to our people at home protection at great personal sacrifice to themselves when our National Guard ... was at war."[8]

The 37th Division Meets the U.S. Army Supply System (May 1918)

Even before they arrived in France, the well-trained soldiers of the 37th Division would have an encounter with the U.S. Army's supply system which would leave them shaking their heads—and not for the last time. With their training complete at Camp Sheridan, Alabama, soldiers belonging to the four infantry regiments of the 37th Division had one more stop before they could be loaded onto the ships which would carry them to France. Moving by train, they were dispatched to Camp Lee, Virginia, for target practice on the rifle ranges, more instruction in gas defense in the huge Camp Lee trench complex, and the integration of even more new soldiers into their ranks. This was also the last opportunity to ensure each soldier was fully equipped with all of the personal gear he would need in France. Each man was inspected in turn for completeness of personal and field kit. It was soon apparent that no one in the 145th Infantry Regiment had been issued a serviceable set of the overalls required by Army policy. The Camp Lee quartermaster staff in the 155th Depot Brigade quickly remedied this shortfall by providing each soldier a set of brown denim overalls. The soldiers had barely enough time to pack away their new overalls when they received orders to dig them out and turn them back in; Army regulations stated brown overalls were only for engineer units—not infantry units. So they were issued blue overalls the day after turning in the brown ones. Two days later they were inexplicably directed to turn in their recently issued blue overalls. The day before the 145th was scheduled to leave Camp Lee and head to the port of embarkation, they were again informed no soldier would be permitted to deploy without a set of overalls. Now completely out of time for a meaningful issue, the soldiers were given a set with no attention to size or fit, and some received theirs as they were marching in formation to the train.[9]

Colonel Miller Sets the Record Straight (August 1918)

On 6 July 1918, Private Henry H. McGilvery, a soldier of the 162nd Depot Brigade, was given an order to join a workgroup in clearing some brush at Camp Pike, Arkansas. McGilvery twice refused on the grounds that it was Saturday and he was a Seventh Day Adventist to whom Saturday was the Sabbath. He was later ordered to clean a latrine. Again he refused and stated his objection to working on a Saturday. He also added, for good measure that he was a conscientious objector.

As a result of these episodes, McGilvery was charged with three counts of refusing to obey an officer's legal order. He was found guilty on all three charges, each of which carried with it a five-year sentence of imprisonment at hard labor. However, one of the senior officers reviewing the case, Colonel Miller, saw things differently. His research showed that while the 87th Division had been training at Camp Pike, their commanding general had issued a policy memorandum which excused Seventh Day Adventists from performing duties on Saturdays, unless absolutely necessary. The important wording in the case was "military necessity," and in Colonel Miller's view, clearing brush was not a military necessity. Since the "Sabbath Memorandum" had never been rescinded,

This unusual image shows the austere compound at Camp Meade, Maryland, where the prisoners and conscientious objectors were held. The conditions of these men's imprisonment often depended on the local commander's personal beliefs and level of interest. Undoubtedly the worst conditions were found at Camp Funston and Fort Riley, Kansas, where General Leonard Wood commanded (private collection).

McGilvery was therefore innocent of the charges relating to clearing brush on the Sabbath and disobeying lawful orders.

And here's where Colonel Miller showed his wisdom. Although McGilvery had never provided any proof or certification of his membership in a Seventh Day Adventist congregation, Miller accepted it based on McGilvery's statement. However, the memorandum exempting soldiers of that faith from working on Saturdays did not give those soldiers any more rights than soldiers for whom Sunday was the Sabbath. More importantly, because cleaning the latrine was not a military necessity but instead a health and welfare duty it had to be performed daily for the safety of the overall command. By refusing to clean the latrine, McGilvery was disobeying a lawful command. The five years at hard labor sentence for this charge was upheld and McGilvery was sent to the prison at Fort Leavenworth, Kansas.[10]

Rumors of War and Rumors of Rumors of War (August 1917–November 1918)

All armies exist on rumors, well-intentioned or otherwise. There is no way to stop the "underground wireless" which spreads information and misinformation in equal amounts. The soldiers in France serving in the AEF lived on a steady diet of rumor and gossip about their French Allies, the Germans, the never-ending rain and, of course, the end of the war. Their stateside comrades were much the same. Obviously there was a constant stream of speculation about when their unit would leave for France. While this was a never-ending source of rumors and half-rumors, it is some of the other speculations or beliefs which are certainly the most interesting.

For example, Camp Devens, Massachusetts, was visited by Secretary of War Baker during the winter of 1917. Following his departure, the word was quickly passed that Camp Devens was going to be shut down because it was too cold for the troops to train there.[11] Another great example came as the 37th Division was preparing to depart Camp Sheridan when the stores on post were forbidden to sell any food or drinks which did not come sealed in containers. This action was caused by rumors that the Germans were trying to poison the American soldiers and that poisoned apples had been detected at "another camp."[12]

Clearly these rumors were not true but that never stopped the soldiers from passing them on. And this honored tradition continues today in all U.S. military units.

A Soldier of the 16th Division

Albino Abeyta's time in the Army clearly illustrates the instability and turbulence of service in the United States, as well as the apparent

Albino Abeyta, a farmer in New Mexico, was inducted into the Army in October 1917 and assigned to the 164th Depot Brigade. He was transferred to the 40th Division in Camp Kearny, California, but was left behind when they deployed. After serving for a while as camp tailor, he was transferred to the camp provost guard and at this time he posed for this picture showcasing his MP armband and "billy club" (New Mexico War Service records via Ancestry.com).

randomness of assigning soldiers to units. Abeyta, a farmer from New Mexico, was drafted and entered service on 3 October 1917. He was assigned to the 41st Company, 164th Depot Brigade at Camp Funston, Kansas, for three weeks before being sent to Company D, 143rd Machine Gun Battalion, 40th Division, at Camp Kearny, California. In June 1918, the first men from Kearny began to leave as replacements for overseas units as members of the June Automatic Replacement Draft (ARD). According to Abeyta,

> I Boluntere to go and was transfred to the June ARD. but it happened they wanted only Boy with good Training such as good manual of arms and [I] dint know any thing but machine Gun so they dint let me go at all then I was sint Back to my company again and in a few days I was transfered out of my Regiment and atached to the Q.M.C. [Quartermaster Corps] as a tailor.[13]

Abeyta was still serving in that position when the entire 40th Division left for overseas service; he was left behind in the Quartermaster Corps until four months later when the 16th Division began to organize. Abeyta was then transferred to the Provost Guard (Military Police) of the division until shortly after the Armistice when he was transferred to Fort Bliss, Texas, where he received his discharge on 4 June 1919. In his twenty-month military career, Abeyta served in two different divisions (the 40th and 16th), three different states (Kansas, California, and Texas), three different branches of the Army (Infantry, Quartermaster, and Military Police) and yet never made it east of the Mississippi River.

Captain Whisler Goes Off the Rails (January 1918)

One of the more gruesome and inexplicable events at Camp Funston took place in early 1918. It centered on Captain Lewis R. Whisler, a veteran of the Spanish-American War and several years in the Philippines. Captain Whisler was a highly regarded member of the camp staff and by all appearances he was well liked and respected by the soldiers at the camp. Something, however, went awry, and late one evening, after drawing two hatchets from the supply room, the captain went to the Camp Funston Bank. He knocked on the door and was admitted where he found four bank employees and a local newspaper editor talking. Drawing his pistol, the captain forced one of the bank employees, Kearney Wornall, to tie up the other four men. Whisler then tied Wornall up and removed some money from the safe. As he was leaving, Whisler heard one of the tied men ask Wornall if he recognized the bandit. Wornall answered in the affirmative, that he had. Hearing that said, the captain turned to the first man and asked him directly if he knew him. The tied-up man replied, "I sure do, you black scoundrel!" At which point the captain began to hit all of the bound men with his hatchet. By the time he finished all were dead except for Wornall who was left unconscious and bleeding.

When Wornall regained consciousness a short while later, the captain and the money were gone. The wounded man managed to free his hands and make it to the door. Opening it, he called for help and was heard by a sentry. The sentry immediately informed his superiors, and in short order Camp Funston was locked down.

In the morning, knowing from the one surviving witness to the robbery and murder a captain had committed the crime, all units were ordered to send their captains to the post headquarters. As this order was circulating, two shots were heard coming from Captain Whisler's barracks room. On entering the room, soldiers found Whisler dead with a note beside his body: "I have been thinking of committing suicide for a long time, but I have never had a good reason. Yesterday I went and made myself a reason." The note was addressed to a woman whose name was never revealed. There were blood drops all around the room and two bloodstained towels. With the positive identification of the body in the barracks as being Captain Whisler, the camp authorities recovered the money and closed the case. Later investigations revealed the captain had been in debt, and this drove him to rob the bank. When questioned, Whisler's former wife said she had recently received a letter from him, and from the writing in it, he appeared to have been happy and in good spirits. Perhaps the greater mystery was why and how it took two shots for Whisler to kill himself.[14]

A 164th Depot Brigade Doctor Gets Court Martialed (March 1918)

The War Department announced in March 1918 that Medical Reserve Corps 1st Lieutenant John G. Dwyer, assigned to the 164th Depot Brigade, was dismissed from the service. The dismissal came about after Dwyer, a regimental infirmary surgeon, was charged with violating the 96th Article of War. The text of this article states "all disorders and neglects to the prejudice of good order and military discipline, all conduct of a nature to bring discredit upon the military service, and all crimes or offenses not capital, of which persons subject to military law may be guilty, shall be taken cognizance of by a general or special or summary court-martial...."[15] And what led to this discrediting crime and the court martial? It appears that Dwyer failed to perform a proper physical examination on Private Christie L Gherring, a soldier sent by his company commander to sick call at the hospital. Gherring, a farm laborer from Nuckells, Nebraska, died in October 1917 at Camp Funston. His local paper reported the funeral:

> was of more than usual sadness and pathos. The young man had gone into the war service of his country from Nelson, Nebraska, and shortly after his arrival at Camp Funston was stricken with typhoid pneumonia, which resulted in his death....

It was also noted:

> The stars and stripes were draped over the casket and prominent throughout the church and in the remarks made by Rev. Seidel, he laid great stress upon the fact that the deceased had come to his death in the most honorable service of his country.[16]

The War Department statement gave no details on the failure of Lieutenant Dwyer to perform a proper examination on the sick soldier, but there remains no doubt that because of his negligence. he was held personally responsible for Gherring's death.[17]

Major General George Bell Gets Mad (March 1918)

General George Bell had a long and very distinguished career before he was assigned as the first commander of the 33rd Division. He was energetic and well respected for both his military knowledge and his ability to carry out orders in the face of adversity. All of this led to his nickname throughout the Army being "Do It Now." Despite his many years of Army experience, he soon found one issue in his new command which perpetually drove him to distraction. It was the insufficient number and poor quality of replacements he was receiving at Camp Logan, Texas. Logan itself was no prize, and when Bell's soldiers started to arrive at the camp in later summer and early autumn of 1917, much of the camp construction was incomplete or shoddily built. His own divisional engineers warned him that several of the newly built structures were in danger of collapsing.[18]

Despite the personnel shortfall, Bell persisted in training his soldiers to the required Army standard. Persevere he might with most other problems; the issue of replacements nearly drove Bell over the edge. As happened in many divisions, the 33rd lost some trained men to earlier deploying units. The 33rd therefore required constant replenishment to reach and maintain the mandated divisional war strength of 28,000 men. Bell continuously sent telegrams and messages to the War Department requesting more troops be assigned to him at Camp Logan. When two large groups of soldiers arrived at Logan, 5,600 from Camp Grant and 1,000 from Camp Dodge, it appeared someone in a higher headquarters was finally listening. The bad news followed quickly. After an examination of the new soldiers, the receiving section of the 33rd Division reported back to General Bell that 371 of the men from Grant and 62 of the men from Camp Dodge were physically unfit for Army service. Another 303 from the two camps were deemed either "Unsuited" or "Worthless." Additionally 328 were non–English speaking and 256 were illiterate. Finally the two camps had also sent him 97 men with venereal disease. In short, almost 20 percent of the troops he had received were not acceptable or even deployable.[19]

It was a pattern which was repeated over the next few months, and still the 33rd remained some 3,500 men short. With an imminent departure approaching, Bell finally lost patience and wrote directly to the Army Chief of Staff on 9 March 1918. Along with providing enclosures showing the requests and results, Bell wrote:

> While in France, [General Pershing] personally declared to me that no divisions should be sent overseas unless they were thoroughly disciplined.... I know no royal road to efficiency except through discipline and training. It must be obvious that any division, no matter how efficient, is necessarily greatly weakened by the infusion of raw recruits on the eve of taking the field. For that reason I have made every conceivable endeavor to have the five thousand men needed by this division sent here at once in order that they may be at least partially trained before our departure....[20]

Bell went on to point out that twenty-eight replacements had just arrived at Camp Logan for the African American 370th Infantry Regiment which had already departed en route to France. He wrote, "Such things do not create efficiency." It is in his final paragraph, however, that Bell finally let his feelings and temper show:

> It is requested that this communication be referred to the Chief of Staff himself and not to a subordinate. Having been a Staff officer I know only too well how important communications frequently never reach the officer to whom they are addressed.[21]

This letter must have reached the right person. Just two weeks later Bell was informed that the 33rd would soon receive 2,700 men from the 86th Division, 2,300 from the 88th Division and 1,000 from the 84th Division. Of these soldiers at least a thousand came directly from Camp Grant's 161st Depot Brigade. Over the next four weeks some 7,100 soldiers arrived, and the 33rd was finally beginning to fill out. It was just in

7. The "Spare Parts" Brigades 173

time. By the end of April 1918, the 33rd was moving to the port and on to France.[22]

A Traitor in the 155th Depot Brigade? (September 1918)

One would think that a soldier in the Army who has reached the rank of corporal would know to keep his seditious thoughts to himself. Obviously Corporal Joseph C. Manger, of the 155th Depot Brigade's 2nd Training Battalion, hadn't figured that out because he carelessly made his remarks in front of three other soldiers. They were all very willing to testify against him. Although Manger was born in America, he apparently identified more strongly with his parents' Bavarian heritage. Shortly after the 37th Division finished its last pre-deployment training at Camp Lee, and departed for France, Manger began to tell his fellow soldiers how he had missed his chance to go overseas with the Ohio National Guard Division. He bemoaned the fact the 37th would reach the fighting front soon and if he had been with them he could have crossed over to the German lines with ease. He made his rationale for wanting to change sides very obvious. He said his family came from Bavaria, and they have more property there than they have in this country. I would rather be in the German Army than

CORPORAL SENTENCED TO FIVE YEARS FOR DISLOYAL REMARKS

Similar Punishment Imposed Upon Private Cawley for Disobedience.

Corporal Joseph C. Manger, of the Second battalion, 155th depot brigade, has just been sentenced to five years at hard labor for making disloyal remarks against the United States. Although born in this country, Manger is of Bavarian parentage. He was forwarded to Camp Lee form Uniontown, Pa. The alleged disloyal utterances are said to have been made in the presence of Privates Milton T. Harris, of Gloucester, Va.; John Pugh, of Wilkesbarre, Pa., and Howard S. Fitzhugh.

From the Camp Lee newspaper *The Bayonet* comes this story of Corporal Joseph C. Manger, 155th Depot Brigade. Unable to keep his treasonous thoughts to himself, Manger soon discovered that the Army had very little patience with NCOs who couldn't keep their mouths shut (U.S. Army Quartermaster Museum).

in the American Army. The German Army is a real army. ... I hope this war lasts for some time for when it ends I will lose my job.[23]

Unfortunately for Manger, the court martial board members considered themselves to be part of a "real" army also and sentenced him to five years at hard labor at Fort Jay, New York. In fairness to Manger, he had tried to be exempted from the draft by claiming he was the sole support for his mother. He also claimed he was a self-employed businessman. On the other hand, and in fairness to the Army, Manger only served some sixteen months of his five-year sentence before he was released from prison in March 1920.

It is interesting to note that the same board also ruled on Private Clarence Cawley of the 155th Depot Brigade's 2nd Development Battalion. Private Cawley was accused of willfully disobeying a lawful order and sentenced him to the same five years at hard labor as Corporal Manger. Cawley refused to report to the rifle range for duty and was reported by his lieutenant. From records it appears that Cawley, a draftee from Pittsburgh, had first been assigned to the 80th Division and then to the 2nd Development Battalion. Perhaps an indication Cawley had other problems as well can be seen in the fact that when he died just ten years later in 1928 the official cause of death listed on his record was "Chronic Alcoholism." Nevertheless, with the heavy sentences handed down in these two cases as evidence, it is obvious that Camp Lee and the 155th Depot Brigade was not the place to either run your mouth or refuse to obey an order.

Someday I'm Going to Murder the Bugler: Doughboy Humor

Perhaps more than soldiers of any other period in U.S. military history, the Doughboys of the U.S. Army were able to poke fun at themselves and their unusual circumstances. Often underestimated by their German enemies, and considered unsophisticated amateurs by their allies, the American officers and enlisted men paid little attention to the critics. Instead, they honed their self-deprecating humor on themselves and the soldiers in their own units. One soldier who had been demoted in rank from private 1st class, wrote home to his parents that he had been "promoted from private first class to private second class."[24] Another common saying among the engineer units was that if they had known how many miles of trenches they would dig during the war, they would have turned them westward and dug all the way home.

7. The "Spare Parts" Brigades   175

Even the hospitals got caught up in the act, as evidenced by the sign in Base Hospital Number 6 in Bordeaux: "Only Pro-Germans spit on the floor." Many of the Doughboys arrived in France determined to speak the language. To encourage this attitude, in the training camps and transit camps there were a number of "Teach yourself French" pamphlets and handbooks. After quickly mastering a few of the easier words and phrases, some soldiers dug deeper into the phrasebooks. They then attempted to communicate with the locals in their language. It was often noted, after several failed attempts to successfully communicate, the soldier usually gave up and told his buddies how disappointed he is to learn that the French "can't understand their own language."[25]

A prime example of the Doughboy sense of humor is found in their popular songs. Along with the many sentimental ballads with roots back to the Civil War, there were such favorites as Irving Berlin's "Oh! How I hate to get up in the morning," which was written while he was serving in the 152nd Depot Brigade at Camp Upton. Another favorite was written by Geoffrey O'Hara, an Army song leader assigned to the training camps. His song "K-K-K-Katy" gently mocks a young soldier suffering from a stuttering problem; yet in the end, the soldier wins the girl and goes off to fight in France and "make the Kaiser dance." It ends with his unique promise that "when the m-m-m-moon shines over the cow shed, I'll be waiting for you at the k-k-k-kitchen door."

Another example of Doughboy humor was exhibited at Camp Devens during the Thanksgiving holiday in 1917. Many of the citizens living near the camp opened their homes to soldiers and wanted to provide them with a good home-cooked holiday meal. They would contact the camp, give their address, and say how many soldiers they could feed. The staff of the camp stayed busy keeping track of the invitations and making sure that the right number of soldiers was sent. One of the more generous invitations came from a well-to-do lady who offered to feed forty soldiers. The officer receiving the call was more than happy to accept her exceedingly kind offer but was surprised when she added an unexpected caveat; she said she didn't want any "Hebrew or Irish" men. Always willing to oblige a request which would get forty soldiers a good meal, the officer made sure that when the day came, forty African American soldiers recently arrived from Florida were transported to the dinner. Returning to camp later, the men told the officer they all had a great meal and a very good time even though they never saw their hostess. It appears she came down with an unexpected and "sudden illness."[26]

Better Late Than Never (November 1918)

The War Department drafted men right up to the Armistice. Indeed, a great many men were drafted in the last two days of the war. Most of the men drafted before November served for at least a couple of months. Men taken during the last draft call in late October started training, and many were assigned to units until their discharge in December. Most of the men drafted in November, however, were discharged very soon after the Armistice. Some never even arrived at their designated training camp.

We can get an idea of the nature of the service that these late draftees provided while forming a picture of the draft process as it stood in November by examining the records of men from Racine County in southeast Wisconsin. According to *Racine County in the World War*, a large number of men reported for duty on 11 November:

> The first entrainment by Racine boards was on September 6, 1917, when eleven men were sent to Camp Custer. The last contingent entrained was on November 11, 1918, (the day the armistice was signed) when 191 men were started for Camp Logan, Texas, by the city [draft] boards. They did not get quite as far as Chicago, however, being stopped by a telegram from the war department, and they returned to Racine the same day, a disgusted lot of "raw" recruits. They were discharged on November 13th, and given three days pay.[27]

An analysis of the records yields slightly different dates and numbers, yet it still gives us a picture of the state of the draft and military service in November 1918. At least 294 men entered the Army from Racine in November. A breakdown by date of induction and date of discharge follows:

   1 November (to date unknown): 1
   2 November (to date unknown): 1
   4 November (to various dates from 18 December 1918 to 25 July 1919): 5
   5 November (to various dates from 13 December 1918 to 27 June 1919): 4
   6 November (to various dates from 13 November 1918 to 9 June 1919): 6
   7 November (to 13 November 1918): 3
   8 November (to various dates from 11 November 1918 to 16 April 1919): 3
   9 November (to various dates from 12 November 1918 to 18 December 1918): 4

7. The "Spare Parts" Brigades 177

10 November (to 10, 11, or 12 November 1918): 158
11 November (to various dates from 11 November 1918 to 20 November 1918): 73

Men who were among the last to be drafted were, generally, among the first to be discharged. In these examples, most of the men inducted between November 1 and 9 served for anywhere from a few weeks to a few months before their discharge, while those drafted on November 10 and 11 were discharged within a day or two of their induction.

One can immediately see that 10 and 11 November were large draft days, with 158 reporting on the 10th and 73 on the 11th. The vast majority of the men who served from 10 to 12 November were discharged while en route to Camp Logan, Texas; others were en route to Camp Custer in Michigan. Many of the records imply that the men actually arrived at Camp Logan. If so, they were immediately discharged there and sent back to Racine. As for the men who reported on 11 November, an idea of their brief service is shown by the record of Walter R. Cook: "Nov 11–18 (10 a m) [to] Nov 11–18 (7:30 p m)." Since the Armistice went into effect at 11:00 a.m. France time (about 5:00 a.m. in Racine), the war was technically over by the time these men showed up for their induction.

An examination of the abbreviated service records of these men yields some interesting observations. Many of the men who served for more than a few days were in U.S. Air Service units. They were assigned to units such as the 673rd and 674th Aero Supply Squadrons, the 677th Aero Squadron, and the 53rd Balloon Company. Men who served into December and beyond were sent to such places as Camp Dodge, Iowa; Fort Ethan Allen, Vermont; Camp Grant; Illinois; Camp Greene, North Carolina; Camp Meigs, Washington, D.C.; Morrison Field, Florida; Camp Shelby, Mississippi; and Camp Wheeler, Georgia. They also served at other locations such as a Quartermaster Corps office in Chicago, Illinois, and in a motor transport unit in Hoboken, New Jersey. Apparently recruiting for the Students' Army Training Corps (SATC) was also ongoing until the very end. For example, Layton E. Perkins enlisted in the SATC at Racine College on 8 November; he was discharged on 11 November.

There seems to have been some effort to classify men on their first, and only, day in service. Alvin Waters, who reported and was discharged on the 11th of November, was to have been assigned to the Corps of Engineers; others were assigned to the infantry.

Francis R. Mura had an atypical service stint. Mura enlisted in Battery C, 121st Field Artillery Regiment, 32nd Division, on 15 July

```
Wilfand, Aaron                              618,244         4/5        1
        (Surname)        (Christian name)     (Army serial number)    * White * Colored.
Residence: 885 Jennings St.,    Bronx                        NEW YORK
        (Street and house number)  (Town or city)  (County)        (State)
* Enlisted * R. A. * N. G. * E. R. C. *Inducted at New York N.Y.           on Oct. 25, 1918
Place of birth: Odessa Russia              Age or date of birth: 21 10/12 yrs.
Organizations served in, with dates of assignments and transfers: 30 Regt CAC to disch.

Grades, with date of appointment: Corp Nov 11/18.

Engagements:       xx

Wounds or other injuries received in action: None.
Served overseas from †  No      to †          , from †         to †
Honorably discharged on demobilization Dec 3/18.          , 19
In view of occupation he was, on date of discharge, reported  0        per cent disabled.
Remarks:

Form No. 724-1, A. G. O.    *Strike out words not applicable.  †Dates of departure from and arrival in the U. S.
   Nov. 22, 1919.
```

Typical of the men drafted very late in the war, Aaron Wilfand, an immigrant from Odessa, Russia, was inducted into the Army on 25 October, promoted to corporal on 11 November and discharged on 3 December 1918, a complete military career in 40 days (New York State World War I Service Abstracts, via Ancestry.com).

1917, and was discharged the next day. On 18 April 1918, Mura went to Toronto and enlisted in the Canadian Army. His period of service there is unknown, but according to his United States record, Mura had a "Second 'hitch' Nov 11–18 [to] Nov 13–18." Mura's exact total service times and dates are difficult to determine.[28]

Twenty-seven men were inducted and discharged on 12 November, the day after the Armistice, and one man served from 12 to 13 November. These men probably would not have earned the status of World War I veteran even though their friends who had served for only one day on 11 November would have enjoyed whatever benefits might have accrued from such a designation. This brief study focuses on men from one moderate-sized city; figures for other towns probably reflect much the same relative numbers given here for Racine.

To be considered a U.S. veteran of World War I, a person had to have served in the U.S. military any time between 6 April 1917, and 11 November 1918. This would entitle the individual to the award of the Victory Medal and eligibility for bonuses or benefits paid by the federal government and by some states. Even those men drafted on November 11 and reporting a few hours after the guns fell silent in France, swore an oath to support and defend the Constitution of the United States. Like other soldiers who went before them, some were willing and others were not; but they all served, even if only for one day.

Those Darn Overseas Stripes

One of the most contentious issues in the U.S. Army was earning, and the right to wear, overseas stripes on a soldier's left sleeve. There were any number of different rumors as to eligibility and awarding of these simple "V" shaped gold stripes. Originally, War Department General Order Number 6, dated 12 January 1918, called for a stripe to be worn for each six months of duty in the Zone of Advance in France. The start date for each soldier was deemed to be when he arrived in the Zone of Advance, although his overseas service started upon arrival in France or England, for example. This order was amended several times; eventually the start of overseas service creditable for the overseas stripe was considered the day when the soldier entered international waters, basically they day their troopship departed the United States.[29]

In theory, this was a fairly straightforward rule and soldiers were justifiably proud of their overseas stripes. In practice, however, it turned into a much bigger problem than anyone ever expected. During the occupation of the German Rhineland, the issue became even more prominent. The veteran Doughboys who had marched to Germany were extremely proud of their accomplishments and the number of gold-colored overseas stripes on the left sleeve of their uniforms. Newly arrived military police soon realized the soldiers with three or four overseas stripes resented taking orders or directions from "one stripers."[30]

It quickly became necessary to augment the enlisted police patrol units with a number of officers to maintain order. Making the matter worse was the persistent rumor the United States Congress was looking to abolish the use of the gold-colored "overseas" stripe because its use was considered discriminatory against those soldiers who had not actually deployed overseas.

In March 1919, even the 3rd Division's *Watch on the Rhine* newspaper got into the act with an editorial criticizing both the Congress and the "jealous stay-at-homes." The paper opined that Congress should be focusing on more important things such as economic or social issues rather than trying to deny the overseas veteran the gold "V" stripes on his left sleeve. It concluded: "The idea of so much waste of time causes one to think, 'Can women do any worse?' The idea of Women Congressmen causes laughter, but they can't do any worse...."[31]

Sergeant Ernest Goforth served his entire enlistment, from 17 September 1917 until 26 April 1919, in the United States, mostly assigned to Auxiliary Remount Depot #326 at Camp Cody, New Mexico. In this 1919 photograph, Goforth displays three silver service chevrons, indicating at least eighteen months of stateside service, on his lower left sleeve (New Mexico War Service records via Ancestry.com).

7. The "Spare Parts" Brigades

Proud of his service and his four large silver stateside service stripes, the soldier in this portrait has an infantry collar disk with an "S" below the crossed rifles, perhaps indicating his assignment to the Service Company in an infantry unit (courtesy Brian Stewart).

The 308th Engineers Meet the U.S. Army's Supply System (May 1918)

One of the Army's premier bridge-building combat engineer units, the 308th Engineer Regiment had originally been assigned to the 83rd Division while undergoing training at Camp Sherman, Ohio. Whether by fate or just luck, the Doughboys assigned to the 308th were apparently some of the very best draftees to come out of the central Ohio region. During training at Sherman, the soldiers of the regiment consistently out-marched and out-shot the infantry units of the 83rd and even Major General Edwin Glenn, commander of the 83rd, claimed the 308th was the best "infantry" regiment in his division. In spite of these accolades, it soon became obvious that the 308th was not going to deploy to France as part of the 83rd but instead was assigned to the U.S. First Army for use as a stand-alone, non-divisional engineer unit.[32]

The 308th was so highly regarded they were assigned to the U.S. Third Army as part of the Army of Occupation in Germany in December 1918. It was during this time in Germany that the 308th gained a great measure of more fame when they beat the pre-war German Army's time-record for laying a 1,440-foot-long pontoon bridge across the Rhine River. Making this accomplishment doubly impressive was that they used unfamiliar German Army bridging equipment to do so.

In late May 1918, however, they were just another unit deploying to France and were crowded into Camp Merritt to make the final preparations for the move. At this point in the war, the American industrial complex was producing well and the Quartermaster Corps was regularly providing new equipment and clothing to deploying units. When the 308th checked into the Camp Merritt facilities, each soldier's equipment and personal clothing was carefully inspected and "all equipment which was not in perfect shape had to be turned in and new equipment issued."[33]

Just before the 308th's departure from Camp Sherman, each soldier had been issued one long, ankle-length, woolen overcoat. However, recent communications from France had reported that these overcoats were too long and cumbersome for troops living and fighting in the trenches. In response, the Army Quartermaster Corps had quickly designed and ordered a newer, shorter model from the civilian uniform manufacturers. Now at Camp Merritt, the 308th was ordered to turn in their bulky Camp Sherman-issued coats and standby to receive newer ones. When the huge boxes containing a regiment's worth of new overcoats were delivered to the 308th, they were surprised to find the "new coats" were actually older and longer than the coats they had just turned in. Shortly thereafter, when the soldiers went to receive a new issue of shoes, they were equally perplexed to find the only sizes available for them were abnormally large or small sizes, and none of the sizes they needed.

It didn't matter to the soldiers' morale; the 308th survived their encounter with the Army supply system with their sense of humor intact. A short while later, they were in France serving in the first of the three campaigns they earned credit for: the Aisne-Marne, Oise-Marne, and Meuse-Argonne. In spite of all their wartime accomplishments, the 308th ultimately selected "We Bridged the Rhine" for their motto. And no one made a single suggestion about the long overcoat or off-size shoe episodes.

A Question of Murder (August 1918)

The 18 August 1918 edition of the official Camp Lee newspaper, *The Camp Lee Bayonet*, reported on the disposition of a legal case at nearby Camp Meade, Maryland. In order to maintain the Army's good reputation, the name of Private Charles D. Gamble was officially stricken from the rolls of the 154th Depot Brigade by camp commander, Brigadier General Joseph A. Gaston. Gamble, a draftee, had been tried and found guilty of murdering a Washington, D.C., taxi driver. Accompanied by another soldier and an unidentified female, Private Gamble had a dispute with the driver of a cab and had beaten the man to death with a beer bottle. The two soldiers quickly obtained civilian clothes and attempted to flee the area but were caught by civilian authorities. After his trial Gamble was sentenced to death by electrocution.[34]

The Slavic Legion (August–November 1918)

On 8 August 1918, one of the more unique Army formations in U.S. military history was officially brought to life by the War Department. By this point in the war the U.S. Army had recognized that members of some of the "oppressed people" from the Austro-Hungarian Empire might make good soldiers to fight against that empire. The French and Italian Armies had already reached this conclusion and outfitted large numbers of Czechoslovaks to serve with them against the Germans and Austrians. The Russians had formed a large Czech Legion from prisoners of war and deserters from the Austrian Army. The American Army saw that fielding potential Slavic Legion units in the front line across from their former countrymen might also serve to "stimulate the endemic revolutionary activity" in the enemy units.

There were, however, problems with the American version. Many enemy aliens had already been drafted. Thus many of the potential recruits for the Slavic Legion were already in other training camps or awaiting orders to report. It was decided the first members of the unit were to be Yugoslavians, Czechs, Slovaks, and Ukrainians. Unfortunately, a very large portion of these ethnic groups were working in coalmining districts in the United States. The coal supply of the country was considered critical war material, and recruiters for the Legion were expressly prohibited from recruiting in these districts.[35]

There was a compromise. Recruiting could take place among recently arrived immigrants from these ethnic groups who were not already employed in the coal industry, had not yet been drafted, or who were interested in volunteering to serve in the Army. Another source of manpower came from soldiers already in uniform. Draftees with birthplaces in Germany, Austria-Hungary, or Bulgaria were considered "enemy aliens" but were sometimes caught in the draft like American citizens and non-enemy aliens. After being drafted and sent to training camps, their status and continued service in the Army were investigated on a case-by-case basis. While some Army units had welcomed the presence of these "enemy aliens" into their ranks, others had not. Unit commanders in this second group firmly believed this category of foreign-born recruits were not to be trusted and relegated them to menial labor or camp maintenance duties.

The U.S. Army expected many of these men would gladly transfer to the Slavic Legion for a chance to fight. With this in mind, the Army established Camp Wadsworth as the training site for the American Slavic Legion. The Army announced that the Legion "will be organized, armed and equipped as infantry regiments. Companies will, if practicable, be composed of members of the same race.... At present, there will be no units larger than regiments."[36]

The Army knew in advance finding officers for these units was going to be difficult. The requirement for the company-level officers was that they spoke English and the language of the soldiers in their assigned company. If not already an officer serving in the U.S. Army, they were to be provided basic officer training at an Officer Training School at Camp Lee. "Properly qualified" enlisted men would also be given the opportunity to attend the Camp Lee course and, if successful, would be appointed as officers in the Legion.[37]

The prospective officers were also required to provide some form

7. The "Spare Parts" Brigades

of proof of their loyalty to the United States and their desire to fight the "Imperial Governments of Germany and Austria-Hungary." Finally, they were required to swear an oath to serve loyally and faithfully in the Slavic Legion of the U.S. Army. As one concession to the unusual nature of the Legion, because many of the soldiers' next of kin were still living in the Austro-Hungarian Empire, the men were allowed to make out their War Risk Insurance paperwork and list beneficiaries "without restriction as to the citizenship of the allottees...."[38] Provisions were also made to simplify the process for soldiers of the Slavic Legion to become American citizens.

Ultimately, the plan came to naught. When the Armistice was declared, the Slavic Legion was still at Camp Wadsworth and could only count 114 enlisted men and 16 officers on the unit rolls.

They Almost Made It Overseas

At the peak of America's involvement in the war an average of ten thousand soldiers per day were disembarking in France. This pace was kept up right to the end of the war. Some ships which left the U.S. bound for France during the last few days before the Armistice turned around mid-ocean and returned to the United States upon receiving news of the cessation of fighting. And at the ports of embarkation there awaited thousands of other men, ready to board vessels to join their brothers in arms in France. These men were almost universally bitterly disappointed as they turned and boarded trains for the journey back to the camps from which they had recently come, so full of youthful enthusiasm for joining the AEF in France. Some elements of the 8th Division made it to France a few days before the Armistice, while some of the infantry regiments of the division turned back in mid-ocean. The advanced detachment of the 10th Division arrived in France on 9 November while those of the 11th and 12th Divisions made it to England before the Armistice intervened and made moot the deployment of the rest of those divisions. The advanced detachments of several other divisions were either at or en route to Camp Mills, New York, when the Armistice put an end to further movement towards France.[39]

Private Leonardo Gonzales, 62nd Infantry Regiment, 8th Division, was with his regiment at Camp Mills, New York, waiting to board a ship for France when he "heard the glad news the armistice was signed." Instead of sailing to France, Gonzales and his unit sailed to Virginia and further transport by rail and barge to Camp Lee. They were then moved to a camp near their homes for demobilization. Although Gonzales may have been disappointed in not getting overseas, his disappointment was assuaged by his return to home and loved ones: "I came back to my old New Mexico, but believe me I am glad to be home oh boy oh joy where do we go from here?"[40]

Fellow New Mexican Gilberto Gonzales also wrote about his near-overseas experience. Drafted on 2 September 1918, Gonzales was sent to an infantry replacement battalion at Camp MacArthur, Texas. After six weeks of training, Gonzales, now in the 46th Company, October Automatic Replacement Draft (OARD), was ready to head overseas when an outbreak of influenza among the soldiers delayed departure. On 4 November Gonzales and his company were finally "given the great privilege To go out and sail across To take part on the great war." On the morning of 11 November the men were actually aboard the British transport HMS *Cedric* ready to sail when news of the Armistice reached them. Gonzales and his fellow soldiers disembarked and traveled to Camp Merritt, New Jersey. He was discharged at Camp Travis in Texas on 21 December. Gonzales's sadness at missing overseas service is evident in his closing remark when writing about his experiences: "Wish I would have gone further So I could write more but as I was not Lucky to go any further. Hope what I've written is worth reading. Or may be it is worth less."

Ramon Garcia was another member of the 46th Company, OARD, who made it as far as the *Cedric* and no further. During his brief service before proceeding to the port of embarkation, Garcia's unit was quarantined two times, once for three or four weeks. After the disappointing flirtation with deployment, Garcia experienced one final quarantine episode: "About Dec. 3rd a men our Barracks took sick the Docter sead he had the mesles. And from there we wore sent to a quarantine Camp. We had to stay there for 14 days."

Combat in Mexico (1918–1919)

Before April 1917, the main threat to the United States was perceived by almost everyone as coming from south of the Mexican border. Political instability in Mexico caused the United States to pay increased attention to the border area, and there were plenty of reminders of the danger which existed on the Mexican border, even as late as 1918. Cross-border raids by bandits and, on occasion, Mexican soldiers were still threats to the area.

Charles Calarco, an Italian-born factory worker living in Westville, Connecticut, enlisted in the Regular Army on 29 April 1917, about three

7. The "Spare Parts" Brigades

weeks after the United States entered World War I. Calarco served as a corporal in Company F and in Headquarters Company, 37th Infantry Regiment, stationed at Camp McIntosh, Texas, from 13 May 1917 to 11 September 1919. During his service on the Mexican border, Calarco participated in "one small skirmish on the border." Calarco was discharged at Camp Dix, New Jersey, on 16 September 1919.[41]

Of course, the cavalry was well represented among the units seeing some combat in Mexico or on the border. Warren Wells, a native of Connecticut, also got a taste of combat at Juarez, Mexico, in June 1918 while assigned to Troop I, 5th Cavalry Regiment. John Rowe, a native of Liverpool, England, enlisted at the age of eighteen in April 1918. He, too, saw action with the 5th Cavalry Regiment at Juarez, Mexico, on 15–16 July 1918, after only three months in service. Norman Hallsworth enlisted at the age of eighteen in April 1918. Hallsworth a member of Troop E, 5th Cavalry Regiment, carefully recorded his combat: "Engagement with Villastas, Juarez, Mexico, June 15, 1919, Engagements with Villastas, Zaragoza, Mexico, June 16, 1919."

Joe Costa, born in Sicily and working as

Italian-born Charles Calarco was working in a Connecticut factory when war was declared. Assigned to the 37th Infantry Regiment at Fort McIntosh, Texas, Calarco spent the war patrolling the Mexican border (Connecticut World War I records via Ancestry.com).

a bartender in the Café de Beaux-Arts in Bridgeport, Connecticut, wasted little time in joining the Army after war was declared. Enlisting in New York City, he soon found himself serving in Troop H, 7th Cavalry Regiment, in Texas. He stated he was "glad to leave my job as a Bartender to [gain] an Excellent Horsemanship." Promoted to private first class in January 1918, Costa spent most of his military time stationed at Fort Bliss, Texas. Costa recalled his daily training routine: "Continuously Drilling from 7 a.m. to 11 a.m. including 2 p.m. to 3:30 p.m. in the Signal-Squad." Costa participated in what turned out to be one of the last armed clashes between U.S. military forces and Mexican bandits near Juarez and wrote: "River Patrol, Ysleta, Texas, U.S.A., against Villistas in vicinity of Vuarez, Mexico, June 15 to 16, 1919." He was discharged at the Camp Dix Demobilization Center in September 1919 and was later quite proud to report on his Connecticut Military Service Record that he had been promoted from bartender to waiter on his return to the Café de Beaux-Arts.

Another soldier from Connecticut, Warren Wells, takes time out from his cavalry duties to pose for a portrait against a patriotic backdrop. Wells was serving in the 5th Cavalry in June 1918 when he and his comrades were involved in a firefight with some Mexicans near Juárez, Mexico (Connecticut World War I records via Ancestry.com).

7. The "Spare Parts" Brigades

They Needed Men, Fast

By the spring and summer of 1918, the need for men for the AEF was so great that training sometimes was left in the lurch. The experience of Cornelius Mulcahy, a mill worker from Hurley, New Mexico, was not unusual. Mulcahy was drafted on 10 May 1918, and sent to Fort McDowell, a receiving station in California,

> situated on Angel Island (or as we decided Devils Island). We arrived there on May 13th and went through every thing they had in 4 days including two days kitchen police. We were assigned to the Machine Gun Company of the 62nd Inf at Camp Fremont [California] on May 17th remaining there about three months.

On 10 August Mulcahy was sent to the Machine Gun Officers Training School at Camp Hancock, Georgia. The twelve-week course ended on 10 November, the day before the Armistice. Mulcahy was awarded a reserve commission and discharged on 26 November 1918. "So my military career ended without seeing any real service."[42]

Joe Costa left his bartender job and enlisted in the Army in May 1917; he served most of his military tour at Fort Bliss, Texas, in the 7th Cavalry Regiment. Costa, seen here posing in a lightweight U.S. Army uniform, and his fellow troopers were also involved in a firefight at Juárez, Mexico, in June 1919 (Connecticut World War I records via Ancestry.com).

The Inductee Meets the Psychiatrist

Among the more amusing or more irritating aspects of entering the Army at one of the training camps, depending on your viewpoint and sense of humor, was the intelligence test. The early 20th century was a period when many forms of intelligence tests were developed; some of these tended to reinforce whatever social or political point of view the tester wanted to promote. For many of the newly selected soldiers it was just more proof that the Army was crazy. To some of the men being received at Camp Lee by the 155th Depot Brigade, the tests were foolish to the extreme. One test required the soldier to place "the dot in that part of the square that was in the circle but not in the triangle, or in placing the dot in that part of the triangle that was in the square but not in the circle."[43] This was followed by such interesting questions as "How many legs has a Korean?" Keeping in mind that many of the inductees at Camp Lee were drawn from the rural areas of Virginia, West Virginia, and Pennsylvania, there's little doubt many of them had never heard of Korea or Koreans before the test. After the soldiers had completed the tests and moved on to the next station, they usually compared notes but could never determine whether a man's intelligence was signified by a high score or a low score on the test.

Taken at Camp Hancock, Georgia, in November 1918, this photograph shows 2nd Lieutenant Cornelius Mulcahy during his time at the Machine Gun Officers Training School. Mulcahy had been drafted in May 1918 and trained at Camp Fremont, California, with the 8th Division before being selected for officer training (New Mexico War Service records via Ancestry.com).

You're in the Army Now! Or Is It the Navy?

Floating in the vast sea of unusual stateside Army units was Ship Repair Shop Unit Number 301. Activated in May 1918, the unit was based at the Hoboken Port of Embarkation and was responsible for repairs to transport vessels. Since the transports were vital to keeping up the flow of men and material to Europe, the men in the unit performed an important, if unheralded, duty.[44] But not all was smooth sailing for the soldier-mechanics. It seems that a company officer, Captain Thomas D. Barry of the Army Quartermaster Corps, embezzled company funds and officers' mess funds. Captain Barry was caught, prosecuted, and found guilty. He was sentenced to be dismissed from the service and confined at hard labor for ten years, later reduced to five years. Their quasi-nautical duties no longer needed by the War Department, Ship Repair Shop Unit No. 301 was disbanded in April 1919.[45]

Newton Baker—Book Burner? (September 1918)

Newton Baker had seemed to many people a strange choice for Secretary of War. His highest office, prior to his selection by President Wilson, had been as the mayor of Cleveland. He came to the position in Wilson's cabinet with a well-deserved reputation as a pacifist and a firm opposition to militarism of all kinds. Perhaps it was this reputation and support for social causes which influenced Wilson to select him. Baker's peace-loving nature was severely tested immediately as Pancho Villa attacked Columbus, New Mexico, on 9 March 1916, the same day the new Secretary of War was sworn in. Soon Baker was dealing with the problems of the campaign on the Mexican Border while simultaneously trying to oversee the complete reorganization of the U.S. Army. With the declaration of war with Germany in April 1917, Baker the pacifist was now a leader of America's armed forces and military-focused industrial might, second only to the President.

While serving as the Secretary, Baker still tried to espouse some progressive sentiments such as fairer treatment for African American soldiers as well as attempting to mitigate some of the brutal treatment handed out to conscientious objectors in military camps and prisons. As Baker's experience in dealing with military matters grew, he became more engaged in all aspects of training and operations. He also had become convinced the best way to end the war was to win it as quickly as possible. When Pershing was selected to become the leader of the American forces in Europe, Baker wrote him saying:

> General Pershing....
> I have several ambitions, deeply entertained:
> 1. I want the Germans beaten hard and thoroughly—a military victory.
> 2. I want you to have the honor of doing it....[46]

Nevertheless, the action he took in September 1918 to personally provide a list of books to be banned from the training camps must have given him some pause as some of the books were written by well-known pacifists. Even so, he gave instructions that if any of the books were already on the shelves in the many American Library Association (ALA) reading rooms and huts in the camps, they were to be destroyed. Among the list of books were *Approaches to the Peace Settlement* by the famous pacifist Emily G. Balch; *Why War?* by Frederic C. Howe; *Songs of Armageddon* by George S. Viereck, the editor of the very pro–German magazine *Fatherland*; and *The Vampire of the Continent*, an attack on British greed and misdeeds written by Count Ernst zu Reventlow.

In response, the American Library Association noted that over eight million books had already been donated to training camp libraries and while "it is, of course entirely possible that German propagandists have tried to slip their work across to soldiers and sailors … gift books are not placed in camp libraries without going through a process of examination and selection." One of the ALA War Service Committee members who was also on the staff of the New York Public Library, admitted some of the now-banned books might be in that library but only as reference material and for research, but not for checking out. Explaining this policy, he said, "If Satan wrote a pro–German book we should want it for our reference shelves … [where] it might be of use to future historians."[47]

A Drinking Problem at Camp Devens? (October 1918)

During the very worst period of Spanish flu at Camp Devens a number of military and civilian scientists travelled to the camp to attempt to isolate the virus or bacteria causing the sudden and terrible deaths at the camp. Oswald Avery, a scientist from the Rockefeller Institute, was baffled by his inability to recreate in the camp laboratory some of the basic disease tests which had been performed successfully at other sites. One of these important tests was conducted by staining suspected bacteria on a slide with a violet dye, treating it with iodine, washing it with alcohol and then staining it again with a different dye. Bacteria which remained violet in color would be considered not to have the flu bacillus. Try as he may, the samples always remained violet indicating no trace of the flu.

After repeated unsuccessful attempts, he resorted to true scientific methods and checked every possible aspect of the test. It was then that he examined more closely the bottles of alcohol being used as part of the test to clean the slides and samples. It soon became apparent the soldiers who had been working in the lab before the epidemic hit had been drinking the clear-colored alcohol and replacing it with water. Repeating the test with real alcohol, Dr. Avery got the true results and the samples changed color, reflecting the presence of the flu bacillus.[48]

Howard Doesn't Trust the Camp Meade Medical System (11 November 1918)

A young soldier named Howard wrote his mother on 11 November 1918 to share the momentous news that the war had ended and that all the hospital staff had gone into town to celebrate. He wrote of his hope he would be out of the Army soon. That was the last positive note. He wrote:

> Well I am still in bed ... my temperature is around 99 in the mornings and 101 in the evening. [The doctor] yesterday talked like I might have malaria. He said there would be someone around to get a test of my blood but as yet I havnit seen them. I never heard of anybody having malaria this time of year. I wish he would <u>do something</u> for I am getting tired of laying here....
>
> Hope all at home are well and that I soon will be. I don't believe this Dr knows what is the matter, that I have fever like I do, and he don't seem to care to find out. Love to all, Howard.
>
> Until further notice send my mail direct to me, Base Hospital Ward 4, it seems to be <u>to much trouble</u> for them at the Company to mark Hospital on my letters and drop them in the box.[49]

With the benefit of hindsight, we can say Howard should have considered himself lucky to be well enough to write home. Camp Meade was one of the divisional training sites hit hardest by the flu in late 1918, and many of his fellow patients would not have had the strength to write these words, much less underline some of them for emphasis.

The Intriguing Case of Private Lester G. Ott (February 1919)

In February 1919 the *New York Times* carried an article describing a U.S. Congressman's outrage on learning that some conscientious objectors (COs) might soon be released from Army confinement and be given an honorable discharge and back pay for their time served in the military. Representative T.A. Chandler from Oklahoma was beside himself with anger over what he saw as an obvious miscarriage of justice. He pointed out several abuses of the conscientious objector status including one by a man who had previously served an enlistment in the Missouri National Guard and had deployed in 1916 to the Mexican border. The man in question had declared his CO status shortly after arriving at Camp Funston. He reported that he had a "consultation" with God, he was now a CO, and he "did not care who knew it."[50]

Just as aggravating to Representative Chandler was the case of Lester George Ott. Ott, a 23-year-old Ohio draftee, arrived at Camp Sherman in April 1918 and was assigned to the 158th Depot Brigade. A short while later he was assigned to the 331st Infantry Regiment which was part of the 83rd Division. Just seventeen days later he was back in the 158th Depot Brigade, claiming to be a CO. It was all downhill from there. Assigned to a special "Camp of Conscientious Objectors" in the 158th, Ott seems to have had a unique ability to drive the U.S. Army authorities crazy. It reached the ultimate level when a military police sergeant at Camp Sherman was arrested and charged with striking Ott out of frustration due to his unwillingness to obey orders. And here was the crux of Representative Chandler's anger: Sergeant John Bell was undergoing court martial for the attack on Ott, while Ott the troublemaker could possibly be released and given back pay. It had also come to light that Ott had voluntarily enlisted in the Cincinnati Home Guard before he was drafted. In that organization, Ott had served "as an armed sentinel and ... took an oath to support and defend the Constitution against all the enemies of the United States."[51] Neither of these acts appeared to support Ott's claim of being a CO and yet here he was, making that claim and driving his sergeant crazy.

In retrospect, it would probably have been better for the Army to have cut all ties to Ott much earlier. A good indication of Ott's personality can be found in his 5 June 1917 draft registration answers. In response to the question of occupation, the then 22-year-old man claimed to be a lawyer. In response to "By Whom Employed?" and "Where Employed?" he wrote in very large letters "No One" and "No Place." In response to potential reasons for claiming exemption from the draft, he again wrote in very large letters "None."

Ultimately, the last laugh was on Ott as he was transferred to Fort Riley in September 1918 and then to the Disciplinary Barracks at Fort Leavenworth, Kansas, until December 1920 when he was dishonorably discharged from the Army. By the time World War II draft registration came around, Ott was working in a cigar store in New York City and living in nearby New Jersey with his wife and two children. Obviously it was a good job because the Ott family could even afford a live-in maid.

He died in September 1958 and is buried in Florida. His gravestone contains no indication of his military "service."[52]

So Private Butler, What Do You Really Think of the Army? (4 July 1919)

In any military organization there is always a tendency to believe that everybody, or at least somebody, has it better than you. This was certainly true in the U.S. Army of the Great War. There was a strong belief among some soldiers in the AEF that there were a number of shirkers or slackers hiding out in the depot brigades and the development battalions and thereby avoiding frontline service.[53] In some cases immigrants or foreign-born draftees became the easy scapegoats for animosity. Filling out his post-war survey, James V. Butler unleashed his anger at the Army, the war, and foreigners all at the same time.

In response to the question "What was your attitude towards Military Service in general and toward your call in particular?" Butler wrote, "[It] was not done fair. Should make foreigners fight just like us poor boys." Responding to a question about his service overseas, Butler wrote, "No good Poor treatment.... Poor food ... rheumatism in my lower limbs." When he got to the question about the effect or impression actual fighting had on him, he was really warming up: "That we had to finish them [the Germans] so we could get back home and get something to eat and a place to sleep." For the final question which asked how his beliefs had changed from before the war to after, Butler returned to his initial theme: "I have learned what war was and what went with war—to leave all foreigners take our positions [jobs] and none for us."

It is somewhat ironic that Butler served in the 328th Infantry Regiment of the 82nd Division whose nickname was the "All-Americans." The foreword to official history of the 82nd Division in World War I, written in 1920, recounts: "We are glad that the 82nd Division contained men of every blood strain in all the races that make up our nation. This Division has learned that an American is one who is willing to give his life for America."[54] Butler probably never read that section of the book.

8

Lost in the Shadows

Women, African Americans, Patriotic Liars and the U.S. Guards

"Success in battle is the ultimate object of all military training; success may be looked for only when the training is intelligent and thorough."[1]

When a country is building an armed force of four million men, with further plans to expand it to six million, it is impossible not to think, speak, or write in generalities. As we have seen, there were constant large-scale transfers of men between camps, and having eight thousand men show up in a two-day period at a camp was not unusual. Transporting, clothing, equipping, and feeding large numbers of soldiers became a national business, and the sight of troop trains became so commonplace from the Midwest to the East Coast they eventually drew little interest from onlookers. Soon, in this massive sea of olive drab uniforms, the soldiers lose their humanity and become faceless figures wearing campaign hats. And worse, this meant other groups within civilian and military society which already drew little recognition now drew even less. Among those lost in history's shadow are the African Americans serving in labor or engineer battalions building and maintaining the camps' infrastructures, the many female nurses and service organization workers treating the sick and injured, the "less than perfect" men relegated to serve in the U.S. Guards battalions, and the many boys who lied about their age in order to serve their country.

One thing which often tends to be forgotten when the story of the U.S. military in World War I is discussed is the important role played by women. Although there were many men who quickly enlisted when war was declared, the larger majority were drafted through the Selective Service Act. In fact, of "every 100 men who served [in the Army], 10 were National Guardsmen, 13 were Regulars, and 77 were [draftees] in

A common sight during the war: a team of Red Cross volunteers provide drinks and sandwiches to soldiers being shuttled via railroad from one camp to another (Library of Congress).

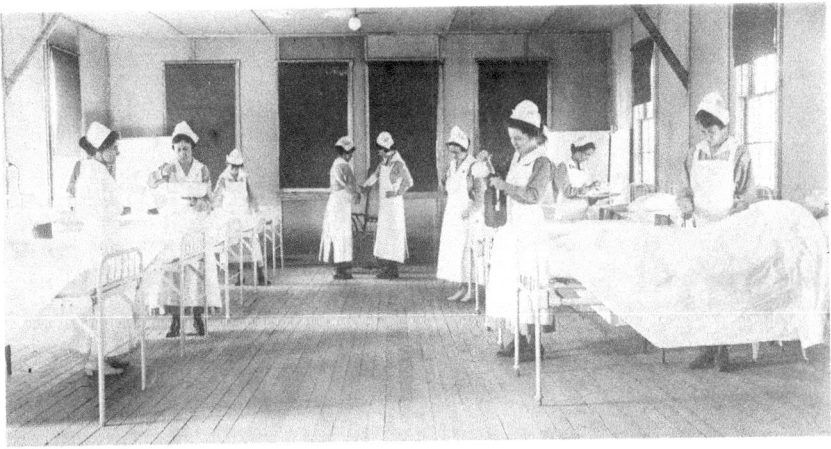

A unique photograph from Camp Wadsworth and a reminder that Army nurses also required training. In the bed on the far right, closest to the viewer, the head of one of the training dummies used by the nurses to practice their skills can be seen (Library of Congress).

the National Army."[2] In stark contrast, every single female who joined the Army as a nurse or Signal Corps telephone operator, or the Navy as a Yeomanette, or the Marine Corps as a Marinette (the women themselves preferred the title: Marine), was a volunteer.[3] There were no draft boards for females, nor were there requirements for them to register. Therefore every woman who came forward to serve in the camps or in France as an Army nurse, or Red Cross, Salvation Army, YMCA, YWCA, Knights of Columbus, or American Library Association volunteer was there of her own accord. So, while some young men were suspected of avoiding the draft by seeking safe duty in one of the service organizations, no woman was ever so accused.

It is an accepted fact that soldiers in training cannot be kept in a training posture all the time; there has to be time for relaxation and entertainment. Unlike the Second World War, during the First World War there was no United Service Organizations (USO) to provide the venues and staff needed for this function. Instead, there was a consortium of the many service organizations. This association included:

Due to its central location on North-South and East-West rail lines, the railroad station in Richmond, Virginia, was particularly busy; in this case the Red Cross ladies appear to be providing drinks and food to soldiers returning from overseas (private collection).

8. Lost in the Shadows 199

The suddenness and violence with which the flu struck the East Coast generated a request to the public that anyone with medical or nursing experience come forward to help with the sick and dying. These African American Red Cross volunteers are representative of those brave ladies who answered that call and helped in the camps as well as the local civilian hospitals (Library of Congress).

The Young Men's Christian Association (YMCA), the Young Women's Christian Association (YWCA), the Salvation Army, the Jewish Welfare Board, the Knights of Columbus and the War Camp Community Service, and the American Library Association. Altogether they became known as the "Seven Sisters."[4] They were tasked by the War Department with providing social, health, and welfare services to soldiers in training camps under the watchful eyes and oversight of the Commission on Training Camp Activities.

Of particular interest to the ladies working in the camps was the YWCA. Although it operated on a much smaller scale than the YMCA, the YWCA played an important role in providing clean, safe lodging for the many female workers in the camps. Although, like the YMCA, it had a strong pacifistic history, it also signed up to support the American effort both in France and at home in the training camps. Duty in the service organizations anywhere near the frontlines in France could be deadly; nine male and two female workers in the YMCA were killed as a result of enemy action. Another 167 were listed as wounded, gassed or shell-shocked. Adding to the casualty lists were the fifty male

Rightfully proud of their service during the twin cataclysms of the war and the Spanish flu pandemic, these Red Cross volunteers participate in one of the many victory parades in the spring and summer of 1919. Note that the ladies on the left are marching with one of the symbols of their trade: a stretcher (Library of Congress).

and twenty-one female YMCA workers who died from accidents or disease.[5]

While the nurses and ladies of the service organizations working in the stateside training camps needed no protection from German bombs or artillery fire, they were faced with what proved to be an even deadlier foe. Camp Devens, Massachusetts, was the first U.S. Army training camp to be hit by the Spanish flu in September and October 1918. By late September the epidemic was so bad that the medical staff was completely overwhelmed. The Red Cross, although busy dealing with the civilian sick and dying, managed to send twelve nurses to the camp to assist. They probably should have saved the effort; almost immediately eight of the twelve were sick or dead. A doctor working there wrote that the camp had been "averaging about 100 deaths per day ... we have lost an outrageous number of Nurses and Drs.... It takes special trains to carry away the dead."[6]

At Camp Grant, Illinois, ten barracks building were used to hold the excess patients for whom there was no room in the hospital as the number of sick and dying quickly climbed to over four thousand. Just five days into the epidemic, thirty-five nurses had been hospitalized. Making the situation worse, the same day as the first cases at the camp were reported, 3,108 soldiers from the camp were transferred by train to Camp Hancock, Georgia, effectively spreading the epidemic there.[7]

When the city of Rochester, New York, and the surrounding Monroe County compiled the list of their war dead, the total came to 609. Of these, a surprising number were Italian-born men, comprising some 12 percent of those lost to combat, disease or accident. Almost invisible in the numbers were four nurses from the Rochester region who died of the Spanish flu while caring for soldiers. Cecil Josephine Cochran was a 24-year-old Red Cross nurse when she was sent to serve at Camp McClellan, Alabama, in September 1918. Upon arrival she was informed the camp was in the midst of the flu epidemic and she was given the opportunity to return home. Instead she went to work immediately in the wards helping to care for the sick soldiers. Just fifteen days after her arrival, she was dead from the flu. Lillian Cupp was also a Red Cross nurse and received orders to report to Camp Gordon, Georgia. Already weakened from exposure to the flu, she insisted on proceeding on 3 October to the camp and hoped her illness would run its course by the time

Cecil Josephine Cochran, a 24-year-old nurse, joined the Red Cross and volunteered to serve in the training camps. In spite of warnings of the danger from the flu epidemic she travelled to Camp McClellan and began working in the hospital. Just 10 days after arrival she contracted the disease and died on 15 October 1918 (private collection).

she arrived. It didn't, and four days later she died. Travelling with Cupp to Camp Gordon was Catherine Rose Connelly. Connelly had joined the Red Cross on 30 September 1918 after completing nursing school. Although healthy while travelling to Camp Gordon, she contracted pneumonia while serving in the wards and died on 16 October. Another Rochester area nurse, Anna Marie Williams, was born in England and completed her nursing training in Buffalo. She signed on with the Army and served with Base Hospital Number 19 which was raised in Rochester. Williams is different from the three other nurses discussed here in that she was serving in an Army hospital in Vichy, France, when she died of pneumonia on 15 October 1918, the very same day as Cecil Josephine Cochran. In fact all four of these nurses died within eight days of each other. By the time the disease had run its course, one out of every sixty-seven soldiers in the Army died from flu or its complications.[8] While it is hard to draw direct comparisons between fighting in

Identified only as the "staff of #8 at Camp Pike," these medical personnel were serving in the frontlines of one of the flu hotspots. At the height of the epidemic over a third of the soldiers in the camp were hospitalized with the influenza or a related disease (private collection).

the trenches and working in a Spanish flu ward in an Army hospital, there can be little doubt that the nurses and volunteers who showed up each day to work exhibited as much courage as the soldiers in France. Yet the medals and accolades were reserved for the AEF, and most of the nurses and nursing volunteers in the stateside camps went completely unrecognized. Ironically, one of the most visible signs of the sacrifice of these ladies came in the form of the black mourning armband worn by Major General Clarence R. Edwards, commander of the 26th Division. Edwards wore the mourning band on his uniform not for the many men under his command who had died in France but instead for his daughter, an Army nurse who died of Spanish flu while serving in the hospital at Camp Meade.

If the ladies serving in the camps were lost in the shadows, they were not alone. A great number of African American soldiers appear to have been drafted at times merely to form a pool of menial laborers. While some truly believed that having the black draftees in uniform will "have given to the white people of our country a new idea of his citizenship, his real character and capabilities, and his 100 per cent Americanism," many of the Army's leaders saw it differently.[9] As we have learned earlier, the odds of a black man being selected for the draft in certain states was greater than that of a white man from the same communities. Obviously, across the country there were many more whites registering and being selected for service than blacks. Looking at percentages, however, tells the other side of the story. The first report from the Provost Marshal stated, "out of every 100 colored citizens called, 36 were certified for service and 64 were rejected, exempted or discharged; whereas out of every 100 whites called, 25 were certified for service and 75 were rejected, exempted or discharged."[10]

Of great interest and much discussion among the senior Army leaders were the questions of where to train the black draftees and then where and how to employ them. In response, the Army Chief of Staff General Tasker Bliss developed six alternatives: (1) Station them in segregated camps at the major training sites; (2) Add a black regiment to each division undergoing training at the 16 National Army cantonments; (3) Station and train them at facilities near the main training sites, but not part of the site; (4) Turn two camps in the South into all-black training camps; (5) Provide them some basic training at eight of the Northern camps and then finish their training in France before using them in battle; and (6) Delay calling into service most of the black draftees and give time for white units training at stateside camps to be gone, then call for their induction at the nearest camps, provide them with basic training, and deploy them to France primarily as "service" troops.[11]

Ultimately, a modified version of the sixth option was chosen. Ironically, the reasons for not choosing the second or third option had little to do with race and a lot to do with War Department economics: it would cost too much money to transport the black draftees around the country and would cost even more if separate facilities were to be built. Of course, the vast amount of troop transfers taking place between the camps certainly weakens part of this seemingly logical argument. The fifth option also hit the economic snag. Since most black draftees were coming from the South, the cost of moving them to northern sites would be prohibitive. Again, with hindsight, it's clear that adding a few thousand more men to the constant rotation of soldiers between camps would not have made the situation that much worse. Or better.

When African American community leaders were informed of the selection of the sixth alternative, they raised an objection, voicing their concerns that the black soldiers would not be given a chance to prove themselves in combat. As a compromise, the War Department agreed to train thirty thousand black soldiers for combat. Another fifty thousand would be trained for service in the depot brigades, from which they might be used as service troops or as replacements to make up for casualties in black combat units. It was a great and well-intended promise but as we have seen, troops assigned to the depot brigades, black or white, had no guarantee of what might be their next unit assignment.

A faded but still valuable photograph of some of the cooks at one of the training camps. By limiting the number of black soldiers in combat units, the Army used many of the African American draftees in logistical support or labor units, ostensibly to allow white soldiers to focus on honing their combat skills (private collection).

Also working against the black inductees was the general perception in the public's mind that most of them had been manual laborers as civilians before the war and so they should "continue to do it for the Army."[12] In fact, one Army memorandum produced by the Army War College was quite explicit in presenting this belief. It said:

> Each southern state has negroes in blue coveralls working throughout the state with a pick and shovel. When these colored men are drafted they are put in blue coveralls (fatigue clothes) and continue to do work with a pick and shovel in the same state where they were previously working.[13]

In contrast to this, however, the same memorandum took the view that whatever solutions with regard to the use and organization of black labor battalions were decided on; the bottom line must continue to be the successful conduct of the war. The memo stated:

> It is understood that no money is to be wasted. But if spending money materially assists in the prosecution of the war, that is what the money is for. If barracks are necessary to

An African American soldier poses with a Model-1898 Krag-Jorgensen rifle. In many camps, the Krag-Jorgensen rifle, obsolete and leftover from the Spanish-American War, had to serve as the training weapon because of serious rifle shortages across the Army (private collection).

> | Reddick, | Frank | 2,464,534 | | 1 |
> |---|---|---|---|---|
> | (Surname) | (Christian name) | (Army serial number) | | *Colored. |
>
> Residence: RFD 5 Box 101   Lynchburg   Campbell   VIRGINIA
> (Street and house number) (Town or city) (County) (State)
>
> ~~Enlisted A. N. G. N. R. C.~~ *Inducted at Bedford Va   on Oct 27, 1917
> Place of birth: Bedford Co Va   Age or date of birth: 25 6/12 yrs
>
> Organizations served in, with dates of assignments and transfers:
> 155 Dep Brig to Mch 15/18; Co H 367 Inf to *June 8/18;
> Co D 431 Serv Bn to disch
>
> Grades, with date of appointment:
> Corp Dec 15/17; Sgt Mch 1/18; Corp Aug 1/18; Sgt Sept 1/18
>
> Engagement:
>
> Wounds or other injuries received in action: None.
> Served overseas from † No   to †   from †   to †
> Honorably discharged on demobilization   *June 27/19   19
> In view of occupation he was, on date of discharge, reported   0   per cent disabled.
> Remarks:
>
> Form No. 724-1, A. G. O.   *Strike out words not applicable.   *Dates of departure from and arrival in the U. S.

The Virginia War Service Record for Frank Reddick, an African American draftee from Bedford, Virginia, who served in the 155th Depot Brigade at Camp Lee, the 367th Infantry Regiment of the 92nd Division at Camp Upton, and finally the Camp Upton 431st Engineer Service Battalion. It is notable that Sergeant Reddick was reduced to corporal when he was transferred to the 367th and then promoted back to sergeant when transferred to the 431st (Virginia National Guard).

> shelter labor battalions and labor battalions help divisions to become trained for overseas service in shorter time, and to be more thoroughly trained, then such expense is entirely justified.[14]

In short, the general policy appears to have been one of trial and error, with drafted black soldiers bearing the brunt of the decisions and with no say in the outcome.

Following these precepts, it is small wonder very few black soldiers received combat training and the appropriate clothing and equipment. Instead, many were issued only overalls and work clothes. One white officer noted that "these men are nothing more than laborers in uniform,

Opposite bottom: Some African American soldiers were selected for duty in combat units and received the appropriate training. In this photograph, a small group is practicing either "drill and ceremony" or "guard mount" procedures under the watchful eyes of two corporals. The corporals were most likely pre-war soldiers from one of the black Regular Army infantry or cavalry regiments (Library of Congress).

8. *Lost in the Shadows* 207

Another common image from the training camps: a group of poorly dressed African American soldiers assigned to a labor unit pose for a postcard photograph. It should be remembered that Camp Lee was a National Army training camp, so the soldiers being trained for combat units lived in wooden barracks while many of the supporting depot brigade soldiers or labor units were relegated to living in tents (U.S. Army Quartermaster Museum).

they do not have colored officers" and that "white men released by them [black labor troops] from day labor work, would be free to spend their entire time being instructed for combatant service."[15] It is this last point which really gets to the heart of the matter. In the large training camps, most of which were still growing and building when the first troops began to arrive, there was no shortage of unskilled and strenuous work that needed to be done. Everything from clearing brush and unloading trucks to digging rifle pits and drainage ditches all required large amounts of labor at each camp. As a result, while few camp commanders sought to have black combat units training at their site, all wanted black labor battalions assigned.

In fairness to the Army leadership, there were also a large number of white labor units performing similar duties both in the States and in France, but again, when looked at in proportion to the total number of soldiers, it is clear that African Americans had a much greater chance of being relegated to labor battalions than their white counterparts. It is small wonder so many draftees became invisible men and received little credit for their inglorious but absolutely necessary efforts in keeping the camps functioning.

Adding to the lack of visibility and recognition was the fact that the Army's treatment of the black inductees was inconsistent across the camps. At some camps, four hours a day were set aside to teach reading, writing, and other basic skills to black draftees. At other camps, no such instruction was provided. It was noted by one observer that Camp Lee's white soldiers in the 155th Depot Brigade received instruction in literacy and soldier skills while black soldiers in the same brigade did not.[16]

Also lost to history in the shuffle of attempting to train and field a four-million-man army, were the surprisingly large numbers of boys who lied about their age to join the military. During World War I, the minimum age for enlistment in the Army without parental consent was eighteen years. Boys between the ages of sixteen and eighteen could enlist with parental consent. Used here, the term "underage" refers to boys who enlisted, with and without parental consent, under the age of sixteen. Thus the "under" part of the term refers simply to boys too young to enlist without parental consent.[17]

A survey of underage enlistees from New York, whose records are easily accessed and searchable, yields some interesting results. Approximately twenty-five young men born in 1902 and 1903 enlisted in the Army and were discharged early due to their underage status.[18] Five boys were between fourteen and fifteen years of age, nineteen were between fifteen and sixteen, and one boy was over sixteen. The youngest to enlist was Nick Ferrara, a native of Caserta, Italy, who enlisted in Company C,

8. Lost in the Shadows

```
Kennedy              Anderson M.      947697           white
(Surname)            (Christian name) (Army serial number)  (Race. White or colored)

Residence:           Imboden                           VIRGINIA.
         (Street and house number)  (Town or city)  (County)  (State)

*Enlisted in RA at Columbus Bks. Ohio on Apr 16/17.
†Born in Sawyers Ky Sept 25, 1900.
Organizations: Co H 36 Inf to June 20/17; Co L 40 Inf to disch.

Grades:  Pvt.

Engagements:

Wounds or other injuries received in action: None.
‡Served overseas: none
§Hon. disch. May 15, 1918 - misrepresentation of age.
Was reported                per cent disabled on date of discharge, in view of occupation.
Remarks: Under the provisions of the Act of Congress approved (over)
```

Remarks (continued): March 16, 1926 (Public 46, 69th Congress) in the administration of any laws conferring rights, privileges or benefits upon honorably discharged soldiers, their widows and dependent children, the above named soldier shall hereafter be held and considered to have been honorably discharged.

Filled with patriotic fervor, Kentucky-born Anderson Kennedy enlisted in the Army at Columbus Barracks, Ohio, just 10 days after war was declared. It appears he managed to hide his true age for a year before the Army caught on and sent him home. In 1926 he was granted an honorable discharge by an act of Congress (courtesy Library of Virginia).

48th Infantry Regiment, at Fort Slocum, New York, on 14 June 1917, at the tender age of 14 years, two months, 15 days. Ferrara was discharged for misrepresentation of age on 15 July 1917, after only one month and one day of service.

Four other New York boys were under fifteen years old when they enlisted. Harry Eliakim, a native of Turkey, enlisted in the 12th New York Infantry Regiment, National Guard (which became the 105th Infantry Regiment), at the age of 14 years, six months, eight days; he was discharged on 23 October 1917, after two months of service. Henry Lincoln, a native of Brooklyn, enlisted in the 47th New York Infantry Regiment, National Guard, on 24 July 1917, at the age of 14 years, 11 months, one day. His regiment soon became the federalized 104th Field Artillery Regiment. Lincoln lasted until 29 March 1918, having served for eight months and five days. Chester O. Siebert, a native of Rochester, New York, enlisted in the 3rd New York Infantry Regiment, National Guard (108th Infantry Regiment), on 20 April 1917, at the age of 14 years, 10 months, 14 days. Siebert's ruse lasted almost a whole year before he was caught and discharged on 3 March 1918. Thomas Gerard Dougherty, whose story is covered below, was the other 14-year-old New Yorker to enlist.

The New York boys served in a number of different types of units. At least three of them started in the National Guard. Thirteen of them were in infantry regiments, and two were in machine gun units. Four boys were in cavalry regiments, one in a field artillery regiment, and the rest in medical or quartermaster units. Five of the boys were immigrants: two were from Italy and one each was from Poland, Russia, and Turkey. It was a rare boy who succeeded in serving for more than a few months. The shortest term of service belongs to Benjamin Harris who managed to hide his true age for only three weeks and three days before being discharged at Fort Slocum, New York, on 4 August 1917.

Paul Krug, a native of Elmira, New York, was one of the first underage New York soldiers to enlist during the war. Krug enlisted in Company C, 22nd Infantry Regiment, at Fort Slocum, New York, on 7 April 1917, the day after the United States entered the war. Krug was just 15 years, two months, 26 days old at the time. He was discovered and discharged on 23 February 1918.

In an effort to get into the "big show," several boys enlisted more than once. Thomas Gerard Dougherty, who was born in Evansville, Indiana, on 23 October 1902, lied about his age and enlisted in the Regular Army under the name Thomas Gerard at Gettysburg, Pennsylvania, on 12 July 1917, at the age of 14 years, eight months, 20 days. Gerard/Dougherty was a private first class in Company D, 4th Machine Gun

8. Lost in the Shadows

Battalion, when he was caught and discharged on 15 November 1917. Not to be deterred, Dougherty enlisted under his actual name at Fort Slocum, New York, on 28 May 1918. Dougherty served stateside as a private first class in Company E, 17th Infantry Regiment, until his honorable discharge on 9 April 1919.

Angelo Favata, a native of New York City, was another young man not to be put off. Favata enlisted in the 22nd Infantry Regiment at Fort Hamilton, New York, on 10 July 1917, at the age of 15 years, five days. Favata was discharged due to his minority on 10 September 1917. But on 16 October, just over a month later, Favata, under the name James Parra, enlisted in the Enlisted Reserve Corps at Governors Island, New York. His fraudulent enlistment discovered, Favata/Parra was discharged again on 20 February 1918.

Irving Posner was born in Brooklyn, New York, on 27 January 1901; he enlisted in the Regular Army on 1 August 1917, at the age of 16 years, six months, five days. Posner was discovered and discharged on 6 September 1917. On 22 November 1917, Posner enlisted again, and this time he got away with it for a longer period of time. In fact, Posner went overseas as a corporal in Supply Company 311, Quartermaster Corps, on 6 June 1918. But he was again found out and sent back to the United States for discharge at the end of July.

Sometimes parents must have felt there was a brotherly conspiracy designed to cause parents much anxiety and exasperation. A case of two brothers from Philadelphia, Pennsylvania, illustrates this nicely. Charles Chiardio was born on 14 October 1900, and his brother Frank was born on 1 September 1901.[19] The boys were the sons of Italian immigrants. Frank lied about his age and, without his parents' permission, enlisted in Company F, 3rd Pennsylvania Infantry Regiment, Pennsylvania National Guard, on 30 March 1917, seven days before the U.S. entered the war. At the time, Chiardio was 15 years, six months, 29 days old. After the U.S. entered the war, the National Guard was federalized, and Chiardio was assigned to the 109th Machine Gun Battalion, 28th Division. With his younger brother gone into the Army, Charles felt the tug of the romance of war, and he enlisted in Company E, 3rd Pennsylvania Infantry Regiment, on 4 September 1917, at the age of 16 years, 10 months, 21 days. Charles was soon transferred to Auxiliary Remount 308, and he was promoted to private first class on 1 February 1918.

Eventually the Chiardio brothers' deception came to light. Charles was discharged on 20 March 1918, and six days later Frank was discharged. Sadly, Frank Chiardio died of pneumonia shortly thereafter, on 15 October 1918, at just over seventeen years of age. Although the precise circumstances surrounding the service of the Chiardio brothers is not known, it can be safely surmised that parental intervention was a factor in the discovery and quick discharge of the young men.

It's important to note that this brief study looks at only those underage men who lied about their age and enlisted without parental permission and who were discovered and discharged before going overseas. Their records bear the notation "fraudulent enlistment," "misrepresentation of age," or some similar notice. There were some young men who apparently received parental permission and served their whole enlistment. Others were discharged for reasons other than fraudulent enlistment. And there were more than a few men who lied, enlisted, and were sent overseas before their true age was discovered. Many of these boys were sent back to the States and immediately discharged. There were even a few men whose records indicate which they were less than sixteen years old when they enlisted but still served their entire term of enlistment. Perhaps these boys succeeded in fooling the authorities until their discharge.

The following notation was stamped upon the service cards for underage soldiers from New York who had been discharged for fraudulent enlistment:

> Under the provisions of the Act of Congress approved March 2, 1929, Public No. 950, 70th Congress, in the administration of any laws conferring rights, privileges or benefits, upon honorably discharged soldiers, their widows and dependent children, the above named soldier shall hereafter be held and considered to have been honorably discharged [date of discharge].[20]

Interestingly enough, as can be seen in our sample record of an underage soldier from Virginia, the authorities in that state called upon the 16 March 1926 Congressional Act (Public 46, 69th Congress) to restore and provide veteran status to the underage but patriotic liars. Regardless of state, all of the boys in this study who were discharged for fraudulent enlistment soon gained legal military veteran status, as indicated in their records. Thus the government recognized the youthful zeal that melded with, or perhaps masqueraded as, patriotism.

Equally missing their share of the publicity and accolades which accompanied the victory in France were the men who served in the United States Guards battalions. The War Department created the "United States Guards, National Army" in December 1917. Organized in battalions, the Guards were not to exceed twenty-five thousand men. Their main duty was to guard various camps, installations, and infrastructure in the United States. These units were manned largely by men who for one reason or another were unfit for active service overseas. Initially, there were forty-eight battalions, numbered 1 through

48, stationed throughout the United States. Each battalion was further divided into companies, and these companies were often geographically separated from others in the same battalion. The Guards units were equipped with "machine guns, Krag-Jorgensen rifles, caliber .30; revolvers, caliber .38, and ammunition for each; and such articles of old model equipment as are available...."[21] Because combat troops slated for overseas service needed the newer machine guns, the Guards units were issued .30 and .303 caliber Lewis, Colt model 1917, and Vickers machine guns. The Ordnance Department also provided each Guards company ten 12-gauge riot shotguns and 100 rounds of buckshot ammunition.[22]

Armed with a M-1917 Enfield, Pvt. Ramon Garcia y Sandoval poses for his portrait. He was assigned to Company A, 25th U.S. Guards Battalion, and most likely stationed at Camp Taliaferro near Fort Worth, Texas, in 1918 (New Mexico War Service records via Ancestry.com).

Beginning in May 1918, the U.S. Guards battalions grew in number. Approximately 18,000 men then in training camps had, "during training, developed minor physical defects or were for other reasons considered unfit for active service abroad. From this number, the enlisted personnel of the United States Guards were largely recruited...." As the number of required Guards locations expanded, other organizations were ordered to transfer men to the newly forming Guards battalions. Camp and unit commanders followed the time-honored practice of using the opportunity to divest themselves of unfit and undesirable men. In one levy of 1,827 men, 826, more than 45 percent, were found to be unfit for even for lighter-duty Guards service and returned to development battalions.[23] In one sampling 1,243 men were returned from eight Guards battalions to development battalions.[24]

By 25 September 1918, there were 1,364 officers and 26,796 men assigned to Guards battalions. These units guarded some 313 points in 29 states and the District of Columbia as follows: shipyards, 101; docks and railroad terminals, 52; arsenals, seven; United States stores, property, and supplies, 86; government buildings, 33; railroad bridges and tunnels, 16; canal locks and waterways, three; waterworks, reservoirs, and dams, 11; and provost guards, four.[25]

The men were supposed to "undergo a course of intensive training embracing the use of machine guns, motor transportation, and instruction in guard duty, detective work, athletics, and riot-duty tactics," in addition to rifle practice.[26] In hindsight this appears to be a rather optimistic syllabus considering that many of the men detailed to the U.S. Guards were suffering some physical or mental malady which prevented them from service in France.

Although much of the work done by Guards battalions was undoubtedly very routine, though necessary, there could be some excitement and an element of danger involved, too. When the T.A. Gillespie Shell Loading Plant in South Amboy, New Jersey, exploded with disastrous results on 4 October 1918, Company B, 15th U.S. Guards Battalion, along with New Jersey Militia troops and U.S. Coast Guard troops, assisted in the difficult duty of evacuation of refugees, crowd control, and casualty clearance. Approximately 100 people were killed and hundreds more injured in the explosion.[27]

Although laboring in anonymity, the U.S. Guards battalions were not without their representation in song. "They'll be Proud of the U.S.G.," written and composed by Lt. Eugene Duffield and dedicated to Major Lucien Wiler, 12th U.S. Guards Battalion, appeared during the war. The song is typical of the ditties written during the war, and it extolls the unsung duty of the Guards:

> Soldier boys are grieving, somewhere over here,
> When they see their comrades leaving for somewhere "Over there."
> Although they can't go over, to help get Kaiser Bill,
> The Fighting 12th Battalion, they'll be there in spirit still.
> Vital work they're doing, somewhere over here,
> Guarding all those dear and precious, to comrades "Over there."
> For night and day they're watching, the spies of Kaiser Bill,
> They'll do their duty here at home, and they'll do it with a will.
> Uncle Sammy, you're sending over all the boys to fight for you.
> We're waiting patiently, the good old U.S.G.,

To go across and take a whack at the doggone Huns,
Beside, beside the boys "Over there."
United we'll stand by you, but if here we must stay,
You can bet they will say they were proud of the U.S.G.[28]

Born in Lorbo Aquila, Italy in 1892, Vincent Pendenza was working as a teamster in New York City when he was selected for the draft. Inducted into the Army on 4 September 1918, he served in the 306th Guard and Fire Company until February 1919. Perhaps a sign of the anonymity in which these soldiers worked, his last name is also recorded as Pentenzo and Pentenza and the 306th is recorded in the Army records as having been active from April 1918 to February 1919 but no location is given (private collection).

Since most of the men in the U.S. Guards battalions were, for some reason, unfit for combat duty, it's not surprising that many of them came to the Guards from various development battalions, those units created to help sub-standard recruits to become fit for some type of military service. Thus, in theory, men in development battalions would receive intensive physical and other training so when they were transferred, "they would be in every respect qualified for the duties in the arm of the service to which they were transferred"[29] In actual practice, this did not always prove to be the case. A study of the 5th, 9th, 13th, 14th, 15th, 16th, 20th, and 26th U.S. Guards Battalions revealed that 1,243 men transferred to those battalions from development battalions proved to be substandard and had to be transferred back to a development battalion at one of the training camp sites. Most of the approximately 110 reasons for transfer were physical; men suffered from a bewildering variety of ailments and conditions to include venereal disease, obesity, tumors, old gunshot wounds, and asthma. The largest category of disqualification—with 183 men—had to do with feet, including flat feet, deformed feet, and bad arches. Of the various non-physical reasons for transfer we find 75 men of "defective intelligence," two men who were enemy aliens, and five who couldn't speak English; 136 were illiterate and 148 were transferred for "inaptitude." The 9th U.S. Guards Battalion had the most transfers with 304. The others had 268 (26th), 255 (5th), 169 (16th), 82 (15th), 81 (14th), 51 (13th), and 33 (20th). Because of the wide disparity in the numbers per battalion in the example, it's difficult to determine an overall average or total, but there must have been close to five thousand men transferred back to development battalions.[30]

Of course men in the Guards Battalions were also subject to the virulent flu epidemic of 1918. Seventy-seven men of the 10th U.S. Guards Battalion on duty at the submarine base at Port Newark, New Jersey, the Foundation Ship Company at Kearney Meadows, New Jersey, and the Federal Ship Company, also at Kearney Meadows, became ill in September 1918 and had to be transferred to the port of embarkation hospital at Hoboken. A detachment of Company C, 15th U.S. Guards Battalion on duty at Newburgh, New York, was hit particularly hard in late October; twenty-eight cases developed over a period of a few days, and two men died. One man from Company B, 15th U.S. Guards Battalion on duty at South Amboy, New Jersey, succumbed to the flu and pneumonia in October.[31]

Just before the Armistice, Company C, 34th Battalion, was deactivated at Fort Niagara, New York, in October 1918. The remaining companies and battalions began to be deactivated in December 1918, and by

8. Lost in the Shadows

The Form 724 War Service Record for Irish-born Hugh Cullen. Originally assigned to the 152nd Depot Brigade at Camp Upton and then to an infantry unit, Cullen ultimately ended up with the 16th U.S. Guards Battalion in Philadelphia. While serving in that unit as a corporal he contracted the flu and died on 9 October 1918 (New York State World War I Service Abstracts via Ancestry.com).

February 1919 the process was almost complete. The last units to deactivate were the companies of the 30th United States Guards Battalion at various posts in Alaska, with Company D at Fort Gibbons being the final unit to disband in November 1919. Perhaps symbolic of the overall anonymity of the Guards battalions, of the 1574 pages of the *Order of Battle of the United States Land Forces*, the U.S. Guards sections runs from page 1566 to page 1570.[32]

As noted earlier, in any organization of the size of the U.S. Army in World War I, it's often easy to overlook even fairly large populations while telling the overall story. It wasn't until the 1970s that the contributions of African American soldiers to the greater war effort were truly recognized. Likewise, the "Hello Girls" of the Army's Signal Corps were not even accorded veteran's status until 1978. Only recently have the contributions and sacrifices of the nearly 800,000 foreign-born soldiers in the U.S. Army become appreciated. So it is no surprise that the dedication and service of the "colored" labor battalions, the female volunteers and Army nurses, the U.S. Guards Battalions, and the patriotism of the underage volunteers have been overlooked and forgotten. Referring back to the quote which opens this chapter, we can see that, for the most part, the men and women described here did not receive the "intelligent and thorough" training necessary for success. Nevertheless, even without it, they too served their country and are deserving of finally having their place in the sun.

9

Biographies from the Hilt of the Sword

"General, I suppose you received your orders to return [from France] to be Chief of Staff with rather mixed emotions.
　I replied, 'No, Mr. Secretary, it made me sick to my stomach.'"[1]

The short excerpt above, from a conversation between Secretary of War Newton Baker and General Peyton March, shows clearly the disappointment felt by many soldiers at being "left behind" in the United States. March was a little more fortunate than others because he had served in France with the AEF, at least for several months. Others did not have this solace. What follows is a series of short biographies of men whose military or civilian service in the Great War was limited primarily to the United States. Some were certainly disappointed to be the "hilt of the sword" instead of "the blade," while others appear to have been content to wait their turn. Most of the names will be familiar to the reader and include such varied celebrities as a famous songwriter, a stage and screen actor, an author from the "Lost Generation," a writer of children's books, a commercial artist, a Medal of Honor recipient who had campaigned against Geronimo, perhaps the greatest dancer and entertainer in American history, and even a World War I armor officer who later became the President of the United States.

Ludwig Bemelmans (27 April 1898–1 October 1962)

　Bemelmans was born in the Tyrolean section of the Austro-Hungarian Empire which today is part of Italy. After moving to Germany with his mother, Bemelmans had trouble adjusting to life in German society and was apparently given a choice between going to reform school or emigrating to America. He chose the latter, and in 1914, at the age of sixteen, arrived in the United States. Bemelmans served stateside in the U.S. Army during the war. After the war, he became an author and illustrator and is best known as the author of the beloved *Madeline* series of children's books. Bemelmans' memoir, *My War with the United States* (Viking Press, New York), published in 1938, is what one would expect from a man of letters. Engaging, articulate, at times light and humorous, Bemelmans' memoir often reads like a diary of his Army service. His illustrations are similar to his later work in the *Madeline* books. From his description of working in mess halls, to his anger at being accused of being a German spy, Bemelmans's book is a pleasure to read. He died in 1962 and is buried in Arlington National Cemetery.²

Already a well-known composer when drafted, Irving Berlin spent the entire war assigned to the 152nd Depot Brigade and then the 9th U.S. Guards Battalion at Camp Upton, New York. He made the most of his time there and composed some of his greatest songs while in uniform (Library of Congress).

Irving Berlin (11 May 1888–22 September 1989)

Born Israel Isidore Baline in Russia, Irving Berlin was a well-known composer and lyricist before he was drafted into the Army. His most famous work to that point was the song "Alexander's Ragtime Band" which became known internationally and was credited with starting a dance craze. After induction into the Army, he was stationed at Camp Upton, Long Island, with the 152nd Depot Brigade. While there, Berlin put his considerable talents to work writing a musical play about Army training. After the war his music career became even more notable, and he was soon considered to be one of the great songwriters of the period. He had an instinctive feel for the kind of music America wanted to hear, and his successes were numerous. Among the most famous of his songs are "Easter Parade," "White Christmas," "There's No Business Like Show Business," "Anything You Can Do, I Can Do Better," and "Blue Skies." Perhaps his most famous song, "God Bless America," was written while he was in the Army although it would not be performed for another twenty years. Berlin even found time to write another military-themed screenplay during World War II called "This is the Army." He died in 1989 at the age of 101.[3]

Raymond Westcott Briggs (19 July 1878–24 December 1959)

Briggs was born in Pennsylvania and enlisted in the Army Hospital Corps in 1898. He applied for a commission in 1900 and was accepted, serving as a second lieutenant, first in the infantry and then in the field artillery. He served in the Philippines in 1901 and by 1907 was a captain. He also served in the Quartermaster Corps. In 1914, while returning from a duty station in the Far East, Briggs was assigned to observe the German Army's annual maneuvers. What he observed instead was the German Army's entry into the First World War. He was in France at the end of the Marne Campaign, and he was the only American officer present at the siege of Antwerp, Belgium. Returning to the United States, Briggs gave a firsthand account of the fighting in Europe.[4]

When Pershing went to France in 1917 to create and command the AEF, he brought Briggs with him as the Chief of the Remount Section. By December 1917, Briggs was back in the States again with an assignment to the 79th Division's 311th Field Artillery Regiment at Camp Meade. When it became apparent that the 77th division was going to be the first National Army division to go to France, Briggs was transferred to the 304th Field Artillery Regiment, 77th Division, at Camp Upton. Very soon, under Brigg's command, the 304th was the first National Army field artillery regiment to deploy to France. Seeing action first in Alsace and then in the Chateau Thierry area, the 304th quickly established a reputation as a competent and effective unit. Shortly after the St Mihiel campaign, however, Briggs was on the move again. This time he returned to the United States to take command of the 18th Field Artillery Brigade which was being trained at Camp Travis, Texas.

Briggs was only in command of the brigade for two weeks when the Armistice was signed, denying him his chance for a fourth trip to the Western Front.

Along with his dynamic leadership, Briggs was well known among the troops for his love of horses and football. Promoted to brigadier general before the age of forty-one, Briggs was also notable for being one of the few senior Army leaders capable of flying an airplane.[5] Briggs is buried in the San Francisco National Cemetery in the Presidio of San Francisco.

The AGO Form 724 reflecting the military service of James Francis "Jimmy" Cagney in the Students' Army Training Corps. Cagney was assigned to Company E of the Columbia University unit in New York City (New York Abstracts of World War I Military Service via Ancestry.com).

James Francis "Jimmy" Cagney (17 July 1899–30 March 1986)

Cagney was born in Manhattan in New York City and graduated from Stuyvesant High School in 1918. He was not required to register for the June 1917 draft because the minimum age was twenty-one, and he was too young. The expanded draft in late summer 1918, however, included all eighteen- to twenty-one-year-olds and Cagney registered. He listed his occupation as "Draughtsman" for a construction

9. Biographies from the Hilt of the Sword

Frank Capra's "Petition for Naturalization" was filled out in 1920 after he was discharged from the Army. It shows that he arrived in the U.S. from Naples in 1903 and served honorably in the Army from August to December 1918 and that his original name was Francesco Capra (Naturalization records via Ancestry.com).

company. Jimmy Cagney's older brother, Harry Vincent Cagney, also fell into the new younger age criteria and registered at the same time. Their father James Cagney, Sr., at age forty-three, was also required to register because now the upper age limit was extended from thirty-one years of age to forty-five. All three men gave 420, East 78th Street in Manhattan, as their address and listed Carrie (Carolyn) Cagney as their next of kin.[6]

Cagney's brother Harry, attending Columbia University as a medical student, encouraged Jimmy to enlist in the Students' Army Training Corps. As Cagney recalled, "I [applied] and they took me. Why, I don't know." According to Cagney, he saw himself as a "98-lb. bum," who "didn't have any military sense at all." Still, his girlfriend, Nellie, took pride in Cagney's status, introducing the erstwhile private to her father as "Lieutenant Cagney." Cagney served in Company E of the Columbia SATC from 1 October to 12 December 1918 when he was discharged. Cagney jokingly referred to the SATC as the "Saturday Afternoon Tea Club."[7] It was also noted that Cagney played the drums in the SATC band at Columbia.[8]

With the war over, Cagney began to work in Vaudeville and then on Broadway, first as a dancer and then as a stage actor. From there he moved onto founding a dancing school and eventually began his extremely successful movie career. Over the years Cagney played many roles including gangsters, U.S. Navy officers, and musical performers. Ironically, one of his more memorable performances was as a World War I Marine in *What Price Glory*. The movie was based on a play which was co-written by the well-known Belleau Wood U.S.M.C. veteran Laurence Stallings. Cagney retired from the movies after 1961. Except for a few small roles he dedicated himself to working on his experimental farm. He passed away in 1986 and is interred in a mausoleum at Cemetery of the Gate of Heaven in Hawthorne, New York. The eulogy at his funeral was given by his close friend and President of the United States, Ronald Reagan.[9]

Frank Capra (18 May 1897–3 September 1991)

Born Francesco Rosario Capra in Sicily in 1897, Frank Capra immigrated to the United States in 1903 with his family. After graduating with a degree in chemical engineering from the California Institute of Technology in Pasadena in June 1918, Capra surprised his family by immediately enlisting in the Army. At the enlistment office, Capra declared his desire to be sent to an outfit destined for immediate service in France.

The Army responded by sending Capra to teach ballistic mathematics to artillery officers at Fort Mason, a small military post established in California in 1863, near the Presidio of San Francisco. After the Armistice, while still teaching mathematics, Capra became ill with influenza. Fearful of dying on an Army base, Capra went absent without leave (AWOL) to his home and the care of his mother. Capra survived both the flu and his AWOL stint to become a successful movie director. During World War II, Capra, and others in the motion picture industry, went back into service. Commissioned a colonel in the Army, Capra directed the *Why We Fight* series of movies for the Army. His 1971 autobiography, *The Name Above the Title* (The MacMillan Company, New York), is extremely detailed, well written, and comprehensive, but it contains only a brief account of his World War I service. Capra passed away in 1991 at the age of 94 and is buried in Coachella Valley Public Cemetery in California.[10]

Dwight David "Ike" Eisenhower (14 October 1890–28 March 1969)

Eisenhower was born in Kansas and graduated from the U.S. Military Academy at West Point in 1915, ranking 61 out of a class of 164.[11] To his great annoyance, he was not sent to France to serve in combat along with his contemporaries. Instead, he spent the war as an instructor at Fort Leavenworth, Camp Meade, and finally at the U.S. Army tank training center located at Camp Colt in Gettysburg, Pennsylvania. Despite his frustration at spending the war in the States, Eisenhower showed his organizational prowess and his ability to get things done. These skills would serve him well in the Second World War as he became responsible for planning and supervising the invasion of North Africa in 1942 and later the successful invasion of Normandy as Supreme Commander of the Allied Expeditionary Force in 1944.[12]

In November 1945, Eisenhower replaced General George C. Marshall as the Army Chief of Staff and served in that role until his retirement. In 1948 he was selected to serve as the President of Columbia University but took a two-year hiatus to serve as the Supreme Commander of the North Atlantic Treaty Organization (NATO). He returned to Columbia but soon became involved in politics and was elected the thirty-fourth President of the United States, serving from 1953 to 1961. After leaving the presidency, Eisenhower retired to his farm in Gettysburg, close to the site where he taught tank tactics during the First World War. Eisenhower was the last U.S. president born in the 19th century.[13]

General Dwight Eisenhower inspects soldiers of the 29th Infantry Division in England prior to the D-Day Invasion in June 1944. Disappointed at not being sent to France during World War I, Eisenhower nonetheless became known as an excellent military trainer and organizer. Walking directly behind Eisenhower is the 29th Division's Commander Maj. Gen. Charles Gerhardt, the son of Brig. Gen. Charles Gerhardt, who was noted for improving the demobilization process after World War I (Virginia National Guard).

F. Scott Fitzgerald (24 September 1896– 21 December 1940)

One of the more famous Americans to be trained at Camp Sheridan, Alabama, was the author Francis Scott Key Fitzgerald. Fitzgerald was born in Saint Paul, Minnesota, and was attending Princeton when he left school to join the Army. He received a commission as a second lieutenant and was assigned to the 67th Infantry Regiment in the 9th Division. Fitzgerald's zeal and wartime enthusiasm, as well as his inexperience, became evident when he pulled his pistol and threatened to shoot a soldier in his unit who refused to drill.[14] The war in Europe ended before Fitzgerald's unit could deploy to France, but the time he spent at Camp Sheridan proved to be important for the future writer. While in training there he met, courted, and married Zelda Sayre, the daughter of an Alabama Supreme Court judge. After he was demobilized in 1919, Fitzgerald began to focus on his writing career and later came to symbolize the "Lost Generation" after the Great War.

Fitzgerald was lured to Hollywood in 1927 with the promise of big money writing screenplays for the movies. Ultimately that job didn't work out and neither did a subsequent attempt to make a career as an actor. With his career as a writer on the ropes as well, he faded from public view, dying in 1940.[15] Virtually unknown and underappreciated during his life, Fitzgerald is now considered by many to be one of the premier American writers of the 20th century.

F. Scott Fitzgerald was attending Princeton when war was declared. He enlisted in the Army and soon was commissioned as an officer assigned to the 67th Infantry Regiment at Camp Sheridan, Alabama. Although his unit never deployed to France, Fitzgerald met his future wife Zelda while in training camp (Library of Congress).

Peyton Conway March (27 December 1864– 13 April 1955)

March was born in Easton, Pennsylvania, the son of Francis Andrew March, a distinguished scholar who is considered to be the principal founder of modern comparative linguistics in Anglo-Saxon culture. March attended Lafayette College, where his father occupied the first chair of English language and comparative philology in the United States. In 1884, he was appointed to West Point, and he graduated tenth out of forty-four cadets in 1888.[16]

On graduation, March was assigned to the 3rd Field Artillery Regiment. In 1894, he was assigned to the 5th Artillery as a first lieutenant. He commanded the Astor Battery (which was personally financed by the American millionaire, John Jacob Astor, IV) when it was deployed to the Philippines during the Spanish-American War. After the Astor Battery returned from the Philippines in 1899, March was assigned as aide to Major General Arthur MacArthur, Jr. Later that year, March was promoted to major. During 1904 and 1905, March was one of several American officers sent to observe the Imperial Japanese Army in the Russo-Japanese

War. In 1916, March was promoted to colonel and led the 8th Field Artillery Regiment during the Punitive Expedition and on the Mexican border.

In June 1917, March was promoted to brigadier general and commanded the 1st Field Artillery Brigade of the 1st Division. March was soon promoted to major general and selected to command all of the field artillery units in the AEF. In March 1918, he was recalled to Washington by the Secretary of War to serve as the acting Army Chief of Staff. The position was made official on 20 May, and March was promoted to general. March was highly critical of President Wilson's decision to send American expeditions to North Russia and Siberia in 1918 in response to British and French requests during the Russian Civil War. These ill-conceived expeditions were given the impossible-to-achieve mission of supporting White Russian forces, recovering the massive Allied military supplies already dispatched to support the Czar's army, providing security for the railroads, supporting the evacuation of the Czech Legion, and stopping the Japanese from exploiting the chaos in order to colonize Siberia. The missions were doomed from the start, and March knew it.[17] Despite his misgivings over the two expeditions, March continued to serve as the Chief of Staff of the Army and maintained the confidence of both the President and Secretary Baker.

March served as Chief of Staff until 30 June 1921. Among his accomplishments as Army Chief were the demobilization of the Army after World War I, the subsequent downsizing and reorganization of the Army, and the acceptance of equality between the National Guard and Regular Army ranks.

Disappointed in having to return to the U.S. after being selected to serve as the nominal head of field artillery in the AEF, Peyton March was appointed the Army Chief of Staff by Secretary of War Newton Baker. March threw himself into the job with energy and enthusiasm. Although he and Pershing had several disagreements over the strategy for supporting the AEF, there is no doubt that March was fully committed to serving the Army and the United States (U.S. Army).

March was also involved in the creation of the United States Army Air Corps, the Chemical Warfare Corps, the Transportation Corps, and the Tank Corps.

As Chief of Staff during the war, he often came into conflict with General John J. Pershing over the question of who was the ultimate commander of a deployed American Army, the commander in the field or the Army Chief of Staff. March died on 13 April 1955 and is buried at Arlington National Cemetery.[18] Among all the books written after the war by high-ranking U.S. Army officers, March's *The Nation at War* is one of the most interesting accounts. Because of his assignment as the Army Chief of Staff, March had unrivalled access to President Wilson and Secretary of War Baker. As a result, March was able to include his perspective on many of the most important wartime decisions made in the White House.

Bill "Bojangles" Robinson (25 May 1878– 25 November 1949)

The legendary actor, dancer, and entertainer was born in Richmond, Virginia, and began his stage career at an early age. It is believed he joined the U.S. Army in 1898 to serve in the Spanish-American War. Whether he was in the Regular Army or in one of the Virginia African American Militia units which were active during the wartime period is still unknown. He later said he was accidentally shot in the leg by an officer cleaning a rifle. What is known is that by the time the United States declared war on Germany in 1917, Robinson was one of the most famous vaudeville performers in the country. His innovative tap and dancing styles changed the manner and style in which many other entertainers of the period performed.

With the war effort reaching into all areas of society in 1917, and at age 40 being too old to be drafted, Robinson offered his services to entertain the troops in the training camps. He quickly proved to be popular with white and black soldiers alike. Adding to his popularity was the well-known fact that he performed for the soldiers in the stateside training camps at no cost. Robinson's entertainment work in the camps was recognized in September 1918 with a War Department Letter of Commendation which stated:

> The War Department, through the Commission on Training Camp Activities, desires to express its thanks for your very kind assistance in entertaining the men in the camps through the volunteer service which you have rendered.[19]

After the war, Robinson went on to greater fame on Broadway and in the movies where he starred with Shirley Temple, Will Rogers, Lena Horne, and Cab Calloway. After his death in 1949, some criticized him for his willingness to accept stereotypical African American roles in movies and on stage. However, over the years most opinions have softened, and today he is recognized as an entertainment pioneer of the 20th century. In light of his willingness to travel to many of the Army training camps and perform for the soldiers, it is appropriate that the viewing before his funeral was held in the New York City armory of the 369th Infantry Regiment in Harlem. A number of well-known World War I veterans including Irving Berlin and Noble Sissle were present at the funeral service. Also in attendance and serving as honorary pallbearers were Bob Hope, Darryl Zanuck, Joe DiMaggio, Duke Ellington, Cole Porter, and Joe Louis. Serving along the funeral parade route was a color guard from the American Legion. The city of Richmond, Robinson's hometown, erected a statue in his honor in 1973.[20]

Set against a patriotic "stars and stripes background, Bill "Mr. Bojangles" Robinson flashes his world-famous smile. A Spanish-American War–era veteran, Robinson was too old to be drafted in 1917 when the U.S. declared war on Germany so he volunteered his services and his talents to entertaining the soldiers in the training camps (Library of Congress).

Charles F. Scholle (28 April 1891–31 December 1987)

Charles F. Scholle was born in New York City to Bohemian immigrants Charles and Anna Scholle. His father was a clock designer who worked as the Chief Superintendent of Clocks at Tiffany and Company. As a child, Charles grew up on the outskirts of Manhattan. He began as an apprentice illustrator for Fauser and Company and was

9. Biographies from the Hilt of the Sword

This YMCA-donated New Testament belonged to Corporal Charles F. Scholle, 49th Machine Gun Battalion, 17th Division. Before the war, Scholle was working in New York City as a designer. After demobilization he opened a commercial studio and became well known for his illustrations, portraits, paintings of city scenes, and landscapes. During World War II, Scholle volunteered as an air raid warden while maintaining his commercial art studio (private collection).

employed there when he registered for the draft in June 1917 at the age of twenty-six. Charles was inducted into the Army in July 1918 and was assigned to a motor transportation unit at Camp Beauregard, Louisiana. He became a machine gun instructor at Camp Hancock, Georgia, in October 1918. Scholle was discharged in February 1919 and returned to New York City to open a commercial art studio. The firm specialized in the design of wallpaper and fabrics until 1927 when Charles began to sketch and paint landscapes and city venues. With the advent of World War II, most of the studio staff enlisted in the U.S. military, and Charles volunteered as the neighborhood air raid warden. He passed away in 1987 at the age of 96 and is buried Riverview Cemetery in Clackamas County, Oregon.[21] Today Scholle is best remembered for his landscape and city life paintings as well as his strong influence on other American artists and illustrators.

Leonard Wood (9 October 1860–7 August 1927)

Wood was born in Winchester, New Hampshire. He attended Pierce Academy in Middleborough, Massachusetts, and Harvard

Medical School, earning his M.D. degree in 1884. He signed on with the Army to serve as a "contracted" doctor, and his first assignment was to Fort Huachuca in the Arizona territory. In 1886 he participated in the final campaign against Geronimo and took command of a leaderless infantry company during a one-hundred-mile trek through hostile territory. For his bravery and leadership, Wood received the Medal of Honor.

Wood served as the personal physician to two United States presidents: Grover Cleveland and William McKinley. He also became well acquainted with Theodore Roosevelt who was serving as the Assistant Secretary of the Navy. This relationship was formalized when Wood assisted Roosevelt in organizing the 1st Volunteer Cavalry Regiment for service in the Spanish-American War. The unit became known as the "Rough Riders" and quickly gained a measure of fame for their exploits in Cuba. Wood was soon promoted to General of volunteers and took over command of the 2nd Brigade of the Cavalry Division in time to lead them during the fighting at Kettle Hill and San Juan Hill. At the conclusion of the Spanish-American War, Wood remained in the Caribbean, serving first as the Military Governor of Santiago and then as the Military Governor of Cuba until 1902.

Leonard Wood was possibly Pershing's greatest rival for command of the AEF. When Pershing was selected to lead the AEF, Wood was sent to command the 89th Division training at Camp Funston, Kansas. Unfortunately for Wood, he was replaced as commander of the 89th when it deployed to France. Again he received a consolation prize, command of the newly forming 10th Division (Library of Congress).

President William H. Taft selected Wood to serve as the Army Chief of Staff in 1910. This was an unusual honor for a medical officer and indicative of the wide variety of skills and knowledge Wood possessed. While in this position, he initiated a number of preparedness programs including the one which eventually became the Reserve Officer Training

Corps. Wood was always closely identified with the Republican Party through his close relationship with Teddy Roosevelt. As a result, he lost out to John J. Pershing for command of the AEF when the United States declared war in 1917. One historian later noted: "Wood himself was livid that he should be replaced by such a relative junior; he remained an enemy of Pershing's throughout the war, doing his utmost to undermine his credibility ... in Washington."[22]

During the summer of 1917 almost all U.S. Army generals were assigned to command divisional units and Wood was given command of the 89th Division. It was a National Army unit which was being formed at Camp Funston. Wood, always known as a strong leader, took the mission of training the 89th Division seriously and drove the officers and enlisted men relentlessly to prepare for combat. One area in which his forceful personality did not serve him well was in dealing with conscientious objectors. Under his leadership, Camp Funston became known as a place where such men suffered some of the worst abuses. Due mainly to Wood's belief they were "enemies of the Republic, fakers, and active agents of the enemy," the conscientious objectors assigned or incarcerated there were guaranteed rough treatment.[23]

Wood made a pre-deployment trip to France to observe the battlefields in November 1917. The *History of the 89th Division* reported that while in France, Wood and his Chief of Staff, Colonel Charles Kilbourne, were "wounded by the explosion of a trench mortar and their return to the Division was delayed until April 12, 1918." Wood's accidental wounding appears to be confirmed by a comment made by Major General Peyton March when he returned from France to assume his new role as the Army Chief of Staff. March reported to the press that General Pershing said Wood was "rapidly recovering from the wound in his forearm."[24] Whether this incident and subsequent wound ever actually took place is open for debate. There is little doubt Pershing did not want Wood, who was perhaps his greatest rival and biggest critic to serve in France in the AEF. So, whether real or contrived, such an accident provided a perfect excuse for delaying Wood's return to France at the head of a division.

On his return to Funston, Wood was surprised to be relieved of command of the 89th Division as the unit made final preparations to depart for France. Now deemed medically unfit to deploy due to age and health issues, Wood was forced to remain at Camp Funston when the 89th departed. Once again Wood was awarded a consolation prize: he was placed in command of another newly forming unit, the 10th Division, and given the mission to train it for eventual service in France. The war ended before the 10th could deploy.

Wood retired from the Army in 1921 after more than 35 years of service. He was appointed Governor General of the Philippines, serving there from 1921 to 1927. He died in Boston, Massachusetts, after surgery for the recurrent brain tumor which had plagued him for almost twenty years. He is buried in Arlington National Cemetery. Fort Leonard Wood in Missouri, current home to the United States Army Combat Engineer School, Chemical School, and Military Police School, is named in his honor.

10

Demobilization

"I reversed in its tracks the military machine which had been going ahead at top speed, and turned the entire energies of the War Department to the work of demobilization."[1]

The fighting in France ended just as the U.S. was preparing to send more divisions to the Western Front and it caught the Army in the United States with nearly two million soldiers in the midst of either training or getting ready for deployment. It had taken almost two years to build the four million-man U.S. Army; the challenge now was to see how quickly it could be dismantled.

As we have seen, a number of the soldiers waiting for transportation almost made it to France. Among them was Clelio Enriquez, a Mexican-born immigrant and newly naturalized citizen who had been trained at Camp Pike. He "went to Camp Upton, then boarded transport for France was out at sea two days when transport was ordered back on account of the signing of the armistice, from Camp Upton [he] went direct to Camp Cody [New Mexico] where discharge was made."[2]

Many thousands more remained at their training camps or transit camps on the East Coast awaiting departure orders which would never arrive. Instead, the U.S. Army needed to demobilize these men as quickly and efficiently as possible to prepare room for the AEF returning from France.

The reason for speed was obvious, every soldier in uniform cost the U.S. Government an average of two dollars a day, as well as all the other costs not related directly to the individual soldiers such as the building of barracks, the construction of aircraft, the production of ammunition, or the shipping of railroad cars to France.[3] Therefore, time meant money. Such a huge task as demobilizing would have to be accomplished systematically; the first men to leave the service were of necessity the recent inductees who were just starting to undergo training. As noted earlier, some of these men had only been in camp one or two days before the Armistice was signed. Others arrived on 11 November 1918 and some even later.

It would be necessary, of course, to retain a cadre of men at the stateside camps to demobilize the stateside forces and then manage the reception and demobilization processing of the roughly two million men from overseas who would soon be arriving by ship on the East Coast. As early as October 1918 the Army Chief of Staff, General Peyton March and his staff pondered the methodology for determining the best way to demobilize the force. Among the potential strategies discussed were:

1. Discharge by longevity of service
2. Discharge by previous civilian occupation and job availability, a method known as "industrial demobilization" which would be used by the British government to demobilize its army
3. Discharge by locality using the more than four thousand local draft boards as the mechanism for returning the soldiers to their civilian lives
4. Discharge by unit[4]

The first option, discharge by longevity of service, was immediately ruled as impractical because so many of the men in the AEF had been in the Army less than a year and therefore sorting out the seniority or time in service of four million soldiers would be an impossible task. The second and third options were equally unwieldy, and each would require a significant amount of time to establish and then execute. It was also recognized that the potential, however slight, remained for the war to start again should the Germans disregard the Armistice and not participate in the ensuing peace talks. Should this happen, complete Army units would be required to continue the war. General March decided the Army would be demobilized by units, based on their availability and the continued need for that unit in the national strategy. What this meant in practice was that the Regular Army divisions and those other units serving in either the occupation of Germany, the expeditionary forces still in Russia, or along the Mexican border would be the last to demobilize. All others would go before them based simply in the order in which they were sent to demobilization centers.[5]

As soon as March was notified of the signing of the Armistice on 11 November 1918, he directed the ongoing mobilization process be discontinued immediately, and all further scheduled draft calls were cancelled. Just five days later he ordered the discharge of the 98,189 men in the 73 development battalions located in camps scattered around the country. Even this common-sense decision would take time since many of the men were in these battalions for physical infirmities and needed some medical care and clearance before being discharged. The development battalion edict was followed in short order by another which discharged all conscientious objectors who were not currently serving prison sentences for military offenses. Next in line were the thirty thousand soldiers assigned to the lumber units in the Northwest who were milling the materials needed for aircraft construction. Another twenty-five thousand "light-duty" soldiers in the United States Guards units were also designated for discharge. Nevertheless, some of the men in the Guards units remained on duty until November 1919 because of their critically needed services as security guards. Altogether these actions quickly removed almost 200,000 men from the Army, but there still remained many thousands more still in the training camps that needed to be sent home.

Staring intensely at the camera, Klamens Joseph Malonis, a Russian citizen from Lithuania, poses for a portrait outside a barracks. He was working as a cook at the Capital Lunch Restaurant in New Haven, Connecticut, when he was drafted and sent to the depot brigade at Camp Dix, New Jersey. In response to a postwar survey about the effects of service on his civilian occupation, Malonis merely noted that he got his job back at the restaurant (Connecticut War Service records via Ancestry.com).

The training and transit camps designated to serve as demobilization centers also received guidance to establish their own demobilization operation using the personnel already serving at their sites. These ad hoc demobilization cells quickly proved to be ineffective, due in most part to their inexperience with the administrative processes required to demobilize a unit or discharge a soldier. It was one thing to receive, feed, and issue items needed to make up clothing or equipment shortages for soldiers on their way to France. It was entirely another thing to receive, feed, determine final pay, conduct individual physicals, purchase train tickets, etc., for the soldiers coming back from overseas.

Another problem which required an immediate solution was determining the amount of back pay owed to wounded men who were being treated in U.S. hospitals and were almost ready for discharge. Many had been hurriedly evacuated from the battlefield, through a series of intermediate hospitals in France, and back to the States. As a result, there were nearly a thousand men in hospitals who had lost their individual service books in which all their payments had been recorded. Under the guidance of General March, the War Department made a bold move and, instead of delaying payment to these wounded soldiers, authorized the finance officers to pay the men based on their sworn statement of what the Army owed them.

In spite of March's efforts and his willingness to try new methods to smooth the demobilization process, it was inevitable that some soldiers were overlooked and were left behind or sent to the wrong location. As seen earlier, a number of states lost track of some of their soldiers as they passed through the transportation and demobilization processes and so resorted to contacting family members to see if their soldier had made it home. Other states, such as Virginia, attempted to reach out to the returning men and ask them to fill out a questionnaire about their experiences in the military, in training camps, and in battle. Although the survey seemed like a good idea at the time, a number of the responses proved to be of little value. Some refused to fill out the survey and others, such as Oswald, Robert, and William Kemp filled them out grudgingly. The three brothers served together in the 117th Military Police Company of the 42nd Division and completed their forms by providing the exact same answers on all three pages of the form.[6]

By May 1919, the Army realized that there were still many problems and dispatched "Demobilization Groups" with the proper skill set and training to make the system work. Unfortunately, until the new groups were available, chaos was a common feature in some of the large camps, and early demobilizations were marked with confusion and many missteps. The previously noted comments by Frederic L. Paxson in *The Great Demobilization and Other Essays* are worth repeating: "During demobilization there was lacking even the madhouse in which the crazy might be incarcerated. They were at large."[7] It appears one of the exceptions to the "madhouse" was at Camp Devens, Massachusetts. There, Captain George Tait, the camp personnel adjutant, devised

10. Demobilization

a demobilization plan and turned it over to a lieutenant to execute. Under this plan "Camp Devens later broke all records in the American Army for the daily discharge of troops. The men signed their final statements, received their discharges, drew their pay and travel money, and bought their railroad tickets all in one building, being passed from window to window in a never-ending stream."[8] It was the exception to the rule.

Further adding to the complications was that on 24 February 1919, President Wilson signed a bill granting a sixty-dollar bonus for all who were in uniform on 11 November 1918. This generous act did not complicate the process for the men yet to be discharged as it was a simple procedure to add the sixty dollars to every soldier's final pay. The problem was with the 1.6 million soldiers already discharged and deserving of the bonus. Each of them would need to file a claim for the money. All of these claims would then have to be processed by the War Department's finance office in Washington, D.C.

Thomas C. Garcia, from Dona Ana County, New Mexico, enlisted in September 1917 in Texas and was assigned to the 164th Depot Brigade at Camp Funston, Kansas. From there he was sent to the 40th Division training at Camp Kearny, California, then to a transit camp near New York City, and finally to France in July 1918. In France he was assigned to the 28th Division and served in three campaigns. Garcia was badly gassed at St. Mihiel, hospitalized, and did not return to the U.S. until May 1919. Arriving at Camp Dix, he was then transferred to Fort Bliss for discharge (New Mexico War Service records via Ancestry.com).

Information on the bonus and how to apply for it went out via newspaper and newsletter to inform the recently-discharged soldiers; very quickly their claims began to pour in, sometimes as many as a hundred thousand a day. The initial staff of sixty clerks working on the bonus checks ballooned to nearly a thousand. A number of timesaving measures were developed including having the sixty-dollar amount pre-printed on each check. Traditionally only the department finance officer could sign these checks but now five clerks were authorized to sign for him and they were further enabled with a machine which signed five checks simultaneously as the clerk wrote his name. The checks were mailed in envelopes with clear windows showing the soldier's name and address, eliminating the time needed to write the address on the envelope.

At the same time as these actions were being taken, General Pershing and the AEF staff were directed by March to prepare for demobilization the units in France and Britain which were "no longer needed" and

Soldiers stand in formation after disembarking from the ship that brought them back to the U.S. in February 1919. From here they will journey to a demobilization camp in preparation for discharge from the Army (National Archives).

10. Demobilization 241

to send them home as soon as "transportation could be secured."[9] While Pershing and his staff did not have to worry about the intricacies of the stateside demobilization process, they would soon find that the redeployment process in Europe was equally filled with pitfalls and "madhouse" denizens. Much of the craziness at places like Camp Pontanezen or St. Aignan has been recounted elsewhere and is beyond the scope of our story. It is enough to say some of the bureaucratic roadblocks at the transit camps and ports in Europe were so bad they required Pershing's favorite operational planner and troubleshooter, George C. Marshall, to personally intervene and solve.[10]

In January 1919, it was reported in the *Stars and Stripes* that thirty-three camps in the United States had been designated as demobilization centers for returning units of the AEF.[11] Some of the returning AEF combat divisions, such as the 27th, 28th, 78th, 79th, 88th, and 91st, disembarked at the ports in the New York City area. After short stays at nearby Camp Mills, Camp Merritt, or Camp Upton, they moved on to their demobilization sites: the 28th to Camp Dix, the 78th and 79th to Camp Meade and Camp Dix, the 88th to Camp Dodge, and the 91st all the way to Camp Lewis on the West Coast. The story was much the same for the other returning divisions. Complicating the process, however, was the fact that the National Army and National Guard divisions by now contained men from many different locations. In many divisions, because of the double factors of combat losses and subsequent heavy influx of replacements, whatever local or regional flavor a division or regiment may have had in 1917 or early 1918 was gone by the end of 1918. To address this issue, when a unit arrived at a demobilization site, such as Camp Mills or Camp Upton, detachments were formed of men from the various regions of the country. They were then dispatched to a camp in that area for demobilization. For example, groups of men who entered service from Illinois, Wisconsin, and Iowa were often sent to Camp Grant near Rockford, Illinois, for final discharge. Aside from this sensible provision, the Army basically followed March's guidance that the soldiers were to be discharged by units, not as individuals. Also in accordance with March's wishes, after the various "locality discharge" detachments were sent on their way, the remaining soldiers in the divisions were moved to demobilization centers closest to where the majority of the men had originally entered the service.[12]

The Army did make some allowance for soldiers who were undergoing officer training, allowing their classes to continue to completion so as to make the candidates eligible to apply for commissions in the Reserve Corps. On the opposite end of this logical process was the almost random movement of some soldiers throughout the stateside camps. The story of Guy Tilghman Hollyday is illustrative of this phenomenon. Hollyday had enlisted in an artillery unit of the Maryland National Guard in December 1915 and was selected for the Officers Training Course at Fort Myer, Virginia, in August 1917. He was appointed a 2nd Lieutenant

Almost home! A soldier from the 29th Division's 111th Machine Gun Battalion breaks ranks to grab his sister's hand. The 111th returned to the United States in May 1919 and demobilized at Camp Dix. From there it was just a short train trip back to Maryland, the original site from which the National Guard unit was raised (National Archives).

of Cavalry in October 1917 and assigned to Camp Stuart, near Newport News, Virginia. After almost a year there, he was transferred to Camp Hancock, Georgia, and served there until December 1918 when he was sent back to Fort Myer to serve in D Troop of the 11th Cavalry Regiment. Shortly thereafter he was transferred to the Machine Gun Troop of the 11th Cavalry and detailed to Camp Stuart as a prison and police officer until March 1919 at which time he again served in the 11th's Machine Gun Troop. In May 1919 he returned to Fort Myer and was discharged there in June 1919. The closest he ever came to deploying to France was his service at Camp Stuart, which was one of the transit camps serving the Newport News/Norfolk ports of embarkation.[13]

Private Girney A. Putney, a New Hampshire soldier who was still in training at Camp Devens when the war ended, wrote home on 23 November 1918 and gave an insider's view of the good and bad in the training camps. Keeping in mind that the Armistice had been signed just twelve days earlier, Putney's multi-day letter paints a vivid picture:

> Dear Folks: ... I had an awful good supper last night. Every thing was cooked perfect. Here is what we had: Chicken & Gravy, mashed white &sweet potato, green peas, celery, olives, bread, cranberry sauce, plum pudding, ice cream, cake, brown sugar to go with pudding I guess, apple pie, 1 banana, 1 pear, 1 orange, sweet cider. Each one [of us] got only a small amount of each thing of course but we were all full when we got thru.
>
> [Sunday] I am feeling O.K. to-day. Was on guard last nite & this a.m. We are S.O.L. here I guess, a man in Co H was taken down with measles a few days ago so now we are quarantined. Don't know how long a time for. May be a few days & it may be weeks & weeks I suppose. Now I can't go to the canteen or Y.M.C.A. just out to the shit house & around close to the barracks unless we're sent out to do something, guard work & etc. [I] have had the measles so I am O.K. but I hate to be caged up in here....
>
> [Monday] I am feeling O.K. this morning. My cold is all right now. Those pills fixed it.
>
> I will close with lots of love to all. Girney.[14]

There was one other consideration by the Army leadership in demobilizing soldiers as close to their homes as possible; by doing so, it meant large numbers of the men would not be discharged in or near the large East Coast cities. It was hoped that by moving the demobilizing men closer to their home areas, the returning soldiers, now financially flush with their final pay settlements, would avoid falling prey to big-city con men and hucksters looking for an easy mark.

On arrival at their actual demobilization centers, the soldiers knew that their Army service was now close to the end. Along with a review of the soldier's administrative records to determine final pay, the medical staff conducted a physical exam and any disabilities were noted on his records. As General March later wrote, some men tried to "conceal physical ailments," fearing they would delay their discharge. He further noted that for most soldiers: "In health he was in general at least as good as when he entered the service; if wounded or in worse health, he was entitled to compensation" and further medical care.[15]

As noted earlier, convalescent centers were established at most large camps in the depot brigades to care for men too sick or wounded to be discharged immediately. Once all physicals, inspections, and equipment turn-ins were completed, the healthy men were at last ready to be discharged. They were given their final pay, plus their sixty-dollar bonus, and railroad fare to return home. Each soldier was also allowed to keep his uniform, an important feature since few men had any civilian clothes left in their possession. This was in accordance with the guidance from General March that every soldier was to be given "a uniform, shoes, and an overcoat or raincoat. In the case of overseas men, helmets and gas masks were issued as souvenirs."[16] After a final inspection, and company formation, the Doughboys were released from active duty and went home.

In spite of criticism in both the press and the Congress about the problems of the demobilization, March stuck to his plan and replied, "I wish to make it clear that demobilization is not proceeding haphazardly, but in accordance with a very definite and considered policy...."[17] He also noted during the period 11 November 1918 to 4 January 1919, the United States had demobilized 732,766 men. This was more than twice the number demobilized by Great Britain in the same period. By 1 May 1919, the U.S. demobilization figure stood at nearly two million. Just seven months later in January 1920, the entire four-million-man force had been demobilized except for the 130,000 officers and men who remained in the Regular Army. It may have looked like a madhouse from the outside, and perhaps even more so for those undergoing the demobilization process, but ultimately it was successful in returning the soldiers to civilian life.

11

"When I leave the world behind…"

> "I'll leave the sunshine to the flowers
> I'll leave the springtime to the trees
> And to the old folks, I'll leave the mem'ries
> Of a baby upon their knees
> I'll leave the night time to the dreamers
> I'll leave the songbirds to the blind
> I'll leave the moon above
> To those in love
> When I leave the world behind."[1]

As of this writing, the Doughboys are all gone, having left the world behind. Yet, for those of us fortunate enough to have known them as family members, family friends, or just the older gentlemen at the 4th of July parade or American Legion hall, they are not really gone. Just as in the 152nd Depot Brigade's most famous soldier, Irving Berlin, wrote in his song "When I Leave the World Behind," they left something behind for each of us. For better or for worse, the results of their service in the Great War remain today. American infantrymen and artillerymen assigned to the "Stabilization Force" in Bosnia in 1997 knew full well how close they were to the city of Sarajevo where the First World War started. They also knew they were serving in the former country of Yugoslavia because of regional hatreds and cultural differences which had been exacerbated by the collapse of the Austro-Hungarian Empire in 1918 and the subsequent creation of Yugoslavia from some of the pieces. And many appreciated the irony of serving with Polish, Czech, and Russian soldiers who but a few years earlier had been their sworn enemies.

Except for some technological terms and currently popular catchphrases, we speak today in words and phrases the soldiers, sailors, and Marines of 1918 would have understood. There is very little we could tell them about racism, poverty, overcrowded barracks, biological and chemical warfare, combat rations, terrorism, viral pandemics, sexually transmitted diseases, post-traumatic stress disorder (although they would have called it "Shell Shock"), or the lure of Hollywood that they didn't already know. Their war invented our wars—as well as the "dogfight," the Stormtrooper, the trench coat, the flamethrower, the tank, the steel helmet, and strategic bombing. Their pilots became "aces," their unexploded bombs became "duds," their observation balloons were called "blimps," and their friends who had seen too much became "basket cases." They had seen and knew all these things and they would father the next generation who would have to fight in the Second World War and Korea. Their grandsons would fight in Vietnam, Grenada, Panama, and the Gulf War.

Unfortunately, while many American soldiers, sailors, and Marines returned home from the Great War and took up their lives where they left off, many could not. Pre-war jobs were now being done by women or by men exempted from military service. The economy which had really started to hum in 1918 with the massive contracts for all sorts

In November 1918, the training camps in the U.S. were still going strong preparing to send more troops overseas. The 11 November Armistice quickly brought that effort to an end, and most of the troops being trained were quickly demobilized and sent home, just like this happy group at Camp Dix, New Jersey (National Archives).

of war-related materials, now slowed again as the orders for weapons, clothing, vehicles and military machines of all kinds, and food services were cancelled or quickly curtailed. In effect, as much of the Army was being demobilized, so too was the American industrial home front. Frederic Paxson wrote the "worker came back to a labor market which hardly needed him. The millions of the demobilized, jostling for jobs, would have upset that market even if the curve of war prosperity had been protracted unbroken into peace."2

It's never easy coming home from a war, even one which was considered a great victory or in which you never left the boundaries of the United States. A surprising number of the soldiers who served as the "hilt of the sword" felt let down because they didn't serve in France. As we have seen, it was especially painful for the professional soldiers and Marines who trained for battle but instead spent the war teaching draftees how to make their bunks, salute, and march in formation.

When we first introduced the reader to the complex world of the depot brigades at the beginning of this book, we promised an interesting ride through a mainly unknown segment of American military history from 1917 to 1919. As authors, we hope we delivered what was promised.

Ultimately, what the American soldiers of the Great War left behind for us was themselves. While little of their personal artifacts remain beyond wrinkled, sepia-colored photographs, dog-eared draft registration cards, and the occasional musty wool uniform, their personality still speaks. You'll hear it Irving Berlin's songs, watch it in Jimmy Cagney's movies, and read it in F. Scott Fitzgerald's books. A few of the places where they trained are still in existence, and the outlines of their trench works are still visible. Some of the best preserved can be found at Fort Lee, Virginia, and Camp Shelby, Mississippi, and worth a visit. That the "war to end all wars" didn't work out quite as planned is certainly not their fault. For the most part they were citizen-soldiers who shared no greater ambition than serving honorably and surviving the war. They were the blade and the hilt of America's mighty sword and certainly gave everything they had for their country.

Chapter Notes

Preface
1. March, *Nation at War*, p. 291.
2. Friedel, *Over There*, p. 83.
3. March, *Nation at War*, pp. 359–360.
4. *Ibid.*, p. 326.

Chapter 1
1. Lyrics to "Oh What a Lovely War" written in 1918 by J.P. Long and M. Scott.
2. Background material for this chapter was from: Stewart, Richard W. *American Military History; Volume I Army Historical Series*, and Stubbs, Mary Lee and Stanley Russell Connor, U.S. Department of the Army, *Army Lineage Series Armor-Cavalry Part I: Regular Army and Army Reserve*, and the *U.S. Army Facts and Insignia* booklet by Paulsen and Hines for Rand McNally & Company.
3. Services School, *Tactics and Technique*, p. 1.
4. Huston, *Sinews of War*, p. 321.
5. Services School, *Tactics and Technique*, pp. 140–141.
6. *Ibid.*, pp. 96–97.
7. Enlistment and War Service Records courtesy Virginia National Guard Historical Foundation Collection.
8. Services School, *Tactics and Technique*, p. 174.
9. *Ibid.*, pp. 180–181.
10. Hagood, *Services of Supply*, p. 69.
11. March, *Nation at War*, p. 272.

Chapter 2
1. Jackson, *Fall out to the Right of the Road*, p. 63.
2. *Wisconsin in the World War*, p. 42.
3. Robinson, *Forging the Sword*, pp. 11–12.
4. Kirby, *How Me and Amos won World War I*, p. 31.
5. Showalter, *Soldier Cities*, pp. 439–440.
6. Robinson, *Forging the Sword*, pp. 27–28.
7. *NYT*, 1 October 1917. Joseph Rigler was severely wounded on 8 September 1918, while serving as a Musician 3rd Class in the 307th Infantry Regiment, 77th Division. Undoubtedly he had figured out whom he was fighting by then.
8. Johns, *Camp Travis*, p .312.
9. Barbeau, *The Unknown Soldiers*, pp. 36–37.
10. *The History of the 318th Infantry Regiment*, pp. 18–22.
11. Official letter to George F. Butler from Local Board No.4, Oakland, California, 25 March 1918.
12. Kilner, *The Cantonment Manual*, p. 8.
13. English, *History of the 89th Division*, p. 27.
14. Johns, *Camp Travis*, p. 225.
15. Jackson, *Fall out to the Right of the Road*, pp. 35–39.
16. *Ibid.*, pp. 35–36. This description brings to mind a veterinarian's examination of livestock.
17. Jackson, *Fall out to the Right of the Road*, pp. 35–36.
18. Letter from Robert Koehn to his mother, 2 June 1918.
19. See the poignant example of Eugenio Scarlato, 23rd Infantry Regiment, 2nd Division, who died of wounds received in action in November 1918 in

Barnes and Belmonte, *Forgotten Soldiers*, pp. 155–160.
20. Divisional Officers. *Official History of 82nd Division*, pp. 2–3.
21. States Publication Society, *History of the Eighty-Sixth Division*, pp. 20–31.
22. Barber, *Seventy-Ninth Division*, p. 37.
23. Faulkner, *Pershing's Crusaders*, P.354.
24. Ayres, *The War with Germany*, p. 64.

Chapter 3

1. Beaver, *Newton D. Baker*, p. 81.
2. *The Official U.S. Bulletin*, Issues 402–451, 5 October 1918.
3. Robinson, *Forging the Sword*, pp. 83–89.
4. *Gas Attack*, April 1918.
5. *NYT*, 9 May 1918.
6. Robinson, *Forging the Sword*, pp. 25–26.
7. Ibid., pp. 44–51.
8. Ibid., pp. 94–101.
9. Ibid., p. 140.
10. Barry, *The Great Influenza*, pp. 187–188.
11. Robinson, *Forging the Sword*, p. 167.
12. *NYT*, 25 Jan 1918.
13. *The United States Land Forces, Volume 3*, p. 796, and City of Rochester, *World War Service Record of Rochester*, pp. 107 and 297.
14. *The United States Land Forces, Volume 3*, p. 274.
15. Letter from Charles Rose to Mother dated 25 Nov 1917, private collection. Both Rose and Sipley would be transferred from the 153rd to the 78th Division and serve in France. Both would survive the war, and Rose would reach the rank of sergeant.
16. Showalter, *Soldier Cities*, p. 451, and *Posts, Camps, and Stations Volume 3*, p. 745.
17. Letter from Ross, 28 Aug 1918, private collection.
18. Letter from Sergeant Warren, 154th Depot Brigade. The song that to which Sergeant Warren is referring was actually written to poke fun at the men serving in the Services of Supply in France.
19. *The United States Land Forces, Volume 3*, p. 742.
20. Wroth, *War Record of Battery A*, unpaginated.
21. Jackson, *Fall out to the Right of the Road*, pp. 45–47.
22. *The United States Land Forces, Volume 3*, pp. 829–831.
23. Divisional Officers, *Official History of 82nd Division*, pp. 1–3.
24. *The United States Land Forces, Volume 3*, p, 821.
25. Showalter, *Soldier Cities*, pp. 455–456.
26. Peck, *Camp Sherman: Ohio's World War I soldier factory*, p. 27.
27. Enscore, *Camp Sherman, Ohio*, p. 14.
28. Ibid., p. 37.
29. Ibid., p. 44.
30. *The United States Land Forces, Volume 3*, pp. 893–895.
31. Ibid., 865–866.
32. Ibid., pp. 1297–1299.
33. States Publication Society, *History of the Eighty-Sixth Division*, pp. 6–24.
34. BG Gerhardt unpublished memoirs, VANG Collection.
35. *The United States Land Forces, Volume 3*, pp. 845–846.
36. *Trench and Camp, The Arkansas Democrat*, 2 July 1918.
37. Barry, *The Great Influenza*, p. 294.
38. *The United States Land Forces, Volume 3*, pp. 870–872.
39. *NYT*, 27 January 1918.
40. *The United States Land Forces, Volume 3*, pp. 870–871.
41. English, *History of the 89th Division*, p. 19. One interesting aspect of Fort Riley is that it is home to the Ogden Monument, a limestone column that signifies the exact geographic center of the continental United States.
42. Ibid.
43. Ibid.
44. Showalter, *Soldier Cities*, p. 462, and *The United States Land Forces, Volume 3*, pp. 884–885.
45. National Peace Museum website: http://www.nationalpeacemuseum.org/history.html
46. John I. Walter, letter to his mother, June 1918, private collection.
47. *The United States Land Forces, Volume 3*, pp. 930–932.

48. *NYT*, 27 January 1918.
49. *The United States Land Forces*, Volume 3, pp. 931–933.
50. Showalter, *Soldier Cities*, pp. 465–466.
51. Cole, *The Thirty-Seventh Division*, p. 224.
52. Dalessandro, *Organization and Insignia*, p. 199.
53. Dickman, *The Great Crusade*, pp. 17–18.
54. *Ibid.*, p. 25.
55. *The United States Land Forces*, Volume 3, pp. 823–824.
56. Showalter, *Soldier Cities*, p. 467.
57. The Spartanburg County Historical Association Homepage: http://www.schistory.net/campwadsworth
58. *The United States Land Forces*, Volume 3, pp. 826–828.
59. Showalter, *Soldier Cities*, p. 471.
60. *The United States Land Forces*, Volume 3, pp. 834–835.
61. Cutchins, *Twenty-Ninth Division*, p. 11.
62. Showalter, *Soldier Cities*, pp. 467–469.
63. *Ibid.*, p. 470, and *The United States Land Forces, Volume 3*, pp. 857–859.
64. *The United States Land Forces*, Volume 3, pp. 857–859.
65. *Ibid.*, pp. 920–922.
66. Huidekoper, *History of the 33rd Division*, pp. 10–13.
67. *The United States Land Forces*, Volume 3, pp. 905–906.
68. *Ibid.*, pp. 928–930.
69. *Ibid.*, pp. 900–902.
70. Bowen, *Activities Concerning Mobilization*, pp. 165–167.
71. *The United States Land Forces*, Volume 3, pp. 900–902.
72. Showalter, *Soldier Cities*, pp. 470–472.
73. *The United States Land Forces*, Volume 3, pp. 852–854.
74. *Ibid.*, pp. 850–852.
75. *Ibid.*, pp. 865–866.
76. *Ibid.*, pp. 947–949.

Chapter 4

(It should be noted that development battalions were designated in a bewildering variety of ways among the different camps. Alpha and numeric designations were used, and one might find Development Battalion A, Development Battalion 1, or 1st Development Battalion at different camps during the war.)

1. Fosdick, *Keeping our Fighters Fit*, p. 158.
2. *The United States Land Forces*, Volume 3, p. 72.
3. Woodward, p. 48.
4. United States Selective Service System website, https://www.sss.gov/About/History-And-Records/Induction-Statistics, accessed 31 October 2015.
5. Bowen, *Activities Concerning Mobilization Camps*, pp. 167–168.
6. South Carolina History Homepage: www.schistory.net/campwadsworth.
7. Robinson, *Forging the Sword*, p. 105.
8. "Morale Work in an Army Camp," Professor Ralph V. D. Magoffin, Johns Hopkins University, in *The Historical Outlook*, Volume XI, January-December 1920.
9. For all information on Adelo, see New Mexico World War I Service questionnaires via Ancestry.com.
10. See service cards for Eugenio Aceto, Paul Tenuta, Pietro Tenuta, and Gaetano Presta, Wisconsin Veterans Museum, Madison, Wisconsin. It should be noted that these examples are cited not to belittle any man's service. On the contrary, these men were called and reported for duty as required. Rather, as stated, they illustrate a problem that occurred nationwide during the war.
11. The figures are taken from an analysis of statement of service cards held in the Wisconsin Veterans Museum, Madison, Wisconsin.
12. For information on Chakmakian, see Connecticut World War I Service questionnaires via Ancestry.com.
13. NY World War I Service Abstracts via Ancestry.com and City of Rochester. *World War Service Record of Rochester*, pp. 320–342.
14. For information on Phillipchuck, see Connecticut World War I Service questionnaires via Ancestry.com.
15. For information on Antonopulo, see Connecticut World War I Service questionnaires via Ancestry.com.
16. Various authors, "How the Army Uses Individual Differences in

Experience," in *Psychological Bulletin*, Vol. 15, No. 6, June 1918, p. 201.

17. Transcript of an interview with Stanley S. Lane, 13 December 2001, Veterans Oral History Project, American Folklife Center, Library of Congress (available on-line, http://memory.loc.gov/diglib/vhp/story/loc.natlib.afc2001001.00156/transcript?ID=mv0001).

18. *The Medical Department of the United States Army in the World War*, Volume XII, Part One, "Physical Reconstruction and Vocational Education," Section IV, "Development Battalions; Convalescent Centers, Washington: U.S. Government Printing Office, 1927, p. 216.

19. *The United States Land Forces, Volume 3*, pp. 1277–1309.

20. For all information on Sedillo, see New Mexico World War I Service questionnaires via Ancestry.com.

21. For each of these men see the appropriate entry in Peter L. Belmonte, *Calabrian-Americans in the US Military During World War I, Volume 1*, 2017.

Chapter 5

1. From the poem "Interned" by Major G.W. Polhemus in the "*Army and Navy Gazette.*"

2. Elements of the 8th, 10th, and 11th Divisions made it to England and France just days before the Armistice. For the 93rd Division, see Barbeau and Henri, *Unknown Soldiers*, p. 70.

3. March, *Nation at War*, pp. 5–6.

4. *Ibid.*, p. 274.

5. Dalessandro, *Organization and Insignia*, pp. 114–118 and Rinaldi, *Orders of Battle*, p. 31 and pp. 74–75.

6. *The United States Land Forces, Volume 3*, pp. 641–642 and the New Mexico World War I Questionnaires via Ancstry.com.

7. *The United States Land Forces, Volume 3*, pp. 643–644.

8. Wroth, *War Record for Battery*, unpaginated.

9. Rinaldi, *Orders of Battle*, p. 34 and pp. 79–80.

10. For information on Wells, see Connecticut World War I military questionnaires via Ancestry.com.

11. *Ibid.*

12. For information on Hachodoorian, see Connecticut World War I military questionnaires via Ancestry.com.

13. For information on Gomez, see Connecticut World War I military questionnaires via Ancestry.com.

14. For information on Smith see Connecticut World War I military questionnaires via Ancestry.com.,

15. Rinaldi, *Orders of Battle*, p. 34, and *The United States Land Forces, Volume 3*, pp. 647–648.

16. Rinaldi, *Orders of Battle*, p. 34.

17. *Posts, Camps, and Stations Volume 3*, pp. 649–650.

18. Rinaldi, *Orders of Battle*, p. 35 and Dalessandro, *Organization and Insignia*, pp. 125–126.

19. Dalessandro, *Organization and Insignia*, pp. 128–130.

20. Rinaldi, *Orders of Battle*, p. 35.

21. USMA pp. 811–812, and *Posts, Camps, and Stations Volume 3*, pp. 655–656.

22. *The United States Land Forces, Volume 3*, pp. 657–658, and *Camp Travis*, p. 71.

23. Rinaldi, *Orders of Battle*, p. 35.

24. Dalessandro, *Organization and Insignia*, pp. 136–138.

25. Rinaldi, *Orders of Battle*, p. 54 and *The United States Land Forces, Volume 3*, pp. 661–662.

26. *The United States Land Forces, Volume 3*, pp. 662–663.

27. *Ibid.*, pp. 663–664.

28. *Ibid.*, pp. 665–666.

29. *Ibid.*, pp. 667–668.

30. *Ibid.*

31. *Ibid.*, pp. 668–669.

32. *Ibid.*, pp. 669–670.

33. *Ibid.*, p. 670.

34. *Ibid.*, pp. 671–674.

35. March, *Nation at War*, pp. 275–278.

36. Rinaldi, *Orders of Battle*, p. 57.

37. *The United States Land Forces, Volume 3*, pp. 627–630 and Rinaldi, *Orders of Battle*, pp. 73–77.

38. *The United States Land Forces, Volume 3*, pp. 614–615 and 1569.

39. *Ibid.*, pp. 625–627, 973–978 and Rinaldi, *Orders of Battle*, pp. 73–77.

40. *The United States Land Forces, Volume 3*, pp. 630–636, 983–992 and Rinaldi, *Orders of Battle*, pp. 73–77.

Notes—Chapter 6

41. *The United States Land Forces, Volume 3*, pp. 630, 991 and Rinaldi, *Orders of Battle*, p. 75.

Chapter 6

(The spelling of the word "Students" as regards the possessive apostrophe varies among the documents. The War Department regulations booklet gives the plural possessive apostrophe, and that is used here unless the word appears differently in a title or quotation.)

1. Kilner, *The Cantonment Manual*, p. 12.
2. *Students' Army Training Corps Regulations*, p. 5.
3. *The United States Land Forces, Volume 3*, p. 556.
4. *Students' Army Training Corps Regulations*, p. 8.
5. *The Students Army Training Corps, Descriptive Circular*, p. 6.
6. Ibid.
7. https://quod.lib.umich.edu/b/bhlead/umich-bhl-87323?view=text.
8. English, *History of the 89th Division*, pp. 28–29.
9. http://bancroft.berkeley.edu/collections/gaybears/bynner/links/satc.html.
10. *SATC of the University of Colorado*. University of Colorado Bulletin, Vol. XVIII, No. 8, General Series No. 129.
11. *SATC of the University of Colorado*. University of Colorado Bulletin, Vol. XVIII, No. 8, General Series No. 129.
12. https://blogs.lib.ku.edu/spencer/tag/student-army-training-corps/.
13. https://www.thedickinsonpress.com/lifestyle/family/4527951-1918-flu-pandemic-claims-27-und-satc-trainees-dunn-countys-john-hledik.
14. http://news.westminster-mo.edu/uncategorized/westeryears-satc/.
15. Wigmore, "The Students' Army Training Corps," p. 61.
16. For information on Cofrancesco, see Connecticut World War I military questionnaires via Ancestry.com.
17. Ibid.
18. For information on Sternberg, see Connecticut World War I military questionnaires via Ancestry.com.
19. https://wp.stolaf.edu/archives/student-army-training-corps/; "Wester-years: A Chapter in Westminster's Wartime Service," http://news.westminster-mo.edu/uncategorized/westeryears-satc/.
20. Connecticut questionnaire via Ancestry.com.
21. "Illinois College in World War I, 1917–1918," https://sites.google.com/a/mail.ic.edu/icinworldwari/home/student-army-training-corps.
22. For information on Cofrancesco, see Connecticut World War I military questionnaires via Ancestry.com.
23. Ibid.
24. Ibid.
25. For information on Seltzer, see Connecticut World War I military questionnaires via Ancestry.com.
26. For information on Thorp, see Connecticut World War I military questionnaires via Ancestry.com.
27. For information on Harrigan, see Connecticut World War I military questionnaires via Ancestry.com.
28. For information on Hyman, see Connecticut World War I military questionnaires via Ancestry.com.
29. For information on Thorp, see Connecticut World War I military questionnaires via Ancestry.com.
30. For information on Price, see Connecticut World War I military questionnaires via Ancestry.com.
31. Information on Church and Rothstein: Connecticut questionnaire via Ancestry.com.
32. Information on Sanford and Barrs: Connecticut questionnaire via Ancestry.com.
33. Information on Conroy, Corsello, Quaile, and Quigg: Connecticut questionnaire via Ancestry.com.
34. Information on Congdon and Biddy: Connecticut questionnaire via Ancestry.com.
35. Information on Dowd and Haberlin: Connecticut questionnaire via Ancestry.com.
36. Barnes, "They also served." pp. 24–26.
37. Information on Hawley and Chaffee: Connecticut questionnaire via Ancestry.com.
38. Letter, Lloyd Lamb to Charles Hormig dated 27 November 2019, private collection.

39. Connecticut questionnaire via Ancestry.com.
40. Information on Renshaw, Midas, Redick, and Gillette: Connecticut questionnaire via Ancestry.com.
41. Information on Andem, Strant, and Parks: Connecticut questionnaire via Ancestry.com.
42. "Illinois College in World War I, 1917–1918."

Chapter 7

1. The Cantonment Manual, p. 2.
2. Johnson, *The Blue Eagle*, pp. 73–81.
3. *Ibid.*, and *NYT*, 28 June 1918.
4. *The Skirmisher*, May 1919.
5. *NYT*, 15 March 1918, and Draft Registration files at NARA via Ancestry.com
6. Rainville, *Virginia and the Great War*, pp. 77–78.
7. Report to Adjutant General of Virginia from State Inspector General, Jo Lane Stern, 2 November 1917, Virginia National Guard archives.
8. Rainville, *Virginia and the Great War*, pp. 77–78.
9. Cole, *The Thirty-Seventh Division*, pp. 394–395.
10. *Trench and Camp*, 6 August 1918.
11. Robinson, *Forging the Sword*, pp. 56–57.
12. Cole, *The Thirty-Seventh Division*, p. 331.
13. New Mexico, World War I Records, 1917–1919, via Ancestry.com.
14. *NYT*, 13 January 1918.
15. Articles of War, Government Printing Office, September 1920.
16. *The Nelson Gazette* (Nelson, NE), Thursday, 1 November 1917, p. 1.
17. *NYT*, 19 March 1918.
18. Huidekoper, *The History of the 33rd Division*, Vol I, p. 5.
19. *Ibid.*, p. 309.
20. *Ibid.*, p. 22.
21. *Ibid.*, p. 23.
22. *Ibid.*, pp. 27–31.
23. *The Camp Lee Bayonet*, 6 September 1918.
24. *The Spiker*, p. 9.
25. *The Messkit. How we learn French*, June 1919.
26. Robinson, *Forging the Sword*, p.81.
27. Data for this section is taken from Walter L. Haight, Racine County in the World War. Racine, Wisconsin, Western Prtg. & Lithographing Co., c. 1920, p. 48 and pp. 471–600. A large number of men are recorded with no additional information regarding dates of service; probably many of these men reported for duty in November. Elsewhere Haight reports 259 men drafted on 11 November 1918, p. 50.
28. See Haight, op cit.; for Mura's Canadian service, see U.S., Residents Serving in Canadian Expeditionary Forces, 1917–1918, via Ancestry.com.
29. "World War I War Service Chevrons," U.S. Militaria Forum.
30. *NYT*, 8 July 1919.
31. *NYT*, 30 March 1919.
32. 308th Engineers, *With the 308th Engineers*, pp. 8–10.
33. *Ibid.*, p. 65.
34. The Camp Lee Bayonet, 18 Aug 1918.
35. *NYT*, 22 September 1918 and 9 August 1918.
36. The Official U.S. Bulletin, Issues 402–451. 5 October 1918.
37. *Ibid.*
38. *Ibid.*
39. The United States Land Forces, Volume 3, pp. 643–648.
40. All references to New Mexico men in this section are from: New Mexico, World War I Records, 1917–1919, via Ancestry.com.
41. All references Connecticut men in this section are from: Connecticut State Library via Ancestry.com. Skirmishes between U.S. Regular Army units and Mexican bandits along the border and even into Mexico occurred in 1918 and 1919.
42. New Mexico, World War I Records, 1917–1919, via Ancestry.com.
43. Unknown, *History of the 318th*, p. 19.
44. Crowell, *The Road to France*, pp. 292–293.
45. *Opinions of the Judge Advocate General of the Army*, pp. 413–414; *The United States Army and Navy Journal, and Gazette of the Regular and Volunteer Forces*, pp. 158–159.
46. Beaver, *Newton D. Baker*, p. 183.
47. *NYT*, 1 September 1918.
48. Barry, *Great Influenza*, p. 289.

49. Howard letter to his Mother, 11 Nov 1918, private collection.
50. *NYT*, 16 February 1919.
51. *NYT*, 16 February 1919.
52. *NYT*, 16 February 1919, and Ohio World War I service records, and NARA Draft Registration Records, via Ancestry.com.
53. Robinson, *Forging the Sword*, p. 105.
54. Divisional Officers, *History of 82nd Division*, p.vi.

Chapter 8

1. Kilner, *The Cantonment Manual*, p. 12.
2. Ayres, *The War with Germany*, p. 19.
3. Marine Corps History Magazine, "The US Marines in World War I," pp. 5–14.
4. American Library Association homepage: www.ala.org.
5. Mayo, *That Damn Y*, pp. 413–416.
6. Barry, *Great Influenza*, pp. 187–188.
7. *Ibid.*, pp. 216–217.
8. City of Rochester, *World War Service Record of Rochester*, pp. 69–95, 441, and Barry, *Great Influenza*, p. 239.
9. Scott, *The American Negro in the World War*, p. 71.
10. *Ibid.*, p. 67.
11. Barbeau, *The Unknown Soldiers*, pp. 42–43.
12. *Ibid.*, pp. 89–90.
13. Memo for Chief of Staff, dated 16 May 1918, unpaginated.
14. *Ibid.*
15. Barbeau, *The Unknown Soldiers*, pp. 90–91.
16. *Ibid.*, p. 98.
17. The Legal Genealogist, https://www.legalgenealogist.com/2012/01/24/a-doughboys-age/. Due to the fact that the Navy accepted boys as young as fourteen years of age, this section will only consider Army enlistees. Likewise, the Marine Corps recruited a number of young men around the age of sixteen to serve as trumpeters and musicians.
18. All data relating to the men cited in this underage soldiers section is from New York State World War I service abstracts via Ancestry.com, unless otherwise noted.
19. All information about the Chiardio brothers is from: Pennsylvania, World War I Veterans Service and Compensation Files, 1917–1919, 1934–1948; Pennsylvania, Death Certificates, 1906–1967 via Ancestry.com.
20. New York State World War I Service abstracts via Ancestry.com.
21. *War Department Annual Reports, 1918*, Volume I, p. 1156.
22. *Ibid.*, p. 1160.
23. *Ibid.*
24. *Ibid.*, pp. 1165–1167.
25. *Ibid.*, p. 1163.
26. *Ibid.*, p. 1162.
27. *Reports of the Adjutant General of New Jersey, 1918–20*, pp. 63–68.
28. Library of Congress, music published by M. D. Swisher, Philadelphia, Pennsylvania.
29. *War Department Annual Reports, 1918*, p. 1165.
30. *Ibid.*, pp. 1165–1167.
31. *Ibid.*, p. 2998.
32. *The United States Land Forces*, pp. 1566–1570.

Chapter 9

1. March, *Nation at War*, p. 366.
2. Arlington National Cemetery: www.arlingtoncemetery.mil; see also Bemelmans, *My War with the United States*.
3. Rubin, *Last of the Doughboys*, pp. 241–243.
4. Johns, *Camp Travis*, p. 158.
5. *Ibid.*, and *NYT*, 24 August 1919.
6. U.S. World War I Draft Registration Cards via Ancestry.com.
7. Angelos. *Conversations with Cagney*, unpaginated copy.
8. McCabe. *Cagney*, unpaginated copy.
9. Reagan Eulogy, James Francis "Jimmy" Cagney, Valhalla, New York: Waymaking.com.
10. United States Naturalization Files via Ancestry.com; Capra, *The Name Above the Title*, pp. 9–10.
11. USMA, *Alphabetical Locator*, p. 196.
12. Miller, *Two Americans*, pp. 22–48.
13. *Ibid.*, pp. 374–381.
14. Farwell, *Over There*, p. 53.
15. Bryson, *One Summer*, pp. 513–514.
16. USMA, *Alphabetical Locator*, p. 52.

17. March, *Nation at War,* pp. 113-119.
18. Arlington National Cemetery: www.arlingtoncemetery.mil.
19. Haskins, *Mr. Bojangles,* pp. 97-98.
20. *Ibid.,* pp. 16-25.
21. New York Abstracts of World War I Military Service via Ancestry.com.
22. Mead, *The Doughboys,* p. 119.
23. Farwell, *Over There,* p. 53.
24. *NYT,* 2 March 1918.

Chapter 10

1. March, *Nation at War,* p. 255.
2. New Mexico, World War I Records, 1917-1919, via Ancestry.com.
3. Crowell. *Demobilization,* p. 67.
4. CMH PUB 104-8, *Personnel Demobilization,* p. 12-13.
5. March, *Nation at War,* pp. 310-316.
6. Library of Virginia World War I Military Service Records and Virginia Army National Guard Archives.
7. Paxson, *The Great Demobilization,* p. 7.
8. Robinson, *Forging the Sword,* p. 147.
9. March, *Nation at War,* p. 318.
10. Marshall, *Education of a General,* pp. 194-195.
11. *Stars & Stripes,* 31 Jan 1919.
12. Burton, *600 Days' Service,* p. 80.
13. Wroth, *War Record of Battery A,* unpaginated.
14. Letter from Private Girney A. Putney to family, East Andover New Hampshire, dated 23 November and postmarked 25 November 1918, private collection.
15. March, *Nation at War,* p. 321-323.
16. Reynolds, *115th Infantry U.S.A.,* p. 195, and March, *Nation at War,* p. 323.
17. March, *Nation at War,* p. 327.

Chapter 11

1. Lyrics to "When I leave the World Behind," by Irving Berlin, B Feldman and Co. Ltd., 1915.
2. Paxson, *The Great Demobilization,* p. 18.

Bibliography

U.S. Government Publications

American Armies and Battlefields in Europe. Washington, D.C.: Center of Military History, U.S. Army, 1995.

Ayres, Col. Leonard P., compiler. *The War with Germany: A Statistical Summary.* Washington, D.C.: Government Printing Office.

Bowen, Maj. Albert S., U.S. Army. *The Medical Department of the United States Army in the World War,* Volume IV, *Activities Concerning Mobilization Camps and Ports of Embarkation.* Washington, D.C.: Government Printing Office, 1928.

Center for Military History PUB 104–8, *History of Personnel Demobilization in the United States Army* (DA PAM 20–211), 1994.

Commission on Training Camp Activities Report. Washington, D.C.: Gaylord Bros. Makers, 1918.

Crane, Maj. A. G., U.S. Army. *The Medical Department of the United States Army in the World War,* Volume XII, Part One, *Physical Reconstruction and Vocational Education.* Washington, D.C.: Government Printing Office, 1927.

Ford, Col. Joseph H., U.S. Army. *Medical Department of the United States Army in the World War,* Volume II, *Administration American Expeditionary Forces.* Washington, D.C.: Government Printing Office, 1927.

The General Services School. *Tactics and Technique of the Separate Branches.* Specially prepared for the correspondence course. Fort Leavenworth, Kansas, 1922.

Government Printing Office. *Articles of War.* September 1920.

Histories of Army Posts. Recruiting Publicity Bureau, Department of the Army. February 1924. Reprinted from "*The Recruiting News.*"

Influenza 1919—Miscellaneous Reports. Department of the Navy Annual Report of the Secretary of the Navy. Washington, D.C.: Government Printing Office, 1920.

Instructions Concerning Operation of Development Battalions. War Department, Office of the Adjutant General. Washington, D.C.: Government Printing Office, 1918.

MacDonald, Charles B. *American Military History: Army Historical Series.* Volume 1. Washington, D.C.: Office of the Chief of Military History, U.S. Army, 1989.

"Memorandum for the Chief of Staff, Subject: Disposal of the colored drafted men." Dated 16 May 1918, Army Heritage and Education Center.

The Official U.S. Bulletin, Issues 402–451. 5 October 1918.

Opinions of the Judge Advocate General of the Army. Washington, D.C.: Government Printing Office, 1919.

Order of Battle of the United States Land Forces in the World War Zone of the Interior. Volume 3, Parts 1, 2, and 3. Washington, D.C.: Center of Military History, United States Army, 1949.

Stewart, Richard W. *American Military History: Volume I Army Historical Series.* Washington, D.C.: Center of Military History, U.S. Army, 2005.

Bibliography

Stewart, Richard W. *American Military History: Volume II Army Historical Series. The United States Army in a Global Era, 1917–2008.* Washington, D.C.: Center of Military History, United States Army, 2010.

Stubbs, Mary Lee, and Stanley Russell Connor, U.S. Department of the Army. *Army Lineage Series Armor-Cavalry Part I: Regular Army and Army Reserve.* Office of the Chief of Military History, United States Army, Washington, D.C., 1969.

The Students Army Training Corps, Second Edition, Descriptive Circular, corrected to October 14, 1918. Washington, D.C.: Government Printing Office, 1918.

Students' Army Training Corps Regulations, 1918. Special Regulations No. 103. Washington, D.C.: Government Printing Office, 1918.

Training Regulations for Depot Brigades. War Department Document No. 859. Washington, D.C.: Government Printing Office, 1918.

United States Army in the World War, 1917–1919, Organization of the American Expeditionary Forces, Volume I. Washington, D.C.: Center of Military History, U.S. Army, 1988.

United States Military Academy. *Alphabetical Locator of Graduates and Former Cadets.* Volume IX, 1950.

War Department Annual Reports, 1918. Volume 1. Washington, D.C.: Government Printing Office, 1919.

War Department Annual Reports, 1919. Volume 1. Washington, D.C.: Government Printing Office, 1920.

Published Works

Angelos, Bill. *Conversations with Cagney: The Early Years.* Albany, GA: BearManor Media, 2019.

Barbeau, Arthur E., and Florette Henri. *The Unknown Soldiers: Black American Troops in World War I.* Philadelphia: Temple University Press, 1974.

Barber, J. Frank. *History of the Seventy-Ninth Division A.E.F. During the World War: 1917–1919.* Compiled and edited by the History Committee 79th Division Association. Lancaster, PA: Steinman & Steinman, undated.

Barnes, Alexander F., and Peter L. Belmonte. *Forgotten Soldiers of World War I: America's Immigrant Doughboys.* Atglen, PA: Schiffer, 2018.

Barnes, Alexander F., Peter L. Belmonte, and Samuel O. Barnes. *Play Ball! Doughboys and Baseball during the Great War.* Atglen, PA: Schiffer, 2019.

Barry, John M. *The Great Influenza.* New York: Penguin, 2004.

Beaver, Daniel R. *Newton D. Baker and the American War Effort, 1917–1919.* Lincoln: University of Nebraska Press, 1966.

Belmonte, Peter L. *Calabrian-Americans in the US Military During World War I,* Volume 1. CreateSpace, 2017.

Belmonte, Peter L. *Chicago-Area Italians in World War I: A Case Study of Calabrians.* Charleston, SC: Fonthill Media, 2019.

Bemelmans, Ludwig. *My War with the United States.* Illustrated by the author. New York: Viking Press, 1937.

Brown, Arthur H., and Frank Wade Smith. *The Call to Arms: A Manual for Men Preparing for the National Army Camps.* New York: The Abingdon Press, 1918.

Bryson, Bill. *One Summer: America 1927.* London: Black Swan Publishing/Random House, 2014.

Burton, Harold H. *600 Days' Service: A History of the 361st Infantry Regiment of the United States Army.* University of Michigan Library, 1 January 1919.

Capra, Frank. *The Name Above the Title.* New York: The MacMillan Company, 1971.

City of Rochester. *World War Service Record of Rochester and Monroe County, New York, Vol I, Those Who Died for Us.* Rochester: The Du Bois Press, 1924.

Cole, Ralph D., and W.C. Howells. *The Thirty-Seventh Division in the World War 1917–1918.* Volume 1. Columbus, OH: The Thirty-Seventh Veterans Association, 1926.

Crowell, Benedict. *Demobilization: Our Industrial and Military Demobilization After the Armistice, 1918–1920.* New Haven: Yale University Press, 1921.

Crowell, Benedict. *The Road to France, Volume I: The Transportation of Troops and Military Supplies, 1917–1918.* New Haven: Yale University Press, 1921.

Cutchins, John A. *A Famous Command:*

Bibliography

The Richmond Light Infantry Blues. Richmond: Garrett and Massie Publishers, 1934.

Cutchins, John A. History of the Twenty-Ninth Division "Blue and Gray" 1917–1919. Philadelphia: McCalla and Company, 1921.

Dalessandro, Robert J., and Michael G. Knapp. Organization and Insignia of the American Expeditionary Force 1917–1923. Atglen, PA: Schiffer, 2008.

Davis, Arthur Kyle. Virginia Military Organizations in the World War, Source Volume V. Richmond: The Executive Committee of the Virginia War History Commission, 1927.

Dickman, Joseph T. The Great Crusade: A Narrative of the World War. New York: D. Appleton and Company, 1927.

Dienst, Captain Charles F. History of the 353rd Infantry Regiment, 89th Division National Army September 1917 to June 1919. Wichita: The 353rd Infantry Society, 1921.

Divisional Officers. Official History of 82nd Division American Expeditionary Forces 1917–1919. Indianapolis: The Bobbs-Merrill Company, 1920.

English, George H. History of the 89th Division U.S.A. Denver: War Society of the 89th Division. 1920,

Enscore, Susan I., Adam D. Smith, and Megan W. Tooker. Camp Sherman, Ohio: History of a World War Training Camp. Final Report for the Adjutant General Department, Ohio National Guard, U.S. Army Engineer Research and Development Center, December 2015.

Farwell, Byron. Over There: The United States in the Great War 1917–1918. New York: W.W. Norton and Company, 1999.

Faulkner, Richard S. Pershing's Crusaders: The American Soldier in World War I. Lawrence: University Press of Kansas, 2017.

Fosdick, Raymond B., and Edward F. Allen. Keeping our Fighters Fit—For War and After. Published by the War Department Commission on Training Camp Activities, The Century Company, 1918.

Friedel, Frank. Over There: The American Experience in World War I. Short Hills, NJ: Burford Books Inc., 1964.

Haskins, James, and N. R. Mitgang. Mr. Bojangles: the Biography of Bill Robinson. New York: William Morrow and Company, 1988.

The History of the 318th Infantry Regiment of the 80th Division 1917–1919. Richmond: The William Byrd Press Inc., 1919.

Horne, Charles H., editor. Source Records of the Great War, Volume VII. Indianapolis: The American Legion, 1931.

Huidekoper, Frederic Louis. The History of the 33rd Division, Volume I-III. Springfield, IL: Illinois State Historical Library, 1921.

Jackson, Edgar B. Fall Out to the Right of the Road. Verona, VA: McClure Printing Company, Inc., 1973.

Johns, E. B. Camp Travis and Its Part in the World War. New York: E.B. Johns, 1919.

Johnson, Hugh S. The Blue Eagle from Egg to Earth. Garden City, NY: Doubleday, Doran & Company, Inc., 1935.

Kilner, Maj. W. G., and Lt. A. J. McElroy. The Cantonment Manual. New York: D. Appleton and Company, 1917.

Kirby, Dr. Lelias E. How Me and Amos won WWI. Birmingham, AL: Commercial Printing Company, 1976.

March, General Peyton C. The Nation at War. Garden City, NY: Doubleday, Doran & Company, 1932.

Marshall, George C. Education of a General: 1880 to 1939. New York: The Viking Press, 1963.

Mayo, Katherine. That Damn Y: A Record of Overseas Service. Boston: The Riverside Press Cambridge, 1920.

McCabe, John. Cagney. New York: Alfred A. Knopf, 1997.

Mead, Gary. The Doughboys: America And the First World War. Woodstock, NY: Overlook Press, 2000.

Miller, William Lee. Two Americans. New York: Alfred A. Knopf, 2012.

Paulson, Valdemar, and Major Lucius A. Hine. U.S. Army Facts and Insignia. New York: Rand McNally & Company, 1918.

Paxson, Frederic L. The Great Demobilization and Other Essays. Madison: University of Wisconsin Press, 1941.

Peck, G. Richard. Camp Sherman: Ohio's WWI soldier factory. Chillicothe, OH: G. Richard Peck, 2014.

Pershing John. J. My Experiences in the World War. Volume II. New York: Frederick A. Stokes Company, 1931.

Rainville, Lynn. Virginia and the Great

War: Mobilization, Supply and Combat, 1914–1919. Jefferson, NC: McFarland, 2018.

Reports of the Adjutant General of New Jersey, 1918–20. Trenton: The State of New Jersey, 1920.

Reynolds, Chaplain F.C., and Chaplain William F. McLaughlin 115th Infantry U.S.A. in the World War. Baltimore: The Read-Taylor Company, 1920.

Rinaldi, Richard A. *The United States Army in World War I; Orders of Battle: Ground Units, 1917–1919.* Tiger Lily Publications LLC., 2005.

Robinson, William J. *Forging the Sword: The Story of Camp Devens, New England's Army Cantonment.* Concord, NH: The Rumford Press, 1920.

Rubin, Richard. *The Last of the Doughboys.* New York: Houghton Mifflin Harcourt, 2013.

Scott, Emmett J. *The American Negro in the World War.* Chicago: Homewood, 1919.

States Publication Society. *The Official History of the Eighty-Sixth Division.* Chicago: States Publication Society, 1921.

Thisted, Moses N. *Pershing's Pioneer Infantry of World War I.* Hemet, CA: Alphabet Printers, 1981.

The 308th Engineers Veterans Association. *With the 308th Engineers from Ohio to the Rhine and Back.* Cleveland: Premier Press, 1923.

Wisconsin in the World War. Milwaukee: The Wisconsin War History Company, 1919.

Woodward, David R. *The American Army and the First World War.* Armies of the Great War Series. Cambridge: Cambridge University Press, 2014.

Wroth, Lawrence C. *War Record of Battery A: Maryland Field Artillery.* Baltimore: The Barton-Gillet Co., undated.

Magazines and Newspapers

Barnes, Alexander, and Travis Shaw. "They Also Served: A Unique Souvenir of Great War Service." *Military Trader,* April 2019.

The Camp Dodger. The official newspaper of the 88th Division. 1918.

The Camp Lee Bayonet. Published in Petersburg, Virginia. 1918.

Fortescue, Maj. Granville. "Training the New Armies of Liberty." *The National Geographic Magazine.* National Geographic Society. Hubbard Memorial Hall, Washington, D.C., Volume XXXII, Numbers 5 and 6, November-December 1917.

Gas Attack. The official magazine of the 27th Division. 1917–1919. Printed at Camp Wadsworth, South Carolina.

Magoffin, Professor Ralph V. D. "Morale Work in an Army Camp." *The Historical Outlook,* Volume XI, January–December 1920.

The Messkit. Published for the soldiers of the AEF, Article: "How we learn French, France, June 1919."

The Nelson Gazette. Published in Nelson, Nebraska, 1917.

The New York Times. 1917–1922.

Polhemus, Major G. W. "Interned." *Army and Navy Gazette.*

Showalter, William J. "The Geographical and Historical Environment of America's 32 New Soldier Cities." *The National Geographic Magazine November—December 1917.* National Geographic Society. Hubbard Memorial Hall, Washington, D.C., Volume XXXII, Numbers 5 and 6, November-December 1917.

Showalter, William Joseph. "America's New Soldier Cities." *The National Geographic Magazine.* National Geographic Society. Hubbard Memorial Hall, Washington, D.C., Volume XXXII, Numbers 5 and 6, November-December 1917.

The Skirmisher. Published by the 4th Division, 1917–1919.

The Spiker. Published by the Men of the Engineers Railway, U.S. Army, France, February 1918.

Star and Stripes. French edition, 1918–1919.

Students' Army Training Corps of the University of Colorado. University of Colorado Bulletin, Vol. XVIII, No. 8, General Series No. 129. Boulder: Regents of the University of Colorado, 1918.

Trench and Camp. The Arkansas Democrat Edition for Camp Pike, Little Rock, Arkansas, July-August 1918.

Trench and Camp. The Greenville Daily News Edition for Camp Sevier, Greenville, South Carolina, April 1918.

The United States Army and Navy Journal,

Bibliography

and Gazette of the Regular and Volunteer Forces. Volume LVII, 1919–1920. New York: Evening Post Building, 1920.

"The US Marines in World War I: Part III Marine Corps Reserve." *Marine Corps History Magazine,* Winter 2016.

Various authors. "How the Army Uses Individual Differences in Experience." *Psychological Bulletin,* Vol. XV, No. 6, June 1918, published by the Psychological Review Company, Princeton, New Jersey.

Wigmore, J. H. "The Students' Army Training Corps." *Bulletin of the Association of University Professors (1915–1955),* Vol. 8, No. 7 (November 1922).

Unpublished Sources

Butler, George F. Correspondence from Draft Board No. 4, Oakland, California, 25 March 1918. Private Collection.

Gerhardt, Maj Gen. Charles. Unpublished memoirs in the Virginia National Guard Collection. Courtesy Gerhardt family.

Koehn, Robert. Collection of letters 1918–1919 from the 83rd Division. Private collection.

Lamb, Lloyd, letter to Charles Hormig dated 27 November 2019. Private collection.

Putney, Girney A. Letter to Laura Putney, 23 November 1918. Private collection.

"Ross." Letter and post cards to his sister Mrs. George Hicks of Succasumma, New Jersey, August-September 1918. Private collection.

Walter, John. Letter to Mrs. William Walter, 14 June 1918. Private collection.

Warren, Sgt Maj. U.S. Letter to Fletcher Slee, 23 Sept 1918. Private collection.

Zolla, Steve. "The Stateside Army—They Also Served." Unpublished article.

Internet Sources

American Library Association homepage: www.ala.org.

Ancestry.com.

The Arlington National Cemetery official website: http://www.arlingtoncemetery.mil/.

Bentley Historical Library, University of Michigan: https://quod.lib.umich.edu/b/bhlead/umich-bhl-87323?view=text.

Books.google.com.

The Dickinson Press: https://www.thedickinsonpress.com/lifestyle/family/4527951-1918-flu-pandemic-claims-27-und-satc-trainees-dunn-countys-john-hledik.

The Fort Jackson Museum Homepage: http://jackson.armylive.dodlive.mil/post/museum/50th-anniversary-history/.

Hathitrust.org.

Illinois College: https://sites.google.com/a/mail.ic.edu/icinworldwari/home/student-army-training-corps.

Kenneth Spencer Research Library, University of Kansas: https://blogs.lib.ku.edu/spencer/tag/student-army-training-corps/.

The Legal Genealogist: https://www.legalgenealogist.com/2012/01/24/a-doughboys-age/.

Library of Congress: www.loc.gov.

The National Governors Association website: http://www.nga.org/cms/home/governors/past-governors-bios/page_rhode_island/col2-content/main-content-list/title_case_norman.html/.

St. Olaf College: https://wp.stolaf.edu/archives/student-army-training-corps/.

South Carolina History Homepage: www.schistory.net/campwadsworth

The Spartanburg County Historical Association Homepage: http://www.schistory.net/campwadsworth.

The University Archives, The University of California, Berkeley: http://bancroft.berkeley.edu/collections/gaybears/bynner/links/satc.html.

The U.S. Army Center of Military History: http://www.history.army.mil/.

US Militaria Forum: USmilitariaforum.com.

Westminster College: http://news.westminster-mo.edu/uncategorized/westeryears-satc/.

Archives

National Archives and Records Administration, Washington, D.C., and St. Louis, Missouri.

Wisconsin Veterans Museum, Madison, Wisconsin.

Index

Numbers in **_bold italics_** indicate pages with illustrations

Abeyta, Albino 168–169
Adelo Samuel (Asaad Abdallah) 90–91
African-Americans 6, 26, 48, 50, 56, 64–65, 70, 73–74, 78, 92, 104, 136, 152, 172, 196, **_199_**, 203–208, 217, 229–231; *see also* Labor Battalions; Pioneer Infantry Regiments
Alaska 3, 135–136, 217
American Library Association (ALA) 192, 198–199
Amherst College 145, **_146_**, 150, **_151_**

Baker, Newton 20, 56, 156–157, 167, 191, 219, **_227_**, 228–229
Bell, George 172–173
Bell, J. Franklin 160
Bemelmans, Ludwig 219–220
Berlin, Irving 220–221, 230
Briggs, Raymond Westcott 221–222
Brown University 153

Cagney, James Francis 222–224
camps (for specialized or technical training): Colt (Gettysburg, Pennsylvania) 225; Franklin (Camp Meade, Maryland) 53; Humphreys (Belvoir, Virginia) 121, 127; Meigs (Washington D.C.) 177; Merritt (Dumont, New Jersey) 182, 186, 241; Mills (Garden City, New York) 50, 110, 185, 241
camps (National Army): Custer (Battle Creek, Michigan) 36, **_42_**, 59–60, 119, **_120_**, 176–177; Devens (Ayer, Massachusetts) 21, **_22_**, 24, **_33_**, 34, 41, **_43–44_**, 46–50, 57, 89, 93, **_94_**, 95, **_96_**, **_108_**, 113–116, 167, 175, 192, 200, 238–239, 243; Dix (Wrightstown, New Jersey) 34, 51–52, 57, 79, 94, **_95_**, 100, **_129_**, 134, 147, 187, **_237–238_**, 241, **_242_**, **_246_**; Dodge (Des Moines, Iowa) 34, 65, 81, 125–126, 172, 241; Funston (Fort Riley, Kansas) 29, 65–68, 110–111, 141, **_166_**, 169–171, 194, **_232_**, 233, **_239_**; Gordon (Atlanta, Georgia) 34, **_35_**, 46, 56–57, 78, 111, **_129_**, 201–202; Grant (Rockford, Illinois) 21, 34, 60–61, 93, 144, 172, 177, 201, 241; Jackson (Columbia, South Carolina) **_55_**, 56, 78, 100, 131, 152; Lee (Petersburg, Virginia) 17, 20, 24, 27, 31, 34, 54–57, 76, **_100_**, 127, 164–165, 173–174, 183–184, 190, **_206–207_**, 247; Lewis (Tacoma, Washington) 44, 54, 70, 100, **_104_**, **_117_**, 118, **_119_**, 241; Meade (Admiral, Maryland) **_30_**, 34–35, 53, 55, 57, 76, 109, 111–113, **_166_**, 183, 193, 203, 225, 241; Pike (Little Rock, Arkansas) **_25_**, 34, 36, **_62_**, 63–64, 100, 144, 166, **_202_**, 235; Sherman (Chillicothe, Ohio) 21, 57–59, 91, 127–128, 182, 194; Taylor (Louisville, Kentucky) 59, 91, 93, 109; Travis (San Antonio, Texas) 24–25, 34, 68–70, **_97_**, **_98_**, 109, 124–125, 186, 221; Upton (Yaphank, New York) 24, 34, **_48_**, 49–51, 57, 94, 109, 159–160, 175, **_206_**, **_217_**, 220, 235, 240
camps (National Guard): Beauregard (Alexandria, Louisiana) 59, 84–85, 122, 231; Bowie (Fort Worth, Texas) 42, 64, 81–82, 87–88, 133–134; Cody (Deming, New Mexico) 65, 81, **_98–99_**, 130–131, **_180_**, 235; Doniphan (Lawton, Oklahoma) 81, **_92_**; Fremont (Palo Alto, California) 71, 73, 89–90, 107, 137, 189–190; Greene (Charlotte, North Carolina) 34, 44, 47, 72–73, 177; Hancock (Augusta, Georgia) 55, 72, 74–75, 109, 231; Kearny (San Diego) 44, 85, 121–122, 129, 134, 168–169, 239; Logan (Houston, Texas) 21, 79–80, 101, 119, 121, 171–172, 176–177; MacArthur (Waco, Texas) 21, 79, 100, 186; McClellan (Anniston, Alabama) 21, 58, 75–77, 82, 93, 97, **_101_**, 114, 131, **_133_**, 201; Sevier (Taylor, South Carolina) 56, 78, 126–127; Shelby (Hattiesburg, Mississippi) 84, 134, 177, 247; Sheridan (Montgomery, Alabama) 21, 82–83, 95, 109–110, 133, 165, 167, 227; Wadsworth (Spartanburg, South Carolina) 21, 41, 73–74, 88, 129, 134, 184–185, **_197_**; Wheeler (Macon, Georgia) 52, 78–79, 133, 177

Index

Capra, Frank *223*, 224–225
China 7, 135, 137
Cofrancesco, Humbert 143–145
Columbia University *222*, 224, 225
conscientious objector(s) 4–5, 47, 67, 166, 191, 193, 233, 237
Cornell University 152–153

Depot Brigades (National Army): 151st (Camp Devens) 33, *43–45*, 46–50, 93, 95, 114; 152nd (Camp Upton) *48–49*, 50–51, 94, 160, 175, *217*, 220, 245; 153rd (Camp Dix) 52, 100; 154th (Camp Meade) *30*, 34, 53, *112*, 183; 155th (Camp Lee) 27, 31, 54–56, 76, *100*, 165, 173–174, 190, *206*, 208; 156th (Camp Jackson) 55–56, 100, 152; 157th (Camp Gordon) *35*, 56–57, *129*; 158th (Camp Sherman) 57–59, 194; 159th (Camp Taylor) 59; 160th (Camp Custer) *41–42*, 60; 161st (Camp Grant) 34, 60, *61*, 88, 172; 162nd (Camp Pike) *25*, *62*, 63–65, 100, 165; 163rd (Camp Dodge) 65; 164th (Camp Funston) 65–68, 169, 170, 172, *239*; 165th (Camp Travis) 25, 68–70, *98*; 166th (Camp Lewis) 44, 70, 100
Depot Brigades (National Guard): 51st (Camp Greene) 44, 72–73, 104; 52nd (Camp Wadsworth) 73–74; 53rd (Camp Hancock) 74; 54th (Camp McClellan) 75–76; 55th (Camp Sevier) 78; 56th (Camp Wheeler) 78–79; 57th (Camp MacArthur) 79; 58th (Camp Logan) 79–80; 59th (Camp Cody) 80–81; 60th (Camp Doniphan) 81; 61st (Camp Bowie) 81–82, 87; 62nd (Camp Sheridan) 82–83; 63rd (Camp Shelby) 84; 64th (Camp Beauregard) 84; 65th (Camp Kearny) 85
Development Battalion 25, 31, 70, 75, 78, 81, 85, 87, 89, *90*, 91–95, 97–101, 174, 216, 237
Dickman, Joseph 73
Divisions (U.S. Army): 8th *90*, 107–109; 9th 77, 109–110, 226; 10th 110–111, 185, 232–233; 11th 111–113, 185; 12th 93, *94*, 113–117, 185; 13th *104*, *117*, 118–119; 14th 119; 15th 119, 121; 15th Cavalry 121, 135; 16th 121–122, 168–169; 17th 122, 231; 18th 123–125; 19th 105, 125–126; 20th 126; 26th 36, 47, 49, 72–73, 104, 203; 27th *27*, 74, 88, 241; 28th 72, 74–75, 211, *239*, 241; 29th 57, 61, 72, 76; 37th 55–56, 83, 109, 165, 173; 42nd 13, 36, 50, 82, 104, 113, 238; 76th 35, 46–48, 104, 113; 77th 50, 160, 221; 78th 241; 79th 34–35, 53, 55, 113, 134, 221, 241; 80th 174; 81st 56, 75; 82nd 34–35, 47, 56–57, 111, 195; 83rd 35, 57, 127, 152, 182, 194; 90th 123; 93rd 63, 104; 94th 127, *128*; 95th 127; 96th 129, 131; 97th 65, *130*, 131, *132*; 98th 131, *133*; 99th 133; 100th 133–134; 101st 134; 102nd 134
Edwards, Clarence R. 203
Eisenhower, Dwight David "Ike" 225, *226*
Enemy Aliens Bureau of New York *159*, 160
Fitzgerald, F. Scott 226, *227*
Fordham University 147

Harvard 147, *149*, 231
Hawaii 3, *62*, *118*, *119*, 135–136, 140
Hodges, Henry Clay 122
Holy Cross College 145

immigrants 5, 24, 92–93, 97, 116, *178*, 235
influenza 142, 153, 186, *202*, 225

Jewish Welfare Board 199

Knights of Columbus (K of C) 198–199

labor battalions 42, 48, 50, 195, 205–206, 208, 217

March, Peyton Conway 1, 5–6, 19, 37, 105, 158, 219, 227, *228*–229, 233, 236, 238, 244
Marine Corps 1, 3, 7, 9, 140, 150–151, 198, 224
Marshall, George C. 225, 241
McCain, Henry 114
Mexican border 8, 12, 36, 55, 72, 80, 86, 125, 135, 157–158, 186–187, 191, 194, 228, 236; *see also* Villa, Pancho
murder 41, 170, 174, 183

New York University 145–146, 150
Northwestern University 142
nurses, Army 15, 36, 88, *62*, 117, 195, *197*, 198, 202–203
nurses, Red Cross 198, *199*, 200–201

Ott, Lester 193–195

Panama Canal Zone 82, 122, 135, 136, 246
Paxson, Frederic L. 239, 247
Philippines 7, 67, 135, 169, 221, 228
Pioneer Infantry Regiments 73–74, 88, 127, 129, *130*, 131, 133–134, 147

Racine County, Wisconsin 92, 176–177
Red Cross *197*, 198–202
Rensselaer Polytechnic 152
Robinson, Bill "Bojangles" 229–*230*
Rochester, New York 51, 94, 201–202, 210

Salvation Army 198–199
Scholle, Charles F. 230, *231*
service/overseas stripes 179, *180*, *181*
Ship Repair Shop Unit Number 301
Simpson, William H. 80

Index

Slavic Legion 74, 183–185
Spanish flu (also influenza) 5, *14*, 31, 36–37, 41, 48, 51–52, 58, 64–65, 80, 82, 106, 113, 116, 121, *133*, 192–193, *199*, 200–203, 216, *217*, 225; *see also* influenza
Students' Army Training Corps (SATC) 138–154
Students' Naval Training Corps 152–153
Syracuse University 149

Trinity College 150

underage soldiers 208–212, 217
United States Guards, National Army 94, *95*, 101, 136, 162, 164, 196, 212–217, *220*, 237
University of Colorado 141
University of Kansas 142
University of North Dakota 142

Villa, Pancho 8, *17*, 67, 191

Whisler, Lewis 169–170
Wilson, Woodrow 3–5, 86, 155, 191, 229, 239
Wood, Leonard 110, *166*, 231–234

Yale 143–144, *146*, 147–148, 150, 152–153
Yeomanette, U.S. Navy 198
Young Men's Christian Association (YMCA) *27*, 28, 31, 198–200, *230*
Young Women's Christian Association (YWCA) 198–199

Zador, George 158–160

www.ingramcontent.com/pod-product-compliance
Lightning Source LLC
Chambersburg PA
CBHW071405300426
44114CB00016B/2190